This is the first book comprehensively to analyze health screening in the workplace. Three major types of testing are examined: genetic screening, in which job applicants and employees are tested for inherited traits that may predispose them to the disease; genetic monitoring, which aims to detect genetic damage among current employees that could indicate exposure to dangerous chemicals; and teratogenic risk, in which laboratory cultures and animals are used to provide evidence of the effects of chemical exposure on humans.

Risky Business explores the way in which industrial screening practices, usually defended as the neutral application of science and new technologies to health hazards, are shaped by ideological, economic, and regulatory factors that extend beyond considerations of technical effectiveness.

The book draws on fieldwork, documents, historical and statistical materials, and 120 in-depth interviews with corporate managers and physicians, government officials, scientists, labor officials, and industrial employees. Professor Draper shows that a major shift has been taking place in the prevailing conception of risk in the workplace – from one that locates risk in hazardous working conditions to one that locates risk in workers themselves.

This book will be of particular importance to sociologists, health professionals, policy analysts, and those concerned with risk analysis and organizational behavior.

Risky business

Cambridge Studies in Philosophy and Public Policy

GENERAL EDITOR: Douglas MacLean

The purpose of this series is to publish the most innovative and up-to-date research into the values and concepts that underlie major aspects of public policy. Hitherto most research in this field has been empirical. This series is primarily conceptual and normative; that is, it investigates the structure of arguments and the nature of values relevant to the formation, justification, and criticism of public policy. At the same time it is informed by empirical considerations, addressing specific issues, general policy concerns, and the methods of policy analysis and their applications.

The books in the series are inherently interdisciplinary and include anthologies as well as monographs. They are of particular interest to philosophers, political scientists, sociologists, economists, policy analysts, and those involved in public administration and environmental policy.

Other books in the series

Mark Sagoff   *The Economy of the Earth*
Henry Shue (ed.)   *Nuclear Deterrence and Moral Restraint*
Judith Lichtenberg (ed.)   *Democracy and the Mass Media*

Risky business

Genetic testing and exclusionary practices in the hazardous workplace

ELAINE DRAPER
DEPARTMENT OF SOCIOLOGY
UNIVERSITY OF SOUTHERN CALIFORNIA

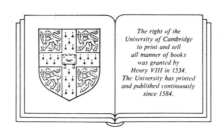

*The right of the
University of Cambridge
to print and sell
all manner of books
was granted by
Henry VIII in 1534.
The University has printed
and published continuously
since 1584.*

CAMBRIDGE UNIVERSITY PRESS
CAMBRIDGE
NEW YORK   PORT CHESTER   MELBOURNE   SYDNEY

Published by the Press Syndicate of the University of Cambridge
The Pitt Building, Trumpington Street, Cambridge CB2 1RP
40 West 20th Street, New York, NY 10011, USA
10 Stamford Road, Oakleigh, Melbourne 3166, Australia

© Cambridge University Press 1991

First published 1991

Printed in the United States of America

Library of Congress Cataloging-in-Publication Data
Draper, Elaine.
Risky business : genetic testing and exclusionary practices in the
hazardous workplace / Elaine Draper.
p.   cm. – (Cambridge studies in philosophy and public policy)
Includes bibliographical references and index.
ISBN 0-521-37027-2 (hard). – ISBN 0-521-42248-5 (paperback)
1. Human chromosome abnormalities – Diagnosis – Social aspects.
2. Occupational diseases – Diagnosis – Social aspects.   3. Medical
screening – Social aspects.   I. Title.   II. Series.
RB155.6.D73   1991
363.11 – dc20   90-28112
CIP

British Library Cataloguing in Publication Data
Draper, Elaine
Risky business : genetic testing and exclusionary
practices in the hazardous workplace.
1. Industrial health & safety
I. Title
363.1163

ISBN 0-521-37027-2 hardback
ISBN 0-521-42248-5 paperback

Contents

Contents

Tables

Foreword

In this pathbreaking book, Professor Draper enriches our understanding of genetic testing by pushing beyond its scientific and legal boundaries into the fertile terrain of sociology and political theory.

It has now been more than a decade since Richard Severo, a veteran science reporter for the *New York Times*, drew attention to the fact that industry was conducting genetic screening of workers for job placement purposes. The articles in the *Times* stimulated congressional hearings on genetic screening in industry, and the Office of Technology Assessment undertook two studies of the subject. A number of legal scholars wrote law review articles and books concerning the screening of workers, and the issue continues to raise new scientific, legal, and ethical questions.

Genetic testing covers not only genetic screening, where workers are examined for possible genetic predisposition to chemically caused disease, but also genetic monitoring, which measures genetic damage caused by exposure to chemicals in the workplace or general environment. Broadly speaking, genetic testing is advocated by industries that wish to focus on the "high-risk worker" and sometimes apply exclusionary employment practices. These practices, of course, may run afoul of constitutional and statutory protections offered under the Civil Rights Act to people who are singled out deliberately or consequentially as a result of their race, sex, or age. In the context of fetal protection policies,

Foreword

the unanimous Supreme Court decision in the *Johnson Controls* case ruled against these practices in March 1991. But after a decade of serious erosion in the area of affirmative action and worker protection, it would not be surprising for the policies of industrial genetics to find increasing acceptance in other contexts.

In this important study, Professor Draper forces us to reexamine the ethical and social basis for discriminating on the basis of genetic makeup or genetic condition, and documents an unsavory political history in this trend. Her book should be required reading for all scholars and policymakers interested in workplace and discrimination issues.

Nicholas A. Ashford
Massachusetts Institute of Technology

Preface

Genetic techniques for identifying high-risk workers have been widely debated but little understood. At a time when an increasing number of corporate employers are using genetic information as a cornerstone of their hiring practices, the ramifications of genetic testing in the workplace deserve closer examination. When workers find their chromosomes considered alongside their résumés, the implications are profound.

The focus on employee screening bolsters the often erroneous belief that the workplace is safe for all but those who are intrinsically vulnerable. Thus, reproductive health policies have focused on screening out women, despite major chemical risks to men. And blacks have been the focus of major screening programs, despite widespread health hazards affecting other racial and ethnic groups. This skewed framing of workplace risk deepens divisions in society based on sex, race, and ethnicity. "Susceptibility policies" also may penalize people without protecting workers at all. The economic burden of disease falls more heavily on workers, their families, and the public, and less on employers who permit health hazards to continue.

Susceptibility policies reflect the broad allure of genetic technology and the widespread belief in genetic explanations for social ills. An important danger of new genetic technologies is that they tend to define workplace risk as an individual problem. They transform work hazards from a collective problem into a matter for fragmented, atomized clusters of individuals who no longer have the capacity to mobilize support for alternative policies. In this way, the use of genetic technologies turns on its head the relationship that C. Wright Mills observed between private troubles and public issues: it converts a social problem into a seemingly merely personal one.

This book analyzes health screening in the workplace in depth. It shows how industrial screening practices, usually defended as the neutral application of science and new technologies to health hazards, are in fact socially created. They are shaped by ideological, economic, and regulatory factors that go beyond considerations of technical effectiveness.

Scholarship ought to explain the ways in which major social forces contribute to susceptibility policies, particularly by shaping the competing conceptions of risk and safety that underlie the use of new genetic technologies. In attempting to construct such an explanation, I have found that present academic models of decision making, risk analysis, and organizational dynamics rarely take account of existing power structures and conflicting conceptions of risk. These models also tend to misjudge the choices that actually confront workers who must deal with the problems raised by new technologies.

I wrote *Risky Business* with several types of readers in mind. First are scholars – particularly in sociology and political science – who are concerned with work and organizations, science and medicine, and social stratification. Second are those in professional schools of law, business, medicine, and public health who wish to move beyond the limited accounts of new technologies and chemical hazards published to date in legal and medical journals. Third are those in philosophy and medical ethics who are interested in choice and equity and may be willing to challenge the rational choice and decision-making models that tend to ignore actual social forces.

Although this book will doubtless find its main audience among scholars within academic disciplines, I hope it will also be read by nonacademics who seek to influence public policy: health professionals, labor leaders, industrial managers, politicians, and government officials, to name a few. In addition, I hope to reach general readers with an interest in health and the environment or trends in the world of work. With their needs in view, I have defined many scientific and legal terms when they first occur in the text, and offered a short glossary of acronyms and other specialized terms. I have also included an appendix on research methods, which explains the interviews and other research I conducted. The research upon which I draw includes fieldwork, documents, historical and statistical materials, and 120 in-depth interviews. To illuminate the social context and meaning of medical screening at the workplace, I have used quotations from the interviews throughout my sociological analysis.

During the long and absorbing process of completing this book, I have been fortunate to have had the support and assistance of many colleagues, friends, and family members.

To Troy Duster at Berkeley, I am especially grateful. His intellectual guidance and enormous encouragement over the years have been invaluable. Arlie Hochschild, David Matza, and Laura Nader all have been thoughtful, incisive critics at several stages of this project. They have provided admirable models in their own work as scholars, teachers, and writers, and each of them has been a generous source of encouragement.

For their perceptive comments on earlier versions of this work, I wish to thank David Plotke, Diane Beeson, Robert Schaeffer, Anne Lawrence, Bill Domhoff, Dick Scott, Terry Lunsford, Vicki Smith, Paul Adler, Kay Sloan, Lillian Rubin, Allen Graubard, Linda Fuller, Angela Bean, Florence Bird, Reva Faver, Lee Draper, and April Wayland.

I have had the good fortune of working with excellent editors and reviewers in preparing this book for publication. Daniel Wikler's careful reading and brilliant criticism of the manuscript challenged me to push my analysis further. I also appreciate Gene Tanke's extraordinarily helpful editorial advice. Nicholas Ashford and the anonymous reviewers at Cambridge offered cogent recommendations that helped me in revising the manuscript. Terry Moore guided the manuscript through the publishing house channels with vision, dedication, and a welcome sense of humor.

The Institute for the Study of Social Change at Berkeley provided a stimulating collegial environment for my research. Its distinguished scholars and numerous major research projects gave me many opportunities to try out ideas. For over three years, I worked as a member of the Social Issues in the New Genetics research group at the Institute. As a group of sociologists analyzing new technologies, we read each other's draft manuscripts carefully, exchanged innumerable references, and met frequently to talk about our related work. In particular, I would like to thank Troy Duster, Diane Beeson, Terry Lunsford, and Judith Ellis for our stimulating meetings and for the rewards of working with a successful research team.

The Stanford postdoctoral program in organizations research offered me the time and vital intellectual community for completing the manuscript. I especially wish to thank Dick Scott, Jim March, and Paul Adler for our spirited discussions and joint projects, which greatly enriched this study.

The professional staffs of several libraries and research organizations were helpful in tracking down elusive sources, including staff members of the Government Documents Library and the Institute of Industrial Relations at Berkeley, the Library of Congress, the House Science and Technology Committee, and the Office of Technology Assessment. Jeffrey Colen contributed exceptionally capable research assistance, and David Fogarty gave me excellent documentary advice. Steve McMahon and Bob Yamashita graciously helped me solve technical and computer puzzles. Janice Tanigawa offered expert coordination of grant support and secretarial assistance.

Some of the central ideas of this study appeared first in articles I wrote for the *International Journal of Sociology and Social Policy* and *Contemporary Sociology,* and in papers I delivered at meetings of the American Sociological Association, the International Sociological Association, and the Society for the Study of Social Problems. The National Science Foundation Sociology Program awarded me grant support, which I greatly appreciate. The National Institute of Child Health and Human Development funded the crucial early stages of this research. A National Institute of Mental Health fellowship contributed to the study by supporting intensive three-year research training in field research methods. A Business and Professional Women's Foundation grant funded research on exclusionary policies affecting women workers exposed to toxic chemicals. Several other research grants and fellowships provided valuable support, including awards by the University of California Chancellor's Patent Fund, the Sigma Xi Scientific Research Society, American Educational Services, Kappa Kappa Gamma, and the Josephine de Karman Research Foundation.

Finally, sincere and deep appreciation goes to the men and women I interviewed, for generously sharing their time and experience with me. These corporate managers, government officials, physicians, scientists, labor officials, and industrial workers spent many hours with me discussing problems of risk that to them are thorny social issues, and often intensely personal ones. For their candid and informative responses I am most grateful. I hope that this study will contribute to an understanding of the conflicts and controversies in which they participate and to the amelioration of risk in the hazardous workplace.

Introduction

OVER the last two decades, reports of chemical hazards to health have risen to front-page status in the world press. Pesticide residues like those in California grape vineyards, toxic waste dumps like the one at New York's Love Canal, and chemical leaks like the 1984 catastrophe in Bhopal, India, killing over two thousand people and injuring many thousands more, are only a few examples.[1] In industry especially, the health risks and costs posed by workers' exposure to the hazards of asbestos, lead, and cotton dust have become matters of concern. The growth in public awareness of such hazards at work has been accompanied by an increased corporate and professional interest in identifying workers who may be especially susceptible to illness from toxic chemicals, and by the spread of genetic testing as a means of identifying them.[2]

In general, scientists regard issues of occupational risk primarily as problems to be understood in technological terms and resolved through biological and chemical investigation. The current interest in identifying high-risk workers thus stems in part from recent scientific research that suggests associations between particular traits and diseases and new information on genetic abnormalities.[3] But the use of a genetic framework for assessing risk to workers has had a major influence on the practice of industrial medicine – with results that stretch far beyond the scientific. It has had a considerable impact on how professionals and policymakers conceive of the workplace, and on their views of who is responsible for what happens there. As the focus of the debate over occupational hazards has shifted away from chemical hazards per se and toward personal characteristics of high-risk workers, certain fundamental questions become more pressing.

First, what political, economic, and cultural forces have converged to make the "high-risk worker" a major focus for research and social policy, and why has this approach gained widespread interest, funding, and credibility? Second, once this orientation toward genetic components of risk becomes prevalent, who comes to be seen as the worker at risk, and

3

why? And third, how can the divergent perspectives toward genetic testing and exclusionary practices in the workplace be explained?

My approach to these questions can be summarized most usefully by explaining how it differs from other approaches commonly found in the literature on risk. Genetic testing and the exclusion of high-risk workers have received considerable attention, but the type of sociological analysis I will present has not previously been brought to bear on these or related practices.

The literature on genetic testing and occupational risk has been expanding rapidly. Some studies review the technical capabilities of genetic technologies.[4] Various analysts – from labor, industrial management, and government – have evaluated the applications of particular testing and exclusionary practices to the workplace.[5] Yet this literature has not exhibited an understanding of the social significance of industrial genetics.

Most studies that claim to analyze the social components of occupational genetics focus rather narrowly on legal or ethical issues, such as whether or not specific industrial practices are legal or socially beneficial.[6] The ethical studies are often misleading sociologically. Although they evaluate genetic testing in terms of the "social good," they typically assume that the benefits to society as a whole provided by workplace practices can be determined by applying a single standard, instead of by assessing many different perspectives and interests. Furthermore, virtually all studies of genetic testing fail to account adequately for the social forces behind what this book will describe as a conceptual shift toward genetic susceptibility and away from workplace hazards.

The burgeoning literature on technological risk has also lacked such a broad perspective. Studies conducted on a "technical-scientific" model of risk tend to celebrate new technologies as dramatic breakthroughs in science, and to minimize associated risks. Or, if the risks are acknowledged, they are examined as if they were exclusively technical and scientific problems.[7]

Studies conducted on an "economic decision-making" model generally approach risks as manifestations of modern industrial society that reflect individual preferences in risk taking. Analysts in this tradition claim to assess technological risks through socially neutral models that quantify and evaluate costs and benefits.[8]

A third major approach is the "cultural bias and technophobia" model. When applied to workplace and environmental hazards, studies of risk from this perspective frequently portray workers as misapprehending risk because of their cultural biases. For example, in *Risk and Culture* (1982), Douglas and Wildavsky ask the question: What values and institutions lead particular individuals and groups to highlight certain risks and not others?[9] In the cultural bias and technophobia view, workers and the public typically overestimate risks from industrial chemicals and nuclear power plants but underestimate risks from smoking, diet, and other personal activities. In many cases, analysts argue that cultural biases cause workers to behave irrationally in response to risks. Terminology that describes employee symptoms and complaints as "psychogenic disorders," "chemophobia," and "technophobia" reflect this cultural bias perspective.[10]

In contrast to these approaches, I will focus on analyzing the social-structural and ideological factors that give rise to different definitions of risk. These factors, after all, are what lead individuals and groups to adopt specific orientations toward risk and to oppose or support specific technologies. Industrial genetics has not yet been viewed through this lens.[11]

I will treat susceptibility tests and exclusionary practices as an important example of the social construction of risk and of the processes by which conceptions of risk are understood differently by various social groups.[12] In the case of health hazards in the workplace, I will examine the ways in which corporate officials, scientists, government officials, industrial employees, and labor officials perceive and respond to them.

I will also treat susceptibility policies as an example of the resurgence of genetic explanations for social phenomena.[13] Increasingly, it is the genetic makeup of workers, not the conditions of the hazardous workplace, that is understood to be the core problem of occupational disease.

Finally, in analyzing industrial genetics, I will emphasize how power relations and conflicting interests influence the ways in which risk is defined and new technologies are employed in the workplace.

The plan of the book is as follows. In Chapter 1, I outline the emergence of genetic testing and susceptibility explanations, discuss their social application, and preview the sociological argument to come. I also describe the major social pattern in the controversy over genetic testing and exclusionary policies in the workplace: the conflict between labor and management over how to define workers at risk from hazardous chemicals.

In Chapters 2 through 6, I examine five social factors that shape the way in which workers at risk have been identified: (1) belief in the efficacy of genetic technology and biological explanations; (2) the stratification of the work force and the particular importance of race and sex as social categories; (3) conflicting conceptions of risk and safety; (4) structures of power and decision making in the workplace; and (5) the legal and regulatory context of conflict over the social costs of occupational disease. These factors help explain how issues of risk are framed and how industrial practices are conducted. They also help explain patterns of support and opposition to genetic testing and exclusionary policies, to which I pay particular attention in examining the social context of industrial genetics.

Chapter 2 examines the resurgence of genetic explanations for social phenomena, and specifically the process by which genetic components of occupational disease have been emphasized. I analyze industrial testing in the context of new developments in genetic technology as well as recent biological explanations for characteristics such as depression, low

6

intelligence, aggression, and maternal behavior. The workplace, besides providing fertile ground for conflicting explanations of human variation and normality, is also the main arena for more specific conflicts over definitions of occupational illness. Examining the way in which risk is defined and debated will help clarify the underlying conflict.

Chapter 3 focuses on the ways in which conceptions of workplace safety shape industrial genetics. At issue is the proper locus of occupational risk: Is it the worker, or the conditions of the industrial workplace? Managers and scientists who adopt the approach of individual susceptibility make it appear that all workers and exposure conditions not considered "high risk" are safe and not of central concern.

Chapter 4 analyzes the stratification of the work force and the particular importance of race and sex as social categories. Although proponents of the new genetic technology claim that it is a neutral approach that therefore protects everyone equally, "susceptibility" often turns out to have a racial or sexual component, for the process tends to single out women and minorities. I show how the search for types of workers at risk often results in the identification of inappropriate biological categories.

Chapter 5 analyzes the use of genetic susceptibility tests within the framework of industrial medicine. I show that power structures and conflicting interests in the workplace influence the ways in which risk is conceptualized and controlled.

Chapter 6 considers the shifting legal environment that both affects and reflects the conflict over responsibility for the costs of occupational disease. I point out how government regulations and liability developments can make it cheaper to maim or exclude particular individuals than to reduce exposure levels.

Finally, Chapter 7 summarizes the argument and major findings, discusses prospects for the future, and suggests policy implications. Throughout the analysis, 120 interviews, documents, published works, and statistical and historical materials provide evidence for the shift in concern

7

from the high-risk workplace to the high-risk worker, and for its social character and consequences.

As the 1990s unfold, genetic testing and susceptibility policies are being applied on what is still a rather limited scale. But with the continued rapid growth of genetic knowledge and the inevitable influence of the ideological, economic, and legal factors that we will examine here, that situation is likely to change dramatically. My analysis of how these factors interact is intended to encourage more insightful studies of risk and of health hazards at work, and to stimulate more cogent debate in this important area of public policy.

Chapter 1

Genetic testing and exclusionary practices in the workplace

Risk, power, and controversy

We are already making the attempt to exclude accident prone workers from certain trades. The principle could perhaps be carried a good deal further.

J. B. S. Haldane (Biologist),
Heredity and Politics (1938:179)

TECHNOLOGIES for detecting genetic traits in individuals and genetic abnormalities that may have resulted from chemical exposure have developed rapidly over the past twenty years. Over the same period, and in part because of the availability of these new genetic technologies, companies have greatly expanded the use of testing policies to exclude high-risk workers from specific jobs.

THE EMERGENCE OF GENETIC TESTING AND SUSCEPTIBILITY POLICIES

Three major types of testing and exclusionary practices will be examined in this study: genetic screening, genetic monitoring, and testing for teratogenic risk (see Table 1).

The first type, genetic screening, involves testing job applicants and employees for certain inherited traits that may predispose them to disease. Companies have conducted genetic screening for markers such as sickle cell trait and glucose-6-phosphate dehydrogenase (G-6-PD) deficiency. These tests are believed capable of detecting increased risk of emphysema or chronic bronchitis for individuals with serum alpha$_1$-antitrypsin (SAT) deficiency, or increased risk of hemolytic reaction for individuals with G-6-PD deficiency, if they are exposed to certain industrial chemicals. Other traits may predispose people to lung cancer or anemia when they are exposed to particular substances.[1] Employers can use the test results in hiring and placement decisions. For example, DuPont has included genetic screening in the regular blood and urine tests it gives job applicants and employees. The tests have been for G-6-PD enzyme deficiency, SAT deficiency, and other genetic traits. They were designed to identify individuals likely to develop anemia, emphysema, or other health problems when exposed to specific chemicals.[2]

The second type of genetic testing is genetic monitoring, which aims at detecting genetic damage among current employees that could indicate exposure to dangerous chemicals.[3] If genetic monitoring reveals substantial chromosome breakage or other abnormalities, an employer may decide to

11

Table 1. *Means of identifying workers who may be at increased risk of disease*

A. *Genetic screening*: Methods for detecting predisposing genetic traits.

Genetic characteristic
Sickle cell trait
Glucose-6-phosphate dehydrogenase (G-6-PD) deficiency
Serum alpha$_1$-antitrypsin (SAT) deficiency
Beta thalassemia trait
Alpha thalassemia trait
Human leukocyte antigens (HLAs)
Inadequate carbon disulfide metabolism
Isocyanate sensitivity
NADH dehydrogenase deficiency
Slow acetylation phenotype
Aryl hydrocarbon hydroxylase (AHH) enzyme inducibility

B. *Genetic monitoring*: Methods for detecting genetic damage and possible exposure hazards.

Monitoring test
Chromosomal aberrations
Sister chromatid exchanges
Mutagens in body fluids (blood, feces, urine)
Somatic cell damage (e.g., lymphocyte transformation, binding of mutagens to hemoglobin, chemically damaged DNA bases)
Germ cell damage (e.g., YFF test and LDH-X variants)
DNA, RNA, and protein adducts
Micronuclei

C. *Testing for teratogenic risk*: Women of childbearing age are excluded due to presumed risk of genetic damage to fetuses through women's job exposures. Indicators of possible fetal damage include results of both in vitro and in vivo laboratory tests.

Substances from which women have been excluded
Lead
Mercury
Benzene
Acrylamide
Vinyl chloride
Carbon disulfide
Carbon monoxide
Carbon tetrachloride
Dimethyl sulfate, and others

reduce exposures.[4] This type of test has also been used outside industry to detect chromosome damage among people who live near toxic waste dumps, such as the one at Love Canal.[5] In 1967 the Dow Chemical Company undertook genetic monitoring of all its production workers, and for ten years it proudly publicized the fact that the test results indicated low levels of genetic abnormalities. But in 1977, after Dow found high levels of chromosome breaks among workers exposed to two of the company's chemical products, the tests were stopped and company officials announced that the tests were unreliable.[6]

The third type of genetic testing is testing for teratogenic risk, in which laboratory cultures and animals are used to provide evidence of the effects of chemical exposure on humans. Laboratory tests can indicate that a substance could produce genetic damage to the fetus when a pregnant woman is exposed to certain chemical hazards, such as those listed at the bottom of Table 1. On evidence from such tests, many companies exclude all fertile women from working with particular toxic substances.[7] For example, General Motors has banned fertile women from work around lead; DuPont has barred women from working with seven chemicals. Beginning in 1978, American Cyanamid barred women of childbearing capacity from production work that entailed exposure to certain chemicals. As a result of this policy, five women chose to be sterilized so that the company would allow them to work in such jobs – which, as it turned out, the company later eliminated altogether.[8]

In all three types of genetic testing, the objective is to identify traits or changes that may increase workers' chances of contracting disease, and exclusion from jobs can result. All three are designed to identify those who are at greater risk because of past or potential exposure to hazardous substances. However, only one type – genetic monitoring – tends to focus attention on chemical risks to an exposed population as a whole. In contrast, genetic screening and teratogenicity testing entail differentiating inherently high-risk workers from those at lower risk. For this reason they are called susceptibility tests.

These three types of testing are most common in the chemical industry, but they also occur in the oil, automobile, steel, textile, electronics, and pharmaceutical industries. Many large companies and some medium-sized ones have the resources in research and testing programs, and the interest in frontiers of medical practice, to conduct their own genetic tests. Generally, they are also engaged in extensive medical surveillance programs. Having fewer such resources, medium-sized companies more often carry out simpler medical examinations. However, companies without their own genetic testing facilities may include these tests in their medical practices by working in conjunction with universities, hospitals, or research institutes. Other companies delegate their genetic testing to contract research firms.[9] The majority of smaller U.S. companies have had little direct experience with genetic screening or monitoring. They also tend to be less interested in advances in medical technology. Most of them simply rely on a medical history.[10]

For the most part, then, genetic screening for employee placement and retention – notably testing programs for sickle cell anemia and trait, SAT deficiency, HLAs, G-6-PD deficiency, and alpha and beta thalassemia – have been conducted by large and medium-sized companies. Monitoring for chromosomal abnormalities has also been found disproportionately in large companies.

Reliable figures indicating the extent of genetic testing and exclusionary practices are unavailable, in part because few company medical practices are made public. A rough indication of the prevalence of testing programs is provided by reports on genetic testing issued by the congressional Office of Technology Assessment. In a 1989 OTA survey, 33 of the 330 "Fortune 500" U.S. companies and major utilities reported using screening or monitoring currently or within the past 19 years. In addition, the OTA found in 1989 that 17 percent of 167 companies with over 10,000 employees and 6 percent of 470 companies with over 1,000 employees reported current or past testing. In a 1982 questionnaire, 59 of the 366 Fortune 500 industrial companies and certain major utilities stated that they were using, planning to use, or considering using in the next five years either screening or monitoring tests, or both.[11] Eighteen reported that they were currently conducting screening and monitoring practices, or had done so within the previous 12 years. Since these OTA studies relied on companies themselves to report their controversial testing policies fully, their findings probably underestimated the extent of testing and exclusionary practices.[12]

Fetal exclusion policies exist in businesses of all sizes, but they are more common in small companies than screening or monitoring, in part because they do not require the company to conduct any medical tests. Companines of any size can choose to bar women from specific jobs. According to the best estimates, at least 100,000 jobs nationwide have been closed to women because of such teratogenic risk policies, and the actual figure may be considerably higher.[13]

OPPOSING VIEWS OF SUSCEPTIBILITY TESTING

The strongest proponents of susceptibility testing have been physicians, researchers, and medical directors in industry.[14] Methods of testing for genetic markers and identifying high-risk workers have also received considerable attention at meetings of trade associations, occupational physicians, and other industry groups. In these circles, proponents of testing have argued that focusing on high-risk workers is effective preventive medicine, because it prevents health damage to individuals or their children by reducing the chemical exposure of certain workers considered to be at risk. Many studies have argued that specific tests offer companies simple and inexpensive means of taking immediate action through job placement, educational programs, or protective equipment to reduce the rate of adverse health effects from certain substances.[15] In the past few years, scientists have frequently assessed the reliability and efficiency of tests to identify workers at increased risk.[16]

This growing interest has by no means been confined to industry, however. Publications on occupational health and social policy regularly include articles on workers at high risk.[17] In the last fifteen years, many books and entire issues of journals have been devoted to the subject.[18] Extensive newspaper coverage of it has appeared in the *New York Times, Wall Street Journal, Washington Post*, and many smaller newspapers and periodicals.[19] It has been the focus of several major conferences as well as congressional hearings, including several days of hearings by a House Science and Technology subcommittee.[20] In addition, government funding for investigation of high-risk workers and research into the genetic bases of occupational disease has risen dramatically in recent years, which both reflects and reinforces the focus on those at high risk.

Despite their increasing use, genetic susceptibility tests have generated extensive controversy.[21] Some advocates of screening emphasize prospects for identifying high-risk workers and for advancing preventive medicine.[22] Others argue that new screening technologies have diverted scarce resources and attention from more effective occupational health practices.[23] Even proponents of the same test often focus on different functions the test performs and on different conditions under which the test should be applied.

Much of the scientific evidence for susceptibility to chronic health effects has received widely varying interpretations by scientific, corporate, union, governmental, legal, and medical authorities. Perspectives concerning the application of specific testing techniques differ sharply. Advocates of genetic screening claim that susceptibility to toxins has an established scientific basis in the case of G-6-PD, sickle cell trait and disease, and SAT deficiency. However, even the data on these heavily researched abnormalities are controversial.[24] A few scientists argue that genetic screening tests in fact do not predict occupational disease very well. Some have pointed to a growing body of evidence that male exposure to many toxic chemicals can cause sperm damage or mutagenic effects in men, so that fetal susceptibility policies that exclude only women from the workplace are discriminatory, leaving men and their offspring vulnerable to genetic damage. Evaluations of test accuracy in identifying individuals who are actually at higher risk vary greatly, and not everyone agrees that focusing on high-risk workers is appropriate in the first place.

Scientists generally argue that the technical nature of industrial genetics accounts for much of the controversy. They suggest that opponents of genetic screening condemn tests out of ignorance or an ideological stance against high technology. But the divergent views represent far more than differences in scientific training. Social and cultural conditions play a crucial hidden role in the debate. Individuals and groups tend to evaluate the use of genetic tests according to their social position and power interest. In other words, divergent perspectives on susceptibility policies reflect the different social locations and often conflicting interests of the various actors. Perhaps nowhere is this fact more apparent than in the case of groups centered around the industrial workplace – industrial managers, research scientists, occupational physicians, union officials, and employees.

Labor–management conflict

The most fundamental contrast in views exists between labor and management, for they assess genetic technology in opposite ways and use different criteria for program acceptability. Neither group is homogeneous, but certain views are clearly dominant in each. Among both groups, for example, views toward genetic monitoring tests are quite distinct from views toward genetic screening.[25] Each group favors the tests that the other group opposes (see Table 2).

As Table 2 indicates, labor is generally critical of genetic screening programs, seeing them as ineffective in identifying high-risk workers or in solving a significant proportion of occupational health problems.[26] Labor argues instead that attention should be shifted to reducing exposure hazards in the high-risk workplace.

17

Table 2. *Conflicting views of labor and industrial management toward genetic screening and genetic monitoring*

	Labor view	Industrial management view
	UNFAVORABLE	FAVORABLE
Genetic screening[a]	Genetic screening is ineffective for detecting significant risk. The dangers of discrimination and employment policies unfavorable to labor are considerable, as long as control over testing, employment decisions, and health information is retained by industrial management.	Screening is more useful than monitoring. Genetic screening enables companies to locate high-risk workers, and thus makes occupational medicine less expensive and more effective.
	FAVORABLE	UNFAVORABLE
Genetic monitoring[b]	Genetic monitoring can detect exposure hazards at low levels and without the need to rely on detection of clinical health effects. Monitoring should be used now for this purpose.	Monitoring tests are expensive and results are of uncertain value. Positive results associated with particular chemicals could lead to publicity damaging to industry.

[a] Screening for traits that may predispose workers to disease (such as sickle cell trait, alpha$_1$-antitrypsin, and G-6-PD).
[b] Monitoring for evidence of genetic damage, presumably from exposure to chemicals (damage such as chromosome breakage and sister chromatid exchange).
Sources: Interviews, literature review, and documentary research (see Appendix).

On the other hand, labor usually views genetic monitoring more favorably.[27] As the president of the AFL-CIO Industrial Union Department has stated:

The case for genetic monitoring is very different. . . . Ideally, such programs promise early warning of toxicity and early

detection of damaged and, therefore, high-risk populations. . . . The potential for the reduction of disease is so great
that a high national priority for rapid research and development of these techniques is justified.[28]

Several unions have advocated the use of chromosomal
studies to locate exposure problems and identify workers
who may be at increased risk for cancer and reproductive
effects. In several cases, labor has cooperated with genetic
monitoring studies by requesting or planning them. For example, the Oil, Chemical, and Atomic Workers International
Union requested that the governmental National Institute
for Occupational Safety and Health (NIOSH) conduct the
ethylene oxide genetic monitoring study undertaken in a
Texas plant.[29]

Although some managers and occupational physicians
have advocated genetic *screening* as a way of protecting individuals thought to be at increased risk, their response to
monitoring for health hazards is largely negative.[30] Corporate officials generally oppose using monitoring studies in
their medical programs. They cite three major reasons. First,
the clinical meaning of monitoring test results is ambiguous;
it is unclear what high rates of chromosomal abnormalities
mean for worker health. Second, positive test findings, even
though inconclusive, could result in political pressure to reduce workplace exposure or to expand government testing
requirements – in short, to stricter regulation. Third, employees could become unduly alarmed about their health
and their exposure to chemicals, or the public could become
unnecessarily aroused over working conditions and product
safety.[31]

The very different views of labor and management toward
genetic testing have been dramatically illustrated in the response to two scientific articles published in the same 1981
issue of the *Journal of Occupational Medicine*. In one article, Jill
Fabricant and Marvin Legator concluded that several techniques for genetic monitoring should be used immediately to
screen workers for damage from industrial chemicals. In the

other, Betty Dabney concluded that in no case should genetic monitoring be employed to test workers except on a very preliminary research basis. The two articles were presented without editorial comment, implicitly inviting readers to evaluate them on the basis of scientific merit alone. In the responses over the next few years, however, labor consistently favored the Fabricant and Legator article and management the Dabney article. A similar pattern exists with respect to the exclusion of fertile women from industrial jobs because of presumed risk to the fetus. Management tends to favor fetal exclusion policies and labor tends to oppose them. In the prevailing climate of scientific uncertainty, how can we explain the rise of susceptibility policies and the patterns of support for them?

My research suggests that ideological and social-structural factors strongly influence perspectives on the use of particular genetic tests. These factors include: values concerning acceptable risks, economic interests, ethnic and racial characteristics of the work force, gender, structures of decision making, and expectations concerning who will control testing programs and the genetic information they produce. Identifying such factors, which can explain patterns of support and opposition to genetic technology, is a major aim of this book.

Who are the workers at risk? By what methods should they be identified and protected? How should the scientific evidence be evaluated? Of what value are genetic screening and monitoring tests, and how should they be used in industrial medicine? This book examines the answers given by industrial physicians and medical directors, nonmedical corporate managers, union officials, industrial workers, scientists, and government officials. More significantly, it offers a sociological explanation for their conflicting answers, and thereby suggests a model for analyzing the social response to other biomedical technologies and for interpreting the genetic explanations offered for other types of variation in society.

Chapter 2

The rise of the genetic paradigm for occupational risk

The heredity/environment issue has become resolved in scientific minds.

Arno Motulsky
(Professor of Medicine and Genetics,
University of Washington)

I think we should do certain [genetic screening] tests because we can.

Paul Kotin
(as Medical Director of Manville Corporation)

RECENT scientific advances and dissatisfaction with existing interpretations of social problems have given genetic theories both a wider hearing and a firmer base of support. It is in the realm of occupational disease, where genetic and environmental conceptions of risk have vied for predominance, that the ascendance of the genetic paradigm has had the most far-reaching implications.

RECENT HISTORY OF ATTENTION
TO GENETIC RISK

One of the earliest proponents of identifying the susceptible worker was the prominent British biologist J. B. S. Haldane. In 1938, observing that potters died from bronchitis at eight times the rate of the general population, he wrote:

> The majority of potters do not die of bronchitis. It is quite possible that if we really understood the causation of this disease, we should find that only a fraction of potters are of a constitution which renders them liable to it. If so, we could eliminate potters' bronchitis by rejecting entrants into the pottery industry who are congenitally disposed to it.[1]

In the first half of the twentieth century, scientists and industry officials occasionally suggested links between workers' disease and predisposing abnormalities. Yet before the 1960s, with the exception of protectionist policies affecting women, concern about workplace health hazards seldom led to a focus on intrinsic characteristics of the individual. As in the case of infectious diseases – even those that were fairly rare – the emphasis was on the infectious agent, not on characteristics of those affected by disease.[2] Early in this century, for example, public health activists favored the concept of disease screening as part of their strategy for combatting tuberculosis, but they did not perceive the disease as one that afflicts only genetically predisposed individuals. Nor was it considered important to determine who was susceptible to measles or to polio so that individuals could be targeted for special preventive measures. The public health tra-

23

dition linked individual risk to social conditions that could be changed.[3]

In the 1960s and 1970s, however, locating genetic characteristics of the worker became a major policy issue and the focus of considerable research attention. Much of the data on genetic predisposition to disease began to come from the field of pharmacogenetics rather than from industry studies. Research on prescription drugs has indicated that biological variability can influence drug metabolism and provoke adverse reactions. Related research has studied the role of genetic constitution in producing different reactions to viruses and bacteria and in increasing risks of heart disease, cancer, and other illnesses.[4] Another area of proliferating genetic research examines variability in response to air pollution, cigarette smoke, and other environmental toxins. Differential susceptibility to chemical hazards has become a widely accepted concept.[5]

In the early 1960s, published evidence of individual traits that may predispose individuals to disease drew attention to special susceptibility.[6] The government scientists Stokinger and Mountain (1963) advocated susceptibility testing for job applicants, which they argued would prevent exposing workers at risk to chemical hazards. They announced: "This is preventive toxicology in its highest form; no previous single development in toxicology has opened such prospects for the medical supervision of workers" (p. 57). Since then, technologies for genetic testing in the workplace have advanced rapidly. New techniques for analyzing genetic abnormalities from blood and urine samples have offered greater possibilities for improving workers' health.[7] Government-sponsored projects within the National Academy of Sciences, the National Institutes of Health, and the National Science Foundation have been set up to study the technologies and to evaluate specific practices.[8] The National Cancer Institute funds the development of industrial genetic screening tests.[9] Genetics laboratories throughout the United States and Europe have engaged in research into links between specific inherited traits and susceptibility to illness. Entire professional conferences have been devoted to the high-risk worker.[10] In addition, biotechnology firms have intensified their research efforts toward identifying genetic markers for vulnerability to cancer and other diseases.[11] This burgeoning research activity draws even more attention to genetic predisposition and further increases pressure to fund susceptibility approaches to occupational disease.

In the case of genetic screening, concern with workers' predisposition is prompted in part by the discovery of *associations* between certain diseases and particular traits, which in turn sometimes come to be seen as *causes* of occupational illness. Examples of such associations reported in the scientific literature include the following. (1) People with SAT enzyme deficiency may have increased susceptibility to emphysema and chronic bronchitis under conditions of exposure to pulmonary irritants. (2) Exposure to certain hemolytic chemicals may trigger sickling crises among individuals with sickle cell trait. (3) Individuals with G-6-PD deficiency may be at greater risk of anemia or hemolytic crisis when exposed to oxidizing chemicals such as nitroamino and nitroaromatic compounds. (4) Aryl hydrocarbon hydroxylase deficiency appears to increase susceptibility to lung cancer among those encountering specific industrial pollutants. (5) Over fifty diseases have been associated with human leukocyte antigens.[12] The major emphasis in genetic screening has been on heterozygous carriers – individuals who carry a single gene that may produce disease under specific environmental conditions.[13] The discovery of these associations, along with more general developments in genetic technologies and biological explanations, has given strong support to the susceptibility perspective.

FAITH IN GENETIC TECHNOLOGY

Proponents of genetic testing assume that these scientific discoveries will improve the human condition, particularly through disease prevention and protective policies. Reports of groundbreaking genetic discoveries and advances in DNA technology have fostered great faith, even blind faith, in the promise of genetics.[14] Scientists allow their excitement over the science of genetics to convince them that it will make a major contribution to occupational health. They extend their belief in the great medical potential of genetics to the workplace. Thus, a physiologist, discussing screening for genetic markers, has said that we now have "a block of genetic information that can be used to create a new chapter in preventive medicine."[15] Similarly, a university scientist argues: "It's a travesty, given our medical knowledge, that we give so little attention to individual susceptibility. We shouldn't ignore the life-threatening problems that confront particular people when exposed."[16] And a geneticist, calling susceptibility testing the wave of the future, has said: "We cannot stop progress. This knowledge is going to come out and it may have very important preventive medicine implications."[17]

When scientists set up criteria for recommending testing programs, they select genetic markers that they believe provide a meaningful basis for estimating an employee's vulnerability to illness. For example, Cooper (1973) suggests that screening tests must meet three conditions to be considered for application in industry: (1) the abnormality that the test detects must be one with a relatively high prevalence; (2) the abnormality must be compatible with an apparently normal life until an environmental stress supervenes; and (3) there should be a logical relationship between the abnormality and potential occupational exposures.[18] Stokinger and Scheel (1973) add a fourth criterion to Cooper's three prerequisites for susceptibility testing: There must be knowledge of detection methods that are relatively simple and inexpensive. On the basis of these criteria, they recommend industrial testing for five disorders: hypersensitivity to organic isocyanates, hyper-reactivity to carbon disulfide exposure, sickle cell trait and anemia, SAT deficiency, and G-6-PD deficiency.[19] They advocate the industrial application of genetic screening "for bettering job assignment, improving coverage of the industrial air limits, and hence reducing risk to worker health."[20]

Scientists still frequently cite these early criteria as conditions that genetic tests should meet, and they favor or reject the industrial application of specific tests on the basis of them.[21] Criteria of this type generally focus on the predictive value of existing screening tests, especially their sensitivity and specificity.[22]

Despite the enthusiasm that often surrounds prospects for susceptibility policies, genetic screening for traits or the exclusion of fertile women may not, in fact, be truly protective. Identifying workers at risk through susceptibility tests has not been very successful to date. Screening for genetic markers in particular still has very limited effectiveness as preventive medicine. Very few diseases and substances have markers clear enough to warrant industrial use, and little is known about the specific biological mechanisms through which chemicals affect individuals. The capacity of screening programs to identify a susceptible segment of the population accurately is questionable.[23]

From time to time, scientists express doubts about the technical capabilities of specific tests and challenge applications of screening in industry.[24] Yet their skepticism about particular tests or employment applications has not diminished the overall support for susceptibility policies.

Edward Calabrese (1984), for example, goes through genetic factors one by one in his study of susceptibility traits affecting vulnerability to environmental contaminants, evaluating the scientific evidence for each. In the detail of his elaborate text, Calabrese describes frailties of the scientific state of knowledge. He refers to industrial testing programs and scientific recommendations for workplace screening that are based on speculative linkages between genetic characteristics and disease susceptibility. Limitations such as confounding variables, murky epidemiologic studies, and the lack of precise dose–response relationships make the scientific basis for genetic screening appear altogether uncertain.

Despite this, Calabrese presents an impressive table of fifty genetic risk factors, titled "Identification and Quantification of Genetic Factors Affecting Susceptibility to Environmental Agents."[25]

In the text of his book, Calabrese concludes that there is little direct evidence of workers' susceptibility. For example, he argues that "no direct evidence" exists that individuals deficient in NADH dehydrogenase are at increased risk to industrial chemicals. He says only that there is a "good theoretical likelihood" that individuals deficient in NADH dehydrogenase represent a potential industrial high-risk group, owing to data pointing to drugs that put them at risk. Nevertheless, he includes NADH dehydrogenase deficiency in his table of fifty genetic risk factors. Sickle cell trait also appears in the table as a genetic factor affecting susceptibility to environmental agents, even though in his text Calabrese notes that the scientific evidence regarding the trait is "controversial and unresolved."

Likewise, Calabrese concludes in the text that for lack of supporting evidence, individuals with erythrocyte porphyria are only "theoretically at increased risk to lead-induced toxicity." Nevertheless, this condition finds its way onto the table as a factor identifying a high-risk group susceptible to environmental agents. The same pattern holds for other genetic characteristics listed as susceptibility factors in the table. These include individuals who are slow acetylators, and thus said to be at "potential increased risk" of disease, although epidemiologic studies are lacking; individuals who are cystic fibrosis heterozygotes, for whom various reports only "suggest the possibility" of predisposition to pulmonary disease; and those deficient in sulfite oxidase, for whom Calabrese hypothesizes sulfur dioxide may present a genetic hazard.

Although the science of susceptibility is distinctly uncertain and its claims widely disputed, Calabrese's table makes it appear that scientists can already identify fifty high-risk groups for whom environmental agents present a problem. His frequent expressions of enthusiasm for concepts of genetic susceptibility tend to strengthen the claims of others that susceptibility policies are truly effective.[26] Moreover, the book is widely cited as evidence of genetic predisposition to workplace chemicals.

Clearly, ambiguous data do not deter scientists from supporting susceptibility testing. They applaud the orientation toward high-risk workers even as they criticize current testing. In part because of excitement over the promise of genetic research, then, scientists and corporate officials are generally enthusiastic about the use of genetic screening in industry.[27] Supporters of susceptibility testing share this enthusiasm, in part because they usually evaluate tests by referring to ideal circumstances and potential applications, not to the reality of workplace medical programs.

BIOLOGICAL EXPLANATIONS FOR HUMAN VARIABILITY: THE NEW GENETIC ORTHODOXY

Recent decades have seen genetic explanations for social phenomena gain a popularity they have not had since World War II. Troy Duster (1990) describes an explosion of popular and scientific journal articles that link several types of social deviance to genetic factors. For the period 1976 to 1982, he finds a 231 percent increase in articles tracing crime,[28] mental illness,[29] low intelligence,[30] and alcoholism to genetic traits.[31] His finding is based on a review of the *Reader's Guide to Periodical Literature* for that period. Between 1983 and 1988, he reports, articles that cite a genetic basis for crime appeared more than four times more frequently than in the previous decade. Strikingly, the data base for much of this literature on genetics and social deviance is institutional registries from the early and mid-1900s rather than scientific breakthroughs in the field of molecular genetics. Other scientists trace particular social problems to genetic roots. Analysts have offered biological explanations for a broad range of behavior, from schizophrenia, aggression, and gender differences to chronic shyness. Scientists have used twin, adoption, and family studies in attempts to demonstrate the genetic character of behavioral disorders such as depression, mania, alcoholism, agoraphobia, panic disorder, antisocial personality, and suicidal tendencies.[32]

Despite proliferating claims linking genes to behavioral disorders, major limitations continue to beset the literature on genetic sources of social problems. Studies of genetic causation have not defined the biological mechanisms of the diseases in question, or explained modes of inheritance, or located genes on specific chromosomes. In addition, much of the genetic causation literature is based on correlational studies that identify similar behavior patterns in adoptive twins raised in separate families, yet these studies typically overlook similar social and environmental influences that are shared even by twins reared apart. A passion for genetic theories often overshadows the weak biological evidence in many such studies.[33]

What this amounts to is the rise of a new genetic orthodoxy. Instead of sociobiology or eugenics, advocates now use terms like "ecogenetics" and "hypersusceptibility" to refer to genetic influences.[34] They acknowledge that both genetic constitution and environmental factors contribute to disease. They believe that in doing so, they are deflecting criticism from environmentalists, social determinists, and others concerned with industrial influences – or more broadly, all social influences – on health. But after conceding that disease is partly environmental, they proceed to explain disease causation largely in a genetic framework. Industry officials and scientists who advocate susceptibility policies frequently adopt this way of thinking and terminology of the new genetic orthodoxy in describing these policies.

Those who subscribe to the new orthodoxy generally do not articulate the susceptibility approach in exclusively genetic terms, for that would trigger criticism by making them appear to be unbalanced or out of date. Thus, while emphasizing genetics, they give a nod to environmental factors, often by way of claiming that for the sophisticated, the nature–nurture controversy has been resolved. For example, in his concluding remarks at a 1983 conference on "Genetic

Variability in Responses to the Environment," one scientist stated: "We have been blessed here with relatively little of the old controversy of 'nature versus nurture.' I hope that dichotomization is finally behind us and that now, as this meeting very nicely reflects, attention can be focused on interactions and mechanisms of interactions."[35] Another scientist, discussing genetic susceptibility policies at a National Academy of Sciences conference, has deplored the influence of "people who are radically against the idea of genetic variation in the population and set up an extreme egalitarianism which is ruinous to very large numbers of people."[36]

The fascination with genetic contributions to disease often diverts interest away from evidence of social and environmental influences. In the case of respiratory ailments, for example, scientists stress the role of $alpha_1$-antitrypsin enzyme deficiency in producing chronic obstructive pulmonary disease (COPD). They focus on individuals who may be genetically predisposed to lung ailments, even though environmental factors have been shown to be correlated with COPD. Although the precise relationships between these factors are unclear, there is no doubt that respiratory disease reflects the influence of socioeconomic status, heavy coffee drinking, smoking, workplace toxins, and air pollution.[37] In other words, individuals may be socially and environmentally susceptible to lung disease. Even in the case of diseases such as PKU that are widely thought to be "genetic," individuals suffer symptoms only when they encounter uncontrolled high levels of specific substances such as phenylalanine in the environment.[38] In this sense, these are clearly "environmental" diseases.

Similarly, spina bifida is described as a genetic disorder even though it is found disproportionately in industrial areas with high levels of toxic exposures that can affect the central nervous system. Environmental factors such as poor diet and low socioeconomic status raise the risk of spina bifida defects, and vitamin treatments reduce the risk. Nevertheless, the disease is conceived as genetic in character and made a target of public genetic screening programs. Re-

search effort, resources, and policy recommendations follow.[39]

In view of the considerable evidence of environmental
health hazards that confront workers in general, the emphasis on genetic markers is particularly remarkable in the area
of occupational risk.[40] Most OSHA standards require industries to apply medical surveillance procedures, which include taking a family medical history. When company physicians record this history, they may interpret the presence of
lung cancer or heart disease in a worker's family as evidence
of genetic abnormality, and therefore as a reason to screen
the worker from a job. Of course, the record may also indicate that the worker's relatives were exposed to chemical
toxins and other environmental hazards.[41] Indeed, one clear
manifestation of the stratification of the work force is that the
children of industrial production workers are often production workers themselves.

Scientists and corporate managers may acknowledge that
industrial chemical hazards exist. But this only makes their
claims concerning genetic risk seem more credible. Even if
workers have a trait that renders them more vulnerable to
disease, referring to their increased risk of damage from occupational exposures as a genetic problem masks the environmental components of disease.

SCIENTIFIC MODELS AND THE
TECHNOPHOBIA ARGUMENT

The strong belief that science in general promotes human
welfare, that genetic technology furthers scientific progress,
and that genetic susceptibility tests are scientifically evaluated to ensure validity and reliability, helps explain why
many advocates of screening react so negatively to criticism
from industrial workers and labor officials. Their responses
amount to variations on a theme: Nonscientists fear science
and its practitioners, for a variety of reasons – ignorance,
lack of scientific education, misunderstanding of the benev-

olent intentions behind medical surveillance procedures, mistrust of management, and above all an unsophisticated fear of technology, fueled by sensational reports in the mass media. Interestingly, scientists accuse labor of technophobia, even though union officials and employees have argued that another type of new technology – genetic *monitoring* – should be used in the workplace instead of screening. In rejecting this position, however, scientists attribute labor's attitude to factors other than technophobia, such as political ideology and antimanagement hostility.[42]

Critics of susceptibility policies who are not identified with labor generally speak from one of two perspectives. In one of those, legal scholars, medical ethics specialists, and research scientists maintain that a screening test's value should not be assessed according to technical criteria alone, but also according to criteria for "informed decisions," which establish requirements for voluntary tests, for the confidentiality of genetic information, and for counseling and education programs.[43] Evaluating industrial screening by these criteria leads to conclusions different from those reached by scientists who analyze testing largely in terms of predictiveness. While a test's level of prediction and its linkage to common exposure problems may make its use advisable under a technical set of conditions, the "informed decisions" criteria may advise against a testing program that does not incorporate informed consent and related provisions protecting the individuals screened.

The other perspective from which critics evaluate the potential of genetic susceptibility testing focuses on occupational health priorities. From this point of view, the important question is different: Given limited resources, what are the most serious problems to be solved? Critics in this camp conclude that the available data are insufficient to warrant job transfers for any genetic trait. They reject genetic screening in industry categorically, maintaining that resources are better spent controlling exposure hazards. Two academic scientists put the case this way:

I am unaware of any real promise for identifying genetic markers. While these matters are of theoretical interest, the prospect of using these tests to prevent occupational cancer is laughable. Especially in view of the overwhelming evidence of detrimental risks that affect very large numbers of workers, these genetic tests and traits appear trivial indeed.[44]

The focus on genetic screening is a tremendous waste of resources.[45]

Both of these approaches – "informed decisions" and "occupational health priorities" – take exception to the predominant technical model and are implicitly critical of the genetic paradigm.

Scientists who hold the dominant "technical criteria" view of genetic testing believe that critics of genetic screening who insist upon tightened informed consent provisions are unduly wary. They generally oppose highlighting political power, economic interests, and other social factors in evaluating applications of technologies. Focusing on social and political concerns appears to them to be a maverick perspective. In fact, however, their own judgments also have social and political dimensions, although these are almost entirely implicit.[46] Scientists who are not considered "pro labor" may be, in fact, "pro industrial management." They often undertake research or submit public testimony on industry's behalf. Frances Lynn (1986) finds that among occupational health scientists, scientific views are closely linked to political values and place of employment. In areas of great scientific uncertainty, scientists choose models and assumptions that correlate strongly with personal political beliefs. Further, compared with scientists in government and academia, scientists employed by industry take positions on questions of health risk very similar to those of corporate executives. This pattern holds true even after controlling for the influence of variables such as age, sex, geographic region, religion, and family background.[47]

In their attempts to discredit opposing perspectives, scientists seldom admit such sources of bias, often portraying themselves as the only objective judge of ambiguous data. They assume the stance of balance and wisdom that adds to the force of their scientific expertise. A good example of this process at work may be found in the recent controversy over the role of genetic predisposition, tobacco, and jobs in producing cancer. In a report on cancer causation, Richard Doll and Richard Peto acknowledge uncertainties in the available data; but they dismiss those who interpret the data as indicating high rates of work-related cancer as misinformed laypersons who "wish to emphasize the importance of the control of occupational and environmental pollutants" and "wish to believe ill of the modern world." They refer to the prominent authors of a major report on occupational health risk as "research workers" rather than scientists.[48] More bluntly, they charge that the authors of that report wrote it "for political rather than scientific purposes."[49] As this case suggests, scientists feel free to accuse critics of new medical technologies of being antiscientific, ideologically driven, or self-interested even though their own judgments of these technologies may allow conjecture, extrapolation, blanket endorsement of the screening approach, or strong identification with managerial goals.

This skewed conception of bias, directed against those whose views on the use of technologies are based in part on explicitly nontechnical grounds or are consistent with labor's perspective, is widespread among scientists. It also can be seen in the often-cited work of Mary Douglas and Aaron Wildavsky (1982), who point mainly to cultural factors that compel critics of new complex technologies to organize in opposition to them.[50] Douglas and Wildavsky characterize opponents of corporate policies as ideologically motivated. They emphasize the weaknesses of scientific studies of risk, and portray evaluations of hazards as reflections of cultural biases. In their view, even those whose concerns about chemical hazards are based on scientific evidence are likely to be misguided and irrational. They also point to what they call a "sectarian" orientation of those who believe that current risks from industrial production are substantial. Yet they do not consider what cultural factors contribute to the confidence that scientists, managers, physicians, and others have in the safety of the industrial environment.[51] Their analysis also misperceives the power dynamics in society that give corporate officials much greater control over knowledge and decisions about risks than labor leaders and workers.

Most scientists have difficulty discussing bias publicly, in part because they believe that to do so might be to discredit the objectivity of the scientific enterprise. And of course, a public discussion of bias in science might reflect unfavorably on their own work as well.[52] Nevertheless, the biases and affiliations of scientists must be taken into account in order to understand the controversy that surrounds genetic testing. Sensitivity to bias is especially appropriate in this area, where the scientific and technological questions are linked to public policy and to social issues of health, decision making, employment, and labor-management relations.

Investigating genetic factors in work-related illness may help prevent disease among employees or inhibit its development. But beyond the issue of the predictive efficacy of genetic explanations lies the question of ideology. As we have seen, the genetic paradigm for explaining workers' disease is in fact an ideological orientation that has gained considerable power to shape conceptions of occupational risk.

Chapter 3

Competing conceptions of safety

High-risk workers or high-risk work?

The dance of death is not random. . . . The adage, "what is one man's meat is another man's poison," is a truism wrapped in genetic foil.

Alexander G. Bearn
(Senior Vice President for Medical and Scientific Affairs,
Merck Sharp and Dohme International)

Now when worker health problems develop, some of us are being told that it's not the dirty workplace that causes the problem, but it's who our ancestors are. The company explains that they're going to protect us by imposing a genetic scarlet letter on us, which will bar us because supposedly we're more susceptible to these poisons that the employer himself introduces into the workplace. So we have this susceptibility factor, which is part of the whole thrust of saying it's the victim whose fault it is by virtue of their genes.

Anthony Mazzocchi
(as Director of Health and Safety, the Oil, Chemical, and
Atomic Workers International Union)

Competing conceptions

I N *Illness as Metaphor*, Susan Sontag (1977) gives an elo-
quent account of the social use of myths about illness –
tuberculosis in the nineteenth century, and cancer in the
twentieth. As we approach the end of this century, the worker susceptible to chemical hazards may be seen as a powerful
symbol of the quest for an individual, genetic explanation for
diseases suffered by many. But that quest is also an ideological extension of a social and political belief in the safety and
benefit of industrial chemicals. The social ills of chemical
hazards are projected onto susceptible individuals, in patterns that reflect dynamics of the workplace and the broader
social structure.

The genetic paradigm in occupational health has been
more appealing to industrial managers and occupational
physicians than to industrial workers and union officials. An
important factor contributing to the rise of the susceptibility
thesis in industry, and to its selective appeal, is the conflict in
ideological orientations toward the extent and locus of risk
on the job. Contrasting assumptions about workplace safety
have been central to the controversy over susceptibility.

Genetic testing and exclusionary practices reflect management's interest in finding individual rather than industrial
causes of problems. Identifying individuals in the work force
who are at risk can be another way of saying that conditions
are in fact safe for most workers. This safety component of
susceptibility policies is the basis for some of the most
sweeping claims by advocates and some of the strongest
objections by critics.

THE WORKPLACE IS SAFE: EMPLOYERS MINIMIZE OCCUPATIONAL RISK

The controversy over genetic technologies parallels the debate over the nature of occupational health hazards themselves. Corporate managers and other proponents of
susceptibility policies tend to believe that health hazards
have been overestimated and overregulated.[1] They generally
believe that risk at work accounts for only a small proportion

Table 3. *Estimates of the contribution of occupational hazards to cancer incidence*

Percent of cancer incidence attributed to work hazards	Source
1 or 2 percent	Handler (1979)
4 or 5 percent	Doll (1981)
5 percent	Peto (1980)
1 to 10 percent	Reinhardt (1978)
Greater than 20 percent	Swartz and Epstein (1981)
From 10 to 33 percent or perhaps higher	Stallones and Downs (1979)
Up to 20 to 40 percent	Bridbord et al. (1978)

of chronic illness in the United States. Thus we see a major effort by industry to show that cancer, for example, is due not to jobs or the environment but to life-style, genetic factors, and naturally occurring carcinogens.[2]

Tracing cancer to its causes – whether in occupation, smoking, or diet – is charged with controversy. Methods for establishing occupational causality vary widely. For cancer incidence, estimates of the proportion due to workplace conditions range from 1 percent to up to 40 percent (see Table 3).[3] Epidemiological and other evidence linking disease to work exposure is complex and equivocal. Doll and Peto, for instance, refer even to their own estimates of work-related cancer as "informed guesses," arguing that deficiencies in data on current exposure and health effects necessarily lead to "rather arbitrary" estimates for environmental carcinogens.[4] Like many others, however, they nevertheless adhere to specific percentages in their arguments for disease etiology.

Analysts who maintain that work exposure is a relatively insignificant factor (1–5 percent) in producing cancer generally use models and other research practices that contribute to the low figures they give for workplace hazards. Three of these practices involve highlighting smoking effects and excluding nonwhites and old people from cancer studies.

First, researchers who cite low percentages of cancer due to occupation typically trace a strong causal link between cancer and tobacco smoking while ignoring ways in which occupation confounds the impact of smoking. There is evidence that smokers are more heavily concentrated in occupations with exposure to carcinogenic hazards. Those who believe work contributes little to cancer causation seldom build such confounding effects into their models. Therefore, they are likely to hold smoking responsible for cancers of the lung and bladder, which are vulnerable to both industrial and nonindustrial exposures.[5]

Second, scientists who see a low incidence of occupational cancer often exclude data on nonwhites from their analysis. Peto (1980) argues that limiting cancer studies to whites is a good idea because improved medical care and cancer identification have made cancer mortality rates appear high for blacks and other "previously poor people" whose cancers have gone undetected due to inferior health care. However, findings by Percy and others (1981) indicate that race does not affect the accuracy of cancer mortality statistics. Improvements in medical care have been uneven, with the quality of health care facilities and services actually declining for many nonwhites. Further, nonwhites perform a higher proportion of hazardous jobs, so that restricting studies to whites falsely depresses occupational cancer rates.[6]

The third research practice is excluding individuals over 65 from calculations of cancer causation on the grounds that mortality figures for individuals under 65 are likely to be more accurate.[7] Yet approximately half of all U.S. cancer occurs in individuals over age 65. Excluding people over 65 removes a large group in which work-related cancer is particularly likely to occur, because of longer exposure histories and latency periods for tumor induction.[8] Since the 1960s, the chemical production of carcinogens and other substances capable of causing chronic health effects has grown substantially. Age-adjusted cancer incidence and mortality rates also have risen over this period. Smoking accounts for only part of these increases.[9] Given the time span between carcinogenic exposure and disease manifestation, the effects of recent production increases of environmental carcinogens will probably not be clear until the late 1990s and beyond, and those effects will be most pronounced in older people. By omitting people over 65 from analysis, excluding nonwhites, and ignoring occupational factors that confound disease rates among smokers, researchers can produce statistics that suggest low work-induced disease rates. Reversing these omissions reveals higher levels of occupational cancer.

With a broad range of estimates available to them, then, corporate officials generally accept the lowest estimate of cancer traceable to workplace hazards.[10] They do the same with regard to birth defects. For example, two scientists at Dow Chemical (Rao and Schwetz, 1981) contend that there has been no significant increase since 1970 in the proportion of birth defects related to chemicals and industrial exposures, which they claim has always been small. As we shall see in Chapters 5 and 6, powerful economic, legal, and regulatory pressures impel company physicians and others in industry to minimize the extent of occupational illness, preferably by identifying a worker's ailment as stemming from personal habits or genetic constitution. In general, company managers believe that chemical risks are less dangerous than does the public. According to a 1980 Harris survey, corporate executives are three times more likely than either the public or federal regulators to say that there is less risk from chemicals today than twenty years ago.[11] This pattern holds true for scientists in industry as well. Lynn's survey (1986) found that scientists in industry are three times more likely than university and government scientists to believe that Americans are overly sensitive to risk and want to be protected from nearly all dangers. This belief that risks from chemical exposures at work are minimal and declining bolsters the susceptibility thesis that the industrial workplace is safe for all but a few.

SAFETY AND SUSCEPTIBILITY

In 1938, the geneticist J. B. S. Haldane wrote: "There are two sides to most of these questions involving unfavourable environments. Not only could the environment be improved, but susceptible individuals could be excluded" (1938, p. 180). While highlighting genetic susceptibility, he nevertheless argued that industrial hygiene standards were "shamefully low." A few decades later, however, most advocates of genetic screening would conclude that the environmental dimension of workplace risk was fairly unimportant. They typically would find that the environment had been improved sufficiently, leaving only abnormally susceptible individuals in danger.

The idea that normal working conditions are safe for everyone except the susceptible can be found in scientific journal articles and books that argue the merits of genetic screening, in conferences and hearings at which medical testing is debated, and in statements by the numerous types of social actors who recommend susceptibility policies for workplace use. This conception of safety also can be seen in the classical medical definition of special susceptibility to illness, sometimes called "hypersusceptibility": "A condition of inordinate or abnormally increased susceptibility to chemicals, infective agents, or other agents which in the normal individual are entirely innocuous."[12] Note that here, chemicals to which only "susceptible" workers are considered vulnerable are assumed to be innocuous. Indeed, this assumption pervades much of the discussion about genetic testing and exclusionary practices in industry.

Proponents of susceptibility screening

Scientists and company officials who advocate genetic screening say that identifying susceptible workers will help protect the whole working population, since only these few individuals are at risk from exposure levels below those that protect everyone else. A former corporate medical director of Celanese, at congressional hearings on genetic testing, articulates this view of the high-risk worker's unique vulnerability to otherwise tolerable industrial exposures: "Concern for an individual who is known to be hypersusceptible to adverse effects from any agent requires protection from exposure beyond that which normal individuals may tolerate readily."[13] A physiology professor at Harvard Medical School concurs with this emphasis on the unusual worker at risk:

> [W]hat we are trying to do, I think, is to explore ways in which genetic information can be used to recognize the occasional person who is outside the normal range of susceptibility and therefore should have any of another kind of job, but not exposure to that particular chemical to which he reacts peculiarly.[14]

The key safety ideas are: the *occasional* person who is outside the *normal* range of susceptibility who reacts *peculiarly*.[15]

An important implication of genetic screening is pointed out by two of its earliest advocates, Stokinger and Mountain: genetic tests enable occupational physicians to rule out work exposures as the cause of disease among employees. They wrote in 1967:

> With specific tests available, the industrial physician is in an advantageous position to decide whether a claimed case of emphysema is job-connected or not. . . . Hypersusceptibility tests are useful in predicting the direct, or indirect but additive effects of some of these chemicals, or in distinguishing between effects due to chemical exposure vs. congenital defect.[16]

They went even further, suggesting that genetic susceptibility will largely explain employee illnesses that arise: "As our understanding of the relationship of disease manifestations to genetic abnormalities grows, a large part of our past bewilderment and surprise at finding workers claiming injury to health under conditions known to be protective will disappear."[17] Thus, injured workers' claims linking their diseases to occupational exposures need not challenge the assumption that current conditions protect normal employees. Greater attention to genetic susceptibility can allow us to remain confident that working conditions are safe.

Chemical safeguards and workers at risk

The focus on the susceptible worker is part of a larger effort to demonstrate that the workplace is safe without stricter regulation. Screening advocates believe that existing government standards such as "threshold limit values" adequately protect all but the unusual worker at risk. Threshold limit values (TLVs) are industry standards for chemicals set by the private ACGIH health organization and in many cases adopted by OSHA.[18] The assumption behind TLVs is that they establish concentration levels of workplace substances to which "healthy" workers may be exposed for a lifetime without becoming ill. Employers, in particular, maintain that most workers are safe once these standards are maintained, and that restricting industrial exposures any further is therefore unnecessary. It was early scientific proponents of screening who proposed this link between TLVs and susceptibility policies. In 1967 Stokinger and Mountain wrote: "Medical advances in the last few years have revealed ways of identifying those presently not fully covered by the threshold limits."[19] Thus it is assumed that if workers *do* develop adverse health effects, these must have been caused by the less protective conditions of many years ago, by non-industrial causes, or by special susceptibility.

Threshold limit values have been the subject of considerable debate, however. Supporters have argued that carcinogens and other disputed substances are safe for normal workers at or below the already low TLV exposure levels. Opponents have argued that no safe exposure level can exist for a carcinogen; that zero exposure should be the goal; and that all persons, not only the susceptible, are at risk from these chemicals.[20] Representatives of organized labor have generally been among the opponents. As a national health and safety official with the AFL-CIO has argued: "Because there are no thresholds for carcinogens, employers are not eliminating the risk by excluding workers considered susceptible."[21]

In recent years, support for the TLV concept has declined, due in part to mounting evidence of cancer risks at very low exposure levels.[22] Lynn's (1986) survey of scientists in industry, universities, and government reveals that whereas 80 percent of scientists in industry agree that thresholds exist for carcinogens, only 37 percent of government scientists and 61 percent of university scientists agree. Some industry officials, in semantic retreat, now maintain that while effective threshold levels may not exist, at least workers will suffer no "significant risk" unless they are susceptible.

Others who support the susceptibility thesis shift their argument to the economic realm. They argue that in the case of toxic chemicals, it is economically and technologically impossible to eliminate exposure. They discount the possibility of substituting safer chemicals or adopting new control technology. Industry, they claim, cannot afford to protect the vulnerable and survive in a competitive corporate environment. There is no doubt that in certain cases, employers might indeed be strained financially if required to reduce exposure levels.[23] But the industry claim is often made as a sweeping general argument: Government regulation and industry standards cannot become more restrictive without putting a great many companies out of business. Employers assert that if they pay increased attention to the few susceptible workers, the coverage of current safeguards could become complete.

Cases of safety claims

If management considers the workplace safe for "normal" workers, then if employees become sick, it must be because they were individually susceptible to that sickness. The focus is on individuals who get cancer, not on industrial poisons that may cause the disease. For example, when industrial workers in a petrochemical plant in Texas discovered eighteen brain tumors within their workforce, one scientist remarked: "Why those eighteen? You need to identify groups of workers at risk."[24] This scientist did not ask why there were eighteen instead of none; he asked why *those* eighteen. In fact, nobody has yet determined why those eighteen individuals, and not others, developed brain tumors. Nevertheless, proponents of susceptibility testing assume that those people must have had something in common beyond the workplace exposure. And if you believe that only certain types of workers will have a problem, you can believe that the others are safe.

Another example of the safety emphasis implicit in the susceptibility perspective may be taken from a large textile firm. Cotton dust is widely believed to be hazardous, and the federal Occupational Safety and Health Administration (OSHA) has set exposure limits. But a corporate official in Burlington Industries, in discussing the company's medical program, stated that only 2 percent of the work force are vulnerable to cotton dust, and that they are protected by not being allowed to work in textile industry jobs with exposure to cotton dust.[25] Clearly, this is also intended to mean that 98 percent of the workers are safe when exposed to cotton dust.

A third example is the case of susceptibility policies affecting fertile women. Companies can identify such women as high risk, just as they screen for sickle cell trait and G-6-PD deficiency. Besides expressing concern for protecting the fetus and avoiding lawsuits for fetal damage, saying that women of childbearing capacity are at risk is another way of saying that the remaining work force is safe once fertile women are eliminated. Yet, as we will see in Chapter 4, there are male reproductive hazards – including sperm damage, low fertility, and birth defects – which are in no way removed by excluding women.

47

PROBLEMS WITH THE FOCUS ON
HIGH-RISK WORKERS

Susceptibility tests and exclusionary policies go beyond the scientific evidence on which proponents claim these practices are based. Problems of evidence, accuracy, and industrial application reduce the medical effectiveness of genetic screening. They also limit the effectiveness of susceptibility policies for fetal hazards. However, the weak association between worker characteristics and occupational hazards has not prevented companies from testing and excluding workers. Proponents of genetic screening and fetal exclusion in industry tend to overlook or attempt to explain away several important characteristics of these practices.

Tautological arguments

Screening advocates claim that existing working conditions assure protection of all workers except the susceptible. This perspective sometimes takes the form of tautological arguments: Those who are susceptible develop disease, and those who do develop disease must have an abnormal predisposing factor and therefore must be susceptible.

Polarized categories

The second limitation of susceptibility policies is the difficulty of differentiating low-risk from high-risk groups. Even when the spectrum of response suggests no clear method for doing so, supporters of genetic screening and fetal exclusion tend to adopt polarized categories of risk and safety. Yet these categories are neither polarized nor distinct. Susceptibility policies that focus on heterozygous carriers frequently rely on vague associations between biological traits, disease, and chemical exposures. Differentiating workers who are at risk from those not at risk, or those who are sick from those who are well, or even those who have a trait from those who do not, is typically a murky process.

Only a few genetic characteristics allow for nearly binary judgments as to whether or not a person has a specific condition. Sickle cell anemia, or hemoglobin S, is such a case. Hemoglobin electrophoresis testing allows one to determine with considerable confidence that a person has sickle cell anemia or does not. But even in these relatively clear, usually homozygous cases, ambiguities abound.[26] For example, the extent to which a person will be affected, and whether testing or interpretation errors affect the outcome, are often unclear.[27]

Most genetic traits present even greater difficulties in making distinctions. Testing for single gene disorders generally relies on quantitative, not qualitative, differences in genetic material, with uncertainties and overlap between those considered heterozygotes and those considered normal. The distinctions rely on statistical probabilities. The best the tests can do is show that someone may be at somewhat greater risk for one type of ailment when exposed to one chemical agent or group of chemicals. What if 49 percent of workers are at higher risk or sicker than 51 percent because of biological characteristics, work exposures, medical history, health background, and other factors? How can one differentiate clearly between low risk and high risk? Where is the dividing line in the continuum of vulnerability? The susceptibility perspective frequently avoids the complexity of these questions by arbitrarily identifying high-risk workers and assuming that they alone are at risk.

Limited predictiveness

Current screening tests suffer from both narrow applicability and low levels of predictiveness for disease.[28] Many of the traits screened for are rare. Those who are identified as high-risk workers infrequently develop ailments. The relationship between specific traits and the exposure problems that workers confront is often unclear. Indeed, most current tests are insensitive to industrial health hazards. A university scientist who is a specialist in the health effects of mineral dusts such as asbestos and silica highlights the difficulty of establishing relationships between biological factors and susceptibility to occupational hazards. In the case of mineral dusts, he explains:

> While certain immunologic markers are noted with increased prevalence in workers who have mineral dust diseases, there is no evidence that these serve to predict the condition rather than appearing after the disease is well established. . . . [T]his is a problem in a number of instances. There may be a marker. The question is, does that marker pre-exist – that is, predate the onset of exposures, or is it simply an attendant consequence of the effects of exposure?[29]

Another factor limiting the usefulness of screening tests is that many of the tests produce high rates of false positives. This leads individuals who in fact do not have the predisposing factor to be classified inaccurately as high risk and then excluded from a job on that basis.

At risk for specific diseases and exposures

Workers screened out of jobs who may be somewhat more at risk for one ailment when exposed to a substance may be less at risk for another substance that is present in the same workplace. They might be at lower risk of developing emphysema, but they may develop bladder cancer from the same substance or from other chemicals to which they are exposed. Further, those who are identified as susceptible to adverse effects from working conditions may be less vulnerable to infectious agents, or drugs, or contaminants in air, water, and food. Certainly, some workers are more vulnerable to particular substances than others are. But the susceptibility perspective tends to be very inclusive. It assumes that this variation is significant and relevant to a wide range of illnesses and working conditions. Thus, employers may screen individuals out as generally unfit for employment, even though the workers' suspected susceptibility may in fact be confined to very specific exposure conditions.

Spreading disease through job rotation

Susceptibility policies can promote harmful job rotation practices. Rotating workers out of jobs and replacing them with workers who do not show damage can spread disease or exacerbate hazards by exposing more people to toxic chemicals.[30] Genetic screening, by facilitating the replacement of workers with signs of damage, can multiply cases of birth defects, mutation, and cancer.

Noncompliance with government standards

Company officials claim that current industrial and government safeguards offer workers adequate health protection. Yet some companies that have screened workers thought to be susceptible have been found to be out of compliance with occupational health regulations.[31] These employers are not in a position to assert convincingly that government regulations and susceptibility policies help ensure that normal workers are safe if the regulations are neither followed nor enforced effectively. In addition, employers' noncompliance with government rules calls into question the meaning of their stated commitment to employee health as motivation for their screening programs.

Stigmatization: the genetic scarlet letter

Testing for particular genetic traits focuses attention on the inborn features of individuals, which can stigmatize workers.[32] It can also improperly shift occupational health concerns away from more general exposure problems. By locating the cause of occupational risk in the worker's unusual biological vulnerability, susceptibility policies shift the blame for disease to the workers. Identifying workers as genetically at risk can diminish their self-esteem, damage their family life and other social relationships, and threaten their ability to find work. For example, railroad companies ask job applicants whether they previously have been rejected from jobs for medical reasons. The burden of occupational hazards thus falls more heavily on employees.[33]

AMBIGUOUS TESTING DATA AND THE BENEFIT OF THE DOUBT

Employers' selective caution in assessing evidence of risk and safety is notable. The benefit of the doubt is given to chemicals, to existing company practices, and to exclusion, not to the possibility of health risks to the work force from industrial chemicals. This is a matter of ideology and a question of power.

Management advocates great caution and strict criteria for restrictions on chemicals. For example, in 1981 congressional hearings, the Chemical Manufacturers Association argued that under the proposed OSHA labeling standard, chemicals would be falsely accused of being carcinogens. Corporate representatives referred to evidence of negative health effects as unproven "allegations." They criticized labeling chemicals with health risk information because not all the evidence was in.[34] In this and other cases, employers have used terminology that suggests chemicals are on trial and should be presumed innocent until proven guilty beyond a reasonable doubt. For management, lack of data becomes an argument for safety or for screening workers.

Employers show considerable tolerance for "beta errors," false negatives that inaccurately indicate that chemical exposures are safe; but they display no similar tolerance for false positives. Managers frequently demand human evidence rather than data obtained from animal studies to prove damage at low exposure doses, but they have used animal evidence to clear chemicals for industrial use.[35]

Employers who have screening programs tend to assume that any abnormal biological characteristics revealed by testing will interfere with work or lead to medical problems. In the cases of employers screening out black military cadets and fertile women, women and blacks have been excluded despite slim evidence. For example, American Cyanamid's

Lederle Laboratories barred fertile women from specific production jobs, on the basis of limited and ambiguous data,
because they claimed that although the workplace chemicals
were safe for adults, they were unable to prove that "more
vulnerable fetuses" could tolerate exposure to them.[36] The
company rejected evidence that their working conditions
posed a threat to workers' health. Like many employers,
they chose to exclude workers they considered susceptible
rather than take the chance of leaving themselves vulnerable
to high medical expenses or aggressive legal action on behalf
of damaged fetuses.

In the case of genetic monitoring – as opposed to screening – the same bias in favor of presumed workplace safety
applies. Employers who conduct monitoring tend to interpret test results showing abnormalities as uncertain findings of little significance. Other employers reject monitoring
outright, for that reason; or, in the process of targeting possible exposure problems, they express concern about studies
that might suggest that a chemical they use is hazardous.

While employers respond to ambiguous data by trusting
in chemical safety, they deny people jobs based on preemployment and periodic screening tests that have undeter-
mined or low levels of predictiveness for disease. The same
standards of evidence and proof do not apply to data in both
cases. It is chemicals that enjoy the benefit of the doubt, not
workers with questionable test results.

Monitoring and environmental hazards

Both those who support and those who oppose genetic
monitoring in industry, in order to identify high-risk workers
and jobs, agree on two points. First, chromosomal abnormalities that the tests detect are not clearly associated with
subsequent clinical health effects. In other words, individuals who have high levels of abnormalities may be no
more likely to develop disease than those who do not. Second, genetic monitoring is a useful research tool. But the
consensus stops there. Beyond that point, opponents and

supporters of monitoring have conflicting concepts of risk and safety in the workplace. The two perspectives may be characterized as follows.

Opposition to monitoring. Opponents of genetic monitoring in the workplace argue that all chromosome studies of worker populations have had major and perhaps insurmountable methodological problems that make useful interpretation impossible. Monitoring, therefore, should not be incorporated into industrial surveillance programs, should not be used for risk assessment, and should not affect regulatory action. Further, advocates of chromosomal testing overstate exposure hazards and too willingly undertake tests of limited value. Accordingly, chromosome studies should be limited to research purposes.

Corporate officials, particularly, subscribe to this view. They emphasize problems of interpreting uncertain results and explaining preliminary findings of high rates of chromosomal abnormalities to workers or the public. An industry scientist states,

> *All* of these short-term tests must be considered *research tools.* They are *not* established clinical tests. . . . Genetic monitoring should not be used to set standards for safe exposures, or to establish conditions for the prevention of occupational disease.[37]

The medical director of a large chemical firm concurs:

> I don't know of any evidence that chemicals in industry are known to cause chromosome breaks or abnormalities. We need to know a lot more about what the hazards are in relation to exposure and genetic abnormalities. We don't want to get involved in doing anything that gives us results where we don't really know what they mean. If you do get high levels of chromosome breaks, what do you tell the workers?

A medical officer at a major steel company articulates the negative assessment other corporate officials share: "I would never recommend using chromosomal aberrations as a monitoring tool."

Support for monitoring. Supporters believe that genetic monitoring is already of considerable value in industrial surveillance. They believe that chromosomal studies of populations exposed to particular industrial chemicals should be conducted now, in order to assess exposure risks before clinical symptoms appear. While admitting that some previous studies have been flawed, they argue that certain techniques are already sufficiently developed for identifying exposure hazards in industry.

Proponents of monitoring also state that those who want to limit genetic monitoring to research purposes either misunderstand or misrepresent the value of these tests. They believe that critics of current chromosomal testing insist on unreasonable, interminable programs of research as a prerequisite for testing in the workplace.[38] Instead, advocates cite academic and government research scientists who support current industrial monitoring:

> [Chromosomal monitoring tests] can be integrated rapidly into a medical surveillance program for workers at risk and can provide the most advanced technology currently available for the identification of genetic damage leading to pre-malignant conditions in man or to permanent germ cell damage, or both, thereby providing an advanced warning system for hazardous chemicals.[39]

> [E]ven though [a genetic monitoring test] cannot predict clinical outcomes, this should not preclude its use as an indicator of exposure to potentially harmful agents.[40]

> The results [of chromosomal studies] cannot be interpreted as an indication of ill health risk or susceptibility but can be used to help determine guidelines for safe exposure levels.[41]

> Genetic monitoring . . . is very important, because this can be used not only to identify specific individuals who might be more sensitive within a given concentration range, but also to

identify hazardous work conditions in work areas and to judge the effectiveness of control technology.[42]

Industry personnel usually oppose genetic monitoring in the workplace and labor people typically support it.[43] The safety dimension of susceptibility policies, which is seldom made explicit, helps explain this split. It also helps explain why monitoring has received such a different response from genetic screening.

Managers and others in industry tend to oppose genetic monitoring because they have an interest in avoiding tests that could point to inadequate government standards or new exposure problems. They also have an ideological commitment to the safety of current industrial working conditions – a commitment shared by politicians and scientists who oppose government regulation.[44] In contrast, advocates of genetic monitoring see it as a valuable tool for monitoring populations, not individuals. They believe that elevated levels of chromosome abnormalities in a working population can serve to indicate an exposure problem that confronts all workers. Therefore, labor tends to favor genetic monitoring as a method of detecting hazardous working conditions at low exposure levels. The same reasoning that leads employees and union officials to oppose genetic screening generally contributes to their support of monitoring techniques. Compared with genetic screening, monitoring is more consistent with labor's view of how workers at risk should be located: through identifying high-risk substances and workplaces.

In general, then, the use of genetic monitoring reflects and reinforces a concern for occupational health that targets work risks, a concern that so far has focused on large groups or populations of workers. But if genetic monitoring that identifies particular workers with an unusually high proportion of chromosome aberrations comes to be widely used in industry, the response will change. If labor representatives, for example, discover that industrial firms have not informed workers of their findings, or have denied jobs to workers on the basis of those findings, they may protest against monitoring for the same reasons they protest against screening.

Company testing

Employers are more likely to pursue testing programs, heed their results, and publicize their findings when they perceive the tests to be in their company's interest. For example, between 1964 and 1977, Dow Chemical carried out cytogenetic studies of all its employees – approximately 3,000 workers. In 1977 company scientists found evidence suggesting detrimental health effects from two of the corporation's biggest selling chemicals.[45] Concerned with these findings, they urged the company to publicize the evidence and change the production process. As one company scientist explained: "We wanted them to tell the workers what we had found, reduce the levels of benzene to which workers were exposed, and inform the appropriate government agencies and the rest of the petrochemical industry."[46] Instead, Dow abruptly cut off the testing, explaining that the tests were not useful.[47] Company officials claimed that the cytogenetic data were ambiguous and difficult to evaluate. As the Dow medical director stated: "Continuing periodic medical examination tells us much more than cytogenetic studies about the health of our people. . . . Cytogenetics is a new and developing tool that someday will probably be useful in medical surveillance, but is not regarded as such today."[48] Another Dow official, in a confidential interview, commented on the problem of whether to explain the chromosomal monitoring results to employees: "We can envision a situation in which our workers become unjustifiably apprehensive that they will develop leukemia or other forms of cancer. . . . We may even be the target of litigation and unfavorable publicity." After cancelling its large-scale monitoring program, Dow studied chromosomal changes in sixty to seventy of its office workers on a research basis only. Company officials described this small monitoring project as very costly but useful for pointing to the methodological complexity and limitations of studying chromosomal abnormalities.

Officials at Dow and other companies argue that Dow's experience with monitoring lends support to their view that it should not be used except for research. They argue that this large-scale program revealed the shortcomings of the technology, the inadequate methods researchers used, and the difficulty of explaining equivocal positive findings. Yet Dow's experience suggests that monitoring tests can successfully point to exposure hazards: The company was clearly unwilling to pursue its cytogenetic tests when they seemed to indicate occupational health risks; and its testing of office workers to study variables that influence normal chromosome breakage may well have been an expensive use of medical resources in an attempt to justify avoiding chromosome studies of production workers.

The disparity in perspective toward genetic monitoring clearly is considerable. There are different assessments of the testing programs already undertaken, and different views of the purpose and value of chromosomal studies for industrial surveillance. Because these differences mirror the power dynamics and conflicting interests within industry at large, they are unlikely to be reconciled soon.

THE FOCUS ON HIGH-RISK WORK

Proponents of susceptibility policies, generally allied with management, usually maintain that finding high-risk workers will help ensure that the population as a whole is protected, because current exposure limits leave only these few individuals at risk. The desire of employers to deflect attention from remaining exposure hazards also contributes to their interest in individual susceptibility.

While management focuses on high-risk individuals, labor targets hazardous working conditions and strongly objects to the safety assumptions implicit in susceptibility policies. Employees tend to believe that industrial poison, and not their own biological makeup, lies at the root of occupational disease. Two statements made in personal interviews illustrate this belief. An industrial worker at a major auto manufacturing corporation said: "For years, companies have been saying that workers' diseases are not caused by what we work with in the plants, but by smoking, diet, lack of exercise, and other problems with our life-style. Now they're saying it's the workers' genetic heritage." And a production employee at a large chemical manufacturing firm, commenting on genetic testing programs, said: "By weeding out the so-called susceptibles, industry will presume the workplace is safe." An industrial hygienist with the United Steelworkers made this comment: "To what extent will industry honestly consider the risks to so-called 'non-susceptibles' as well as the risks to 'susceptibles'? Unfortunately, our experience in that area has not been very good."[49]

In general, labor considers susceptibility policies an ineffective tool for identifying workers at risk or for solving a significant proportion of occupational health problems. As a labor official argued at a National Academy of Sciences Conference on Genetic Influences on Responses to the Environment:

> It is possible to talk of susceptible workers as a distinct subgroup of people who are peculiar because they, and only they, suffer adverse effects from exposure to certain chemicals. In fact, however, we know that there are a lot of exposures where the susceptibles are really simply the tip of the iceberg. . . . When susceptibles are removed, the fact that there is a problem for those who aren't as susceptible may be masked. . . . The removal of susceptibles may in fact be counterproductive to health generally.[50]

The stance the EPA has taken toward certain groups at risk provides an effective counterpoint to the high-risk worker approach that favors genetic screening and fetal exclusion. From time to time, in the process of setting government standards, the EPA has recognized special high-risk groups. One such group is infants who are exposed to nitrates and nitrites in drinking water. Another is individuals with heart and lung disorders who are exposed to carbon monoxides and sulfur dioxides in ambient air. In both of these cases, the EPA has tightened their standards to protect these individuals rather than excluded them from sites with contaminated air or water. EPA officials have considered these groups to be the first but not the only groups to suffer toxic effects, and have framed the question of high-risk groups in terms of reducing general exposure levels for these individuals and the general public as well.[51]

In contrast to employers' concern with removing high-risk individuals, a major concern for identifying and regulating exposure to risky chemicals does more than recognize susceptible workers who need protection. It sees them as an early warning system for hazardous conditions that affect many workers and the community at large. In this view, it is unrealistic to expect that eliminating workers with a few specific genetic markers or with early signs of disease will make a substantial contribution to worker health. Moreover, removing individuals who have particular traits or symptoms instead of reducing exposures to all workers reinforces the presumption of workplace safety and may thereby actually exacerbate occupational health risks, because existing toxic exposure limits and government regulations often provide inadequate protection. From the "risky workplace" perspective, then, susceptibility policies are based on the false idea that if we could locate high-risk workers, we could solve the problems of workplace cancer and reproductive damage.

In any environment, certain employees may reveal specific genetic traits, higher levels of chromosomal abnormalities, or earlier and more severe illness in response to particular substances. But it is not necessarily they, or only they, who are in jeopardy. It is all workers exposed to hazardous substances who are at risk, and those who work with the most hazardous chemicals and with the least effective safeguards are at the highest risk. All workers at risk from hazardous substances should be protected by reducing emissions rather than by excluding the highest risk workers from employment.[52]

Finally, in the risky-workplace view, searching for suscep-tible workers directs resources away from workers truly at higher risk – those who handle hazardous substances in inadequately controlled environments. Even if a worker with SAT deficiency is somewhat more susceptible to chronic pul-monary disease, or a worker with G-6-PD deficiency is more susceptible to hemolytic crisis from exposure to oxidizing chemicals, these problems are relatively insignificant in oc-cupational health. Instead, attention and investment could be focused on the more fruitful task of identifying chemical hazards and determining more effective engineering controls to limit exposure.

The conflicting safety orientations within the two major views of susceptibility policies are highly significant. When recommendations concerning the advisability of genetic test-ing and exclusionary practices are put forward, the underly-ing assumptions about safety should be brought out and made clear. Most often, they are not.

Chapter 4

Sex, race, and genetic predisposition

Companies want to weed out the vulnerable and hire the "superworker," and whoever isn't, whether it be Italians, blacks, Sephardic Jews, or people with some genetic trait – whoever isn't superhardy could be excluded.

International Chemical Workers Union official

Sex is perhaps our most obvious genetic characteristic. It requires no sophistication to detect. We all literally wear our genetic markers.

Albert Gore, Jr.
(as U.S. Representative)

PROPONENTS of the new technologies for identifying high-risk workers believe they are championing a neutral approach to reducing employee health risks, an approach that presumably would protect everyone. In fact, the search for types of workers at risk often results in the use of inappropriate biological categories. "Susceptibility" usually has a racial or sexual component.

To some extent this is true, because certain health hazards affect different racial or sexual groups differently. One example is reproductive teratogens that cause fetal damage through women directly exposed to them. Other examples include G-6-PD deficiency and sickle cell traits, both found disproportionately among blacks.

But more strictly social factors also influence testing practices. Employment patterns and cultural views about women and racial minorities help determine which workers come to be seen as being at risk. Genetic screening and fetal exclusion practices – like prenatal diagnosis, abortion, or sterilization – are not purely technical or scientific matters. To understand the origins and impact of these practices, we must look at institutional arrangements, power relations, and work force stratification by sex, race, and class.

In examining the impact of race and sex on susceptibility, I will emphasize cases of fetal exclusion and genetic screening for markers, for these cases most dramatically affect women workers and specific racial and ethnic groups.

FETAL EXCLUSION AND STRATIFICATION BY SEX

An important example of susceptibility policies is the exclusion of women of childbearing age from jobs because of suspected fetal hazards. The major influence of gender stratification structures becomes clear when we examine the nature and extent of these policies.

Company practices

In U.S. industry, about 65,000 different chemicals are already in use, and over 5,000 new ones are introduced each year.[1]

Most of these chemicals have not undergone extensive testing that would indicate whether they cause long-term health
effects. When we think of damage to reproduction, we usually think of birth defects. But reproductive hazards of chemicals include not only birth defects, but also spontaneous
abortion, low sperm counts, menstrual disorders, stillbirth,
infertility, low birth weight, sexual dysfunction, childhood
mortality, and chromosome abnormalities (see Table 4).

As with carcinogens, substances that cause reproductive
damage are difficult to trace to the source of exposure. These
substances can be found in food additives, groundwater con-
tamination, and air pollution as well as in workplace exposures. They often take years to result in clinical symptoms. In some cases, their effect becomes apparent only in
subsequent generations.

Many companies have responded to chemical hazards by
excluding fertile women from production jobs that involve
exposure to toxins such as benzene, lead, vinyl chloride,
carbon tetrachloride, and carbon monoxide. These corporate
fetal exclusionary policies have become widespread in the
chemical, steel, auto, oil, electronics, and textile industries.
For example, the Bunker Hill Company in Idaho has banned
all fertile women from its lead smelter. Allied Corporation,
too, has barred fertile women from working around lead.
Other large firms that have excluded women from working
with hazardous substances include Gulf Oil, B. F. Goodrich,
Exxon, Firestone, Olin, Dow Chemical, Sun Oil, Goodyear,
Globe Union, BASF Wyandotte, Eastman Kodak, Union Carbide, and Monsanto.[2]

One of the best known examples is American Cyanamid,
which in 1978 announced a new policy in its Willow Island,
West Virginia, plant barring women of childbearing capacity
from production jobs in the lead pigment department. The
company claimed that these jobs entailed exposure to toxic
chemicals that could someday endanger the children of these
women. Only women who could prove they were infertile or
postmenopausal were allowed to keep their jobs. Although
American Cyanamid has since closed its lead pigment de-

Table 4. *Occupational hazards to reproduction[a]*

Substance	Reproductive effects	Occupations and industries at risk
Metals		
1. Lead	1, 2. Menstrual dis-	1. Metal industry
2. Mercury	orders, spontan-	2. Metal industry, hos-
	eous abortion,	pital workers
	birth defects	
Gases		
3. Anesthetic	3, 4. Spontaneous abor-	3. Hospital workers
4. Carbon	tion, stillbirth, low	4. Toll operators, met-
monoxide	birth weight, birth	al industry
5. Vinyl chloride	defects	5. Plastic industry,
	5. Spontaneous abor-	meat wrappers
	tion, stillbirth, birth	
	defects	
Organic solvents		
6. Benzene, xy-	6. Menstrual disorders,	6, 7. Lab workers, tex-
lene, toluene,	spontaneous abor-	tile and petro-
trichloroethy-	tion, stillbirth	chemical indus-
lene		tries, cosmetol-
		ogists, laundry
		workers, printers
7. Chlorinated	7. Stillbirth, birth de-	
hydrocarbons	fects	
Pesticides		
8. DBCP, TOK,	8. Spontaneous abor-	8. Chemical manufac-
2,4-D, 2,4,5-T	tion, stillbirth, birth	turing, agricultural
	defects	workers

[a] These include major known and highly suspected occupational hazards to reproduction.
Sources: Office of Technology Assessment (1985), Zenz (1984), Williams (1981); Hricko (1976), and Hunt (1982).

partment, five women underwent sterilization procedures in order to keep their jobs there after the company introduced this exclusionary policy.[3] Also, two women at Allied Chemical Company in Illinois, at least three women at Bunker Hill Company in Idaho, and another woman at St. Joe's Mineral in Pennsylvania decided to be sterilized in order to keep their jobs.[4]

Excluding fertile women from specific types of jobs is a common practice. At least 100,000 jobs have been closed to women because of such protectionist policies. The Equal Employment Opportunity Commission has calculated that if fertile women were barred from every setting that might be deemed a potential hazard to the fetus, as many as 20 million U.S. jobs would be affected.[5] This approach, despite its apparently benevolent concern for individual women and children, has spawned unprotective and inequitable exclusionary practices. The major problems pertain to the treatment of reproductive hazards as problems of women only, the exclusion of only certain women, and the gender-biased legal and economic framing of reproductive hazards.

Reproductive hazards as problems of women only

Females are associated with reproduction – and hence, with risk to reproduction. Existing data do not support this view. Fertile women are often excluded on the basis of insufficient, inconclusive scientific information. Most of the evidence for teratogens – substances that cause birth defects through direct maternal exposure – is sketchy. And since reproductive effects are generally associated with females only, the very methods of testing chemicals for reproductive damage are skewed. Technicians have used female rats and watched for birth defects; testing animals for reproductive effects through males or through both sexes has been less common.[6] An official at the National Institute for Occupational Safety and Health who was charged with investigating reproductive hazards concurs: "The methods of testing for reproductive damage have been biased toward investigating effects through the mother exclusively."[7] The corporate medical director of DuPont has said: "In-utero exposure of the fetus is of much more concern to occupational physicians than is the preconception exposure of the adult male or adult female."[8]

In fact, the evidence shows that occupational hazards that affect fetuses through maternal exposure alone are rare. Many of the chemicals from which women are excluded can harm future children through male workers by way of sperm damage or mutagenic effects.[9] For example, the children of men working with the pesticide DBCP at an Occidental Chemical plant in California have had high rates of birth defects as well as sterility.[10] Carbon disulfide, too, may damage the children of men who have been exposed to it.[11] There is evidence that men who regularly bring home lead dust, asbestos, or other substances on their clothes may produce an accumulation of these substances in women and others outside the work environment.[12] In some cases, risks through paternal exposure to hazards may be greater than the maternal reproductive risks. For instance, male exposure to ionizing radiation presents a higher risk for genetic mutations and chromosome aberrations leading to prenatal loss and congenitally malformed infants than reproductive risk through female workers, at the same radiation dose.[13]

Many of the substances that may endanger the fetus have been shown to have other toxic effects on both parents. Lead, for example, can cause birth defects through maternal exposure.[14] Yet it is well documented that lead can also cause damage to the heart, kidneys, and nervous system in both men and women. The same is true for benzene, vinyl chloride, and other substances from which women are excluded.[15] Chemicals that can damage the fetus are also usually mutagenic and often carcinogenic to adults – that is, capable of causing genetic damage and cancer – but men and infertile women are not excluded from workplace contact with them. For example, the DuPont company bars women of childbearing capacity from exposure to ethylenethiourea, even though company officials acknowledge that it can cause thyroid cancer. The company also excludes fertile women from exposure to hexafluoroacetone, which its own studies indicate damages sperm.[16]

Thus, policies of banning women from industrial jobs have failed to protect fertile women and the unborn from job-related harm, in part because they leave remaining workers exposed to substances that can cause other reproductive effects, genetic damage, and cancer.

Why do companies pursue these policies? The reason they most often give is that they want to protect the unborn.[17] American Cyanamid officials, for example, claim that when they exclude women from jobs, they are protecting the fetus, which they refer to as "the most helpless member of society."[18] Johnson Controls officials maintain that "The issue is protecting the health of unborn children."[19] Similarly, the corporate medical director of DuPont has said: "When we remove a woman [from a job] it's to protect her fetus."[20] While they generally admit that there are legal and economic incentives for excluding women, corporate officials typically say that they do so in order to follow sound medical practice.[21] Employers who believe they are averting reproductive damage by excluding women are unknowingly pursuing policies that are ineffective medically. As we have seen, fetal protection policies fail to prevent the reproductive damage that results from male workers' exposure to chemical hazards. They also leave remaining workers vulnerable to genetic damage and cancer risks.

In addition, fetal protection policies exclude far too many women. In most cases, not just women planning pregnancy but all women between the ages of 15 to 50 or 55 are barred, as if women are always potentially pregnant and have no control over their reproductive functions.[22] In fact, in advanced industrial countries, most births are planned, and the vast majority of women have finished childbearing by age 39.[23] Industry officials and other proponents of fetal exclusion policies often claim that the fetus is most vulnerable to toxic chemicals early in pregnancy, when the woman may be unaware she is pregnant, but this is not necessarily true. For example, in the case of lead, it has been demonstrated that the fetus is at highest risk during the first trimester.[24] The idea that women should be excluded because of their special capability is clearly at work here. When employers assume that women and motherhood must be protected at all costs, the case for excluding women becomes more compelling than the evidence warrants.

Selective exclusion of women

The second problem with fetal exclusion policies is that they are selectively applied, and thus reflect the stratification of the work force by sex and the related ideologies that reinforce it.[25] Women are usually barred not from all jobs that entail toxic risks but only from the unskilled, relatively high-paying production jobs traditionally held by men. The greatest number of these predominantly male jobs are in large companies, such as General Motors, Gulf Oil, and B. F. Goodrich, although fetal exclusion policies are used in many smaller companies as well.

In general, the issue of special risk and exclusion emerges when a particular group is relatively new to an occupation and a minority, as women are to the chemical industry and to lead battery plants. Employment data bear this out. As the data in Table 5 indicate, the proportion of women workers in production and related jobs has been increasing since 1950 in the chemical, automobile, steel, and rubber industries. Fetal exclusion practices have been particularly strong in these industries. When women move into jobs they had not held previously, their presence becomes a problem and different health risks become an issue. This pattern holds both for male-intensive industries as a whole and for specific jobs traditionally held by men.

The question of exclusion does not come up in jobs where the industry is more dependent on women workers. Those jobs may involve serious health risks, such as exposure to solvents in electronics, or exposure to anesthetic gases in health care work. In cases where women predominate, though, no one advocates removing all fertile women. So when women hospital workers are exposed to ionizing radiation or to anesthesia containing ethylene oxide, a powerful toxin, nobody suggests that they be barred from jobs in hospitals. Similarly, nobody proposes that all fertile women be

Table 5. *Production and related workers in selected manufacturing industries, by sex, 1950–1980*[a]

| Industry | Percent and number female production and related workers of total employed[b] | | | |
	1950	1960	1970	1980
Chemicals and allied products				
Female	12.9%	11.3%	16.6%	20.9%
	49,440	50,479	81,375	130,180
Total	383,610	447,781	491,679	624,167
Rubber and miscellaneous plastic products[c]				
Female	22.3%	26.0%	31.3%	32.6%
	38,100	71,480	117,600	146,459
Total	170,610	275,122	375,514	448,957
Primary steel and iron industries[d]				
Female	2.1%	1.5%	2.6%	4.9%
	16,290	10,463	17,898	33,356
Total	770,250	718,517	676,630	674,098
Motor vehicles and motor vehicle equipment				
Female	9.4%	7.2%	9.9%	15.6%
	63,840	45,298	77,705	133,722
Total	675,750	628,341	783,510	859,948

[a] Figures are based on census population samples.
[b] "Production and related workers" refers to:
  1980: Precision production, craft, and repair occupations; and operators, fabricators, and laborers.
  1970: Craft and kindred workers; operatives, except transport; transport equipment operatives; and laborers, except farm.
  1960 and 1950: craft workers, forepersons, and kindred workers; operatives and kindred workers; and laborers, except farm and mine.
These categories do not include: professional and technical workers, managers and administrators, sales workers, clerical workers, farmers and farm workers, service workers, and private household workers.

(*continued*)

Notes to Table 5. (*cont.*)

^cFor 1950, this category includes rubber products only.
^dFor 1950, 1960, and 1970, this category includes primary ferrous
industries, including blast furnaces, steelworks, rolling and finishing
mills, and other primary iron and steel industries.
Sources:
  Bureau of the Census (1984), Table 1: Selected Characteristics of
    Employed Persons by Occupation, Industry, and Sex: 1980,
    pp. 1–180.
  Bureau of the Census (1972), Table 1: Industry Group of Employed
    Persons by Occupation, Age, and Sex: 1970, pp. 1–80; and Table 2:
    Industry Group of Employed Persons by Occupation, Race, Spanish
    Origin, and Sex: 1970, pp. 81–128.
  Bureau of the Census (1963), Table 2: Detailed Occupation of
    Employed Persons, by Detailed Industry and Sex, for the United
    States: 1960, pp. 7–146.
  Bureau of the Census (1954), Table 2: Detailed Occupation of
    Employed Persons, by Detailed Industry and Sex, for the United
    States: 1950, pp. 12–75.

excluded from handling dangerous solvents in Silicon Valley
electronics assembly plants.

Women are not excluded from female-intensive jobs even
when the chemicals they confront are identical to those in
the traditionally male jobs from which they are barred (see
Table 6). Women have been excluded from chemical plants
that use benzene and toluene, but these same substances are
found in high concentrations in the textile and clothing industries and in laboratory technician jobs, all of which rely
largely on women employees. Similarly, women are seldom
hired in nuclear power plants, but X-ray technicians and
other health care workers are exposed to comparable radiation hazards.

Not only are women considered fit for safer jobs, but the
workplaces in which they have long predominated – beauty
parlors, for example, where they are exposed to many chemicals – are mistakenly declared to be safe. In the few cases
where attention has turned to health hazards in female-
dominated jobs, the question of excluding all fertile women

73

Table 6. *Women employees in female-intensive occupations, 1990*

Occupation	Percent women of total employees[a]
Beauty shops	89.1%
Nursing and personal care facilities	87.5
Private household services	85.3
Health services, except hospitals	77.9
Hospital workers	77.5
Employees in dental offices	74.9
Apparel and other finished textile products	74.4
Employees in physicians' offices	71.2
Knitting mills	66.2
Laundry, cleaning, and garment services	59.1
Leather and leather products	57.8

[a] Employed civilians
Source: Bureau of Labor Statistics (1991), Table 28: Employed Civilians by Detailed Industry, Sex, Race, and Hispanic Origin.

has not come up.[26] Thus, in recent years it has been argued that the use of computer video display terminals may be associated with problems such as miscarriages and birth defects, yet no one has suggested restricting computer use to men. Also, although the textile industry has undertaken susceptibility practices, it has not emphasized the exclusion of fertile women, since women constitute almost half of all production workers and have long been present in the industry.[27] The same is true of the low-paying assembly jobs in electronics. If women were excluded from female-intensive jobs, the low-wage female work force would be difficult to replace.

Occasionally, employers and scientists have identified particular groups of men as high-risk workers and have proposed excluding them from jobs. For example, in response to evidence that DBCP, a pesticide spray, is a known carcinogen and mutagen that causes male sterility and other serious toxic effects, the Peach Growers Association proposed that old men pick peaches.[28] Using similar logic, a scientist has recommended hiring only older people for work with cancer-causing substances: "In older persons, low total doses would be possible over the remaining years of employment since the total lifespan for cancer development would be limited."[29] When United States Steel Corporation sought workers to do welding inside a 45-inch pipe where the decibel levels were extremely high, they hired men who were completely deaf.[30]

A closer look at cases in which high-risk male workers have been identified will highlight how different they are from cases of fetal exclusion policies. First, even a discussion of excluding groups of men to protect them from reproductive hazards is a rare occurrence. Second, in those unusual cases in which employers do discuss removing fertile men from jobs, they consider other *men* – not women – to be the replacement workers. Third, and most important, the idea of excluding fertile men is not implemented. Employers do not actually bar fertile men from employment or require that they show evidence of surgical sterilization in order to keep their jobs. For example, a study of 198 large chemical and electronics companies in Massachusetts found that 54 of them used glycol ethers, which even at very low doses produce toxic effects on sperm. None of these companies excluded men from exposure, but 37 of them restricted the work options of women on the basis of potential reproductive risk.[31]

This pattern of retaining men despite reproductive hazards has also appeared in cases involving DBCP and Kepone, in which male workers were not excluded despite correlations between chemical exposure and male sterility or decreased fertility. In those cases, the substances – not male workers – were banned.[32]

In short, corporate concern with the reproductive risks that workers face in their jobs is both highly selective and gender biased. More specifically, it seems to be activated only on behalf of women who hold "men's" jobs in workplaces where women workers are new and a minority.

Legal and economic framing of reproductive hazards

A third problem with fetal exclusion policies in industry pertains to the legal and economic framework in which they are carried out. While fetal protection practices in the workplace are in some respects similar to other efforts to deal with reproductive hazards, the legal and regulatory context gives fetal exclusion policies in industry a special character. Discriminating against women in general or failing to protect workers sufficiently can lead to government penalties under OSHA and EEOC as well as to private lawsuit awards. But managers generally have not regarded discrimination suits and government penalties for work hazards as a major deterrent to their use of fetal exclusion practices. One reason is cost. As one corporate official in a trade association explained in a confidential interview: "In balancing off EEOC and OSHA's penalties with the cost of a [fetal damage] lawsuit, which can be millions of dollars, there is just no comparison. Industry is concerned with megabucks."

Industrial employees are usually covered by workers' compensation, and so under most circumstances they are barred from suing their employers for adverse effects on their own health. Damage to the fetus, however, is not one of those circumstances. Whereas workers' compensation sets limits on the amount an employee can recover, the potential award in a lawsuit for a damaged fetus is unlimited.[33] Industry officials also fear jury sympathy for the parents who claim that workplace exposure of the mother has caused her to bear abnormal children. Although no lawsuits of this type have yet been tried as of 1991, there have been suits for reproductive damage arising from men's exposure to DBCP, Agent Orange, and atomic weapons testing.[34] Furthermore, all states now recognize the right of an infant to sue negligent third parties for his or her prenatal injuries, and an employer could be considered such a party.[35] Industry officials see ominous trends here.

Employers' concern with legal risks of fetal exposure reflects their typically narrow view of liability for reproductive hazards. They overstate special liability that employing fertile women workers may represent, while understating potential liability for male reproductive damage. This is despite the fact that there have been many known instances of damage through male workers.[36] Some employers believe it is more difficult to prove that damage has been caused by preconception male exposure than by in-utero exposure, so that they are less likely to be held liable for damage to children through the father. This view persists even though male reproductive damage already has led to many lawsuits. In addition, companies that exclude women continue to focus on legal risks of fetal exposure, yet they may be held liable for damage to consumers or the community. In the case of Love Canal, many suits were brought by men and women against Hooker Chemical for reproductive and other health damage to residents. Bunker Hill Company has barred women from working with lead but has been sued for exposing children to lead in the area surrounding company facilities.[37]

Over several decades, restrictive industrial practices specific to women drew attention to health hazards and led to improved standards for all workers. But they also raised the costs of hiring women and hindered their advancement in the work force. The legal context of protectionist policies changed dramatically with Title VII of the 1964 Civil Rights Act and the Pregnancy Discrimination Amendment of 1978, which established rules prohibiting sex discrimination.[38] The 1978 Pregnancy Amendment to Title VII required that company reproductive policies be gender neutral. Employers now have the legal burden of justifying any practice that treats women differently or has special effects on them.

Extensive case law under Title VII limits the conditions under which protectionist policies may be allowed. In general, protective legislation and practices violate equal employment opportunities and Title VII provisions. Yet many areas of employment rights are murky, especially those that pertain to pregnancy and reproductive hazards.

Recent legal battles have been fought over fetal protection

and the exclusion of fertile women from industrial jobs, and many suits against company policies have been filed in the courts. Some of these have charged that fetal exclusionary policies violate Title VII because they deny women as a class equal terms and conditions of employment, deny them employment opportunities, and adversely affect their status as employees. In some cases, suits have been won, while others have been settled out of court or decided in favor of the company and against the excluded women workers.[39]

In a widely publicized case concerning Johnson Controls corporation, a Chicago federal appeals court in 1989 upheld the company's fetal exclusion policy barring fertile women from exposure to lead in battery plants. But a California state Court of Appeal in 1990 struck down the company's exclusionary policy as illegal discrimination. Then in March 1991, the U.S. Supreme Court ruled that the Johnson Controls policy unjustifiably discriminated against women. Despite this important ruling, questions about who is a susceptible worker and whether women can be given special protection against reproductive hazards are not fully resolved.[40] Employer vulnerability to lawsuits for fetal damage also remains problematic.

It is in the area of discrimination and protection that most of the controversy lies. I have emphasized conflict between labor and management over genetic testing and fetal protection policies, but other groups have entered the arena. One such group was the Coalition for the Reproductive Rights of Workers (CRROW), based in Washington, D.C., which worked against fetal protection policies although its members had diverse and often conflicting strategies for responding to them.[41]

One debate over fetal exclusion policies is between those who favor what can be called an "equal treatment" approach and those who favor a "special treatment," or "positive action" approach.[42] The debate over equality and legal strategy concerns whether or not women and men are similarly situated and therefore must be considered the same and treated alike. It also raises the question of how these issues should be pursued legally, if evidence indicates special vulnerabilities of the fetus. Major concerns include whether gender-based policies should ever be upheld, and what policies represent the best approach to equality and protection from health hazards. This dispute draws attention to dilemmas arising from the fact that in some cases the fetus *is* at special risk through women employees. The controversy over what to do about it remains heated.

In summary, company policies of fetal exclusion stem from stereotyped assumptions about women and reproductive risks. Employers have pursued policies that they expect will protect their companies along with fetal health, even though in fact these policies may actually increase their own vulnerability to lawsuits for reproductive damage or sex discrimination. Imagining that reproductive risks are located primarily in female workers in male-dominated industrial jobs may extend employers' liability for health hazards. It may also divert their own attention from real risks to male workers, consumers, and the community.

Reproductive risk and the social good

Industrial managers, health professionals, and ethicists often have justified fetal exclusion practices on the ground that society as a whole has an interest in a certain level of health protection or standard of equality.[43] Employers therefore usually have argued that women must be excluded from industrial production jobs that involve exposure to toxic chemicals in order to safeguard the work force and protect future generations. But attention to social stratification and power differences shows that conflicting interests are involved.

What does it mean for women workers when companies exclude them from jobs because of risks of genetic damage to the fetus? What are women's interests in genetic testing and exclusionary policies? In general, women's interests include: (1) access to jobs with good pay, benefits, and working conditions; (2) good health for themselves and their children;

and (3) control over the timing of pregnancy. Exclusionary policies may undermine these interests in three ways.

Women and industrial management. The first issue of power and divergent interests is conflict between women's interests and employers. Women workers and industrial managers assess risks and benefits very differently, in ways that reflect their different interests.

Both employees and employers would like to avoid fetal damage. But while women workers want access to good jobs with safe working conditions, employers also seek to lower labor costs and to avoid third-party suits on behalf of damaged fetuses. Employers vary in their concern about health hazards. Some are very worried about chemical effects, others are not. Yet management in general is keenly aware that it can be expensive to limit exposure to toxic chemicals through engineering controls.

In cases where the fetus may be at risk through the mother, employers have argued that giving fertile women access to all jobs and making jobs safe enough for a fetus would be prohibitively expensive. By focusing on possible dire consequences of teratogenic exposures to women employees, employers have come to believe that reversing fetal exclusion policies would put the fetus at risk and raise their costs, possibly driving them out of business. They maintain that these concerns dwarf the secondary issues of workplace health hazards and women's access to jobs. Thus, employers often choose to exclude fertile women from jobs rather than reduce exposures so that all workers would be protected.

Women workers and fetal health. The second issue concerning conflicting interests and power is the potential conflict between the fetus and the woman. Companies that exclude fertile women cast the problem of reproductive hazards in a way that pits the employment interests of women against their interest in the health of their offspring. Employers link reproduction to women only and appoint themselves guardians of the fetus. They establish policies designed to ensure that women do not act against the best interests of the fetus, as defined by the company. It is as if the woman and the fetus are in competition, with the company as judge considering fetal health to be paramount. Women are then told that they must be denied jobs in order to protect the fetus. They are treated as mothers who require protection until they are proven sterile. Fetal exclusion policies thus place women's interests as mothers in opposition to their interests as workers.

When hazards to fetal health exist in the workplace, women may be willing to take the chance of fetal damage in order to get or keep a job. Employers then may intervene by excluding women in an effort to protect fetuses from harm. There is considerable social support for the view that fetuses must be protected from the decisions of the mother. Fletcher (1980), for example, argues that the fetus has rights in relation to the mother who smokes, drinks alcohol, uses drugs nonmedicinally, and knowingly puts the fetus at risk for genetic damage. We have seen issues of fetal rights develop in other areas, such as with abortion, fetal surgery, and prenatal abnormalities. In these cases, third parties have intervened, not so much with paternalism toward the woman as to protect the fetus against the woman.[44]

One approach to fetal hazards by government officials, academic scientists, and others has been to argue that women should be able to take this risk of possible fetal harm. For example, an attorney involved in litigation stemming from fetal exclusion policies has argued that once OSHA standards are met, employers should offer men and women the same choices:

> full information and confidential counselling on potential hazards plus *voluntary temporary transfers* during the period of potential risk. An employer minimally must treat similarly situated employees similarly, and either restrict both men and women from areas which pose a potential hazard to their future children or offer both the *right to choose*. (Emphasis added.)[45]

However, the notion of choice in relation to reproductive risk is troublesome. The economic necessity of work, limited job alternatives, and incomplete employee information on reproductive hazards constrain choice in employment. Government regulations such as OSHA standards are based on the fundamental assumption that employees should not be able to assume risks associated with hazardous conditions. Yet in the case of reproductive hazards in industry, major dilemmas of workers faced with losing their reproductive health or their jobs are allowed to exist. This is true when employers respond to chemical hazards by excluding fertile women or by allowing employees to risk reproductive damage in full awareness of the risk.

Women and men. The third issue of conflicting interests and power concerns men's and women's interests in reproductive health. Certainly both women and men benefit by reducing exposure to toxic chemicals. Both women and men also want to avoid reproductive damage. Nevertheless, their interests may diverge in specific areas because of the ways in which fetal exclusion policies have been applied. As we have seen, barring women can expose more men to reproductive hazards and other health risks. Also, the question of excluding women arises when women are new to a job, for exclusion tends to occur in jobs that have been traditionally male, not in predominantly female jobs. Targeting women as risky workers and barring them from normally high-paying jobs can widen the wage gap between men and women. Fetal exclusion policies identifying women as high-risk thus may bolster the division of labor by sex.

The impact of fetal exclusion policies

Fetal exclusion policies are ineffective in guarding against reproductive hazards and other occupational risks. In some ways, they also pit women's interests against those of the fetus, those of industry, and those of men. Employers have framed the problem of reproductive hazards in such a way that women's employment interests may be opposed to the well-being of the fetus, women's health and employment interests clash with employers' interests in reducing the costs of doing business, and the division of labor and wage differentials between men and women are reinforced.

Thus, the way in which industrial management has cast the problem and carried out exclusionary policies not only has not been truly protective but has deepened divisions and already conflicting interests in society. These policies have been neither protective nor equitable.

GENETIC SCREENING AND STRATIFICATION BY RACE

Susceptibility policies raise issues of racial stratification and discrimination as well as more general problems of exclusion based on health. Typically, genetic screening has a dual character: Its purpose is to identify individual susceptibility, but screening programs often focus on gross categories of workers.

Distribution of genetic traits

Many genetic traits and diseases, such as those shown in Table 7, are most common among specific racial or ethnic groups. As the table indicates, genetic traits that are screened for often are found among populations such as blacks, Filipinos, and Mediterranean Jews in the case of G-6-PD, and Italians and Greeks in the case of beta thalassemia. If managers exclude people who have sickle cell trait, for example, then they may exclude 10 percent of the black work force and few white workers. Thus, part of the reason "susceptibility" usually has a racial dimension is that racial and ethnic minorities have more of the targeted genetic traits. Therefore, individuals selected for testing programs or for exclusion from jobs are also more likely to be from those groups.

Selective concern with special risk

The treatment of workers who undergo genetic screening, like the treatment of women who face reproductive hazards,

Table 7. *Frequency of genetic factors that may affect*
exposure risks

Genetic abnormality	Groups with disproportionately high rates	Frequency in subpopulation[a]
G-6-PD deficiency (homozygotes, all males)	Blacks, Filipinos, Mediterranean Jews, also Chinese	13–16% U.S. blacks 12–13% Filipinos 11% Mediterranean Jews 1–8% Scandinavians 2–5% Chinese 1–2% Greek 1% European Jews 0.1% British and U.S. whites
Sickle cell trait (heterozygotes)	Blacks, also Sicilians, Arabs, American Indians, Greeks, and Mexicans	8–13% U.S. blacks 0.1% whites
Alpha$_1$-antitrypsin deficiency (heterozygotes)	Swedes, Danes, Norwegians, Irish, Russians, Germans, English, other Northern and Central Europeans	7–9% Scandinavians, Irish, English, Germans, Russians, and Central Europeans 4–5% French and Belgians 3–4% General U.S. population 2–3% Jews 1–2% U.S. blacks
Beta thalassemia trait (heterozygotes)	Italians, Greeks	2–5% Italian and Greek Americans 2–7% U.S. blacks

[a]The frequencies in subgroups of the population are in dispute.
Estimates vary, and even the estimates for frequency rates among the
population as a whole differ.
Sources: Calabrese (1986, 1984) and Office of Technology Assessment
(1990, 1983).

is influenced by social factors. It does not arise simply from a neutral application of medical technology; it generally emerges when a group is relatively new to a specific workplace or occupation. This effect can be seen in the chemical industry, where blacks have been employed only recently and have been tested for sickle cell trait and G-6-PD deficiency.[46] The employment data in Table 8 reveal that industries that have focused on susceptible workers and have conducted genetic screening have been those in which the proportion of black employment has increased since 1960. From 1960 to 1980, the proportion of blacks has risen in major manufacturing industries that involve significant workplace health hazards, including chemicals and allied products, petroleum and other nondurable goods, steel and iron, motor vehicles, textiles, and rubber and plastic products.

As with women, when members of a racial or ethnic group move into jobs they had not held previously, their presence becomes a problem and their distinctive health becomes an issue for employers. The question of special risk and exclusion arises when they are both new and a minority in relatively high-paying jobs, but not usually when they are a majority. If the majority group were excluded, who would be left for the low-wage work force?

This trend does not necessarily preclude the wholesale exclusion of a previously predominant group in an occupation, however. If employers believed that black workers in certain virtually all-black industrial production jobs were at special risk and could be a costly burden, these workers could be replaced with another minority group or with white workers.[47]

Another way in which genetic screening is similar to fetal exclusion policies is that in deciding whether to exclude those at special risk, company officials seem compelled to choose between job discrimination and health protection.

Table 8. *Production and related workers in selected*
manufacturing industries, by race, 1960–1980

Industry	Percent and number black[a] production and related workers of total employed[b]		
	1960	1970	1980
Chemical and allied products			
Black	6.0%	10.7%	13.8%
	51,573	52,723	86,110
Total	857,786	491,679	624,167
Rubber and miscellaneous plastic products			
Black	6.2%	9.9%	10.8%
	24,083	37,027	48,471
Total	389,602	375,514	448,957
Steel and iron[c]			
Black	12.7%	16.4%	15.7%
	116,482	110,759	106,025
Total	918,535	676,630	674,098
Motor vehicles and motor vehicle equipment			
Black	8.9%	15.7%	16.1%
	74,811	122,665	138,722
Total	838,935	783,510	859,948
Textile mill products			
Black	4.5%	12.7%	20.5%
	43,136	100,520	151,087
Total	963,040	789,772	735,604
Petroleum refining and other nondurable goods[d]			
Black	4.1%	13.9%	11.9%
	11,398	112,617	42,262
Total	281,353	807,776	354,383

Notes to Table 8.

*a*Race categories for 1980 included white; black; American Indian, Eskimo and Aleut; Asian and Pacific Islander; and other race. Race categories for 1960 and 1970 included white, Negro, and other races. People of Spanish/Hispanic origin marked white, black, or others of the race categories.

b"Production and related workers" refers to:

  1980: Precision production, craft, and repair occupations; and operators, fabricators, and laborers.

  1970: Craft and kindred workers; operatives, except transport; transport equipment operatives; and laborers, except farm.

  1960: Includes *all workers employed in the industry*.

  1970 and 1980 figures do not include: Professional and technical workers; managers and administrators; sales workers; clerical workers; farmers, farm managers and farm workers; service workers; and private household workers.

*c*For 1960 and 1970, this category includes primary ferrous industries, including blast furnaces, steelworks, rolling and finishing mills, and other primary iron and steel industries. For 1980, it includes primary steel and iron industries.

*d*For 1960, this category includes petroleum and coal products, including petroleum refining and miscellaneous petroleum and coal products. Figures for 1970 and 1980 may largely reflect employment trends among production workers in "other nondurable goods," rather than petroleum refining.

Sources: Bureau of the Census (1984), Table 1: Selected Characteristics of Employed Persons by Occupation, Industry, and Sex: 1980, pp. 1–180.

  Bureau of the Census (1972), Table 1: Industry Group of Employed Persons by Occupation, Age, and Sex: 1970, pp. 1–80; and Table 2: Industry Group of Employed Persons by Occupation, Race, Spanish Origin, and Sex: 1970, pp. 81–128.

  Bureau of the Census (1963), Table 2: Detailed Occupation of Employed Persons, by Detailed Industry and Sex, for the United States: 1960, pp. 7–146.

  Bureau of the Census (1967), Table 3: Race of the Experienced Civilian Labor Force and of Employed Persons, by Detailed Industry and Sex, for the United States: 1960, pp. 7–9.

Racial restrictions in employment

Despite their similarities, exclusionary policies that focus on fetal hazards and on genetic traits have significant differences. Some of these stem from the fact that reproductive and fetal risks have been associated almost exclusively with women. Protectionist policies for women workers have a long history, whereas such policies for racial minorities have begun to emerge only recently. Instead, the case of black workers and genetic screening reveals a history of eugenic policies.[48] Black workers in low-income jobs are often considered either dispensable or especially resistant to occupational hazards.[49] Both women and racial and ethnic minorities have been regarded as special groups requiring special treatment. Both also have been declared protected classes under the law, due to legislation enacted over the past several decades. But only women have been ideologically protected as well (because of their presumed special medical and reproductive vulnerabilities).

Evidence of health differences and race prejudice

Much of the data on genetically based health differences by race is highly ambiguous. Even apparently special effects by race may be environmental and not genetic in origin, stemming not from heredity but from more dangerous jobs, poorer nutrition, and hazardous housing. Differences in disease and mortality among blacks and whites in the United States are substantial. Life expectancy for U.S. blacks in 1988 was 71.5 years, compared with 75.5 years for whites.[50] The black infant mortality rate in the 1980s was twice the rate for whites.[51] Death rates were higher for blacks than for whites for heart disease and stroke, cancer, cirrhosis, tuberculosis, and diabetes.[52]

Some disease and mortality patterns of blacks and whites may be largely due to genetic differences or other intrinsic biological traits. In the case of skin cancer, blacks are genetically resistant but whites have genes that make them susceptible to it.[53] Blacks have higher rates of pseudofolliculitis barbae (PSB), a skin disorder, but compared with whites they have lower rates of cystic fibrosis, phenylketonuria, and other diseases.[54]

Some of the factors that help account for the differences between blacks and whites in disease and death rates are health practices, such as smoking, drinking, diet, and exercise. Other factors are differences in socioeconomic status that make blacks more likely than whites to develop chronic diseases and to die young – inferior housing, fewer years of schooling, reduced access to health care, and higher poverty levels.[55] Much is known about the different living conditions, employment, and health practices of blacks and whites, but data concerning precisely what causes disease patterns among blacks and whites are uncertain.[56] Yet white people in a racially divided society are predisposed – prejudiced – to believe blacks are not as healthy as whites because of inborn characteristics and not because of different social treatment or different social conditions. This is true whether blacks in an occupation are perceived to be especially hardy or particularly vulnerable to disease.

To give an important example, epidemiological studies showing higher lung cancer rates among blacks in the steel industry have led to many interpretations that blacks are predisposed to disease. In response to early research findings suggesting that blacks might be at greater risk, steel company officials expressed considerable interest in substantiating the health response by race and in demonstrating that certain workers were more susceptible. Yet blacks have had the dirtiest, most dangerous jobs, such as standing on top of coke ovens.[57] As the scientist directing a major study of steelworkers reported:

> It generally might be true that particular racial groups have higher mortality rates in certain branches of industry. But it was economic selection that went on in the steelworker population I studied. The top-side coke oven jobs became black jobs. Blacks were at the bottom of the totem pole and got the lousiest jobs.[58]

Overall, blacks suffer much more from disease and disability caused by their jobs. They have many more of the dirtiest, lowest paying, most hazardous jobs. Robinson (1984) finds that compared with white workers, black workers are in jobs that are from 37 to 52 percent more likely to produce a serious accident or illness. Even when blacks and whites with the same levels of education and work experience are compared, blacks are found in more dangerous jobs.[59]

In a study of 6,631 textile workers, Martin and Higgins (1976) found that 60.2 percent of black workers and only 6.1 percent of white workers worked in the three dustiest departments: opening, carding, and picking. Blacks had much higher rates of byssinosis and other respiratory disease. In a study of the rubber industry by McMichael and others (1976), 27 percent of blacks but only 3 percent of whites worked in the more hazardous mixing and compounding area, located at the front of the production line in rubber plants. Black workers had higher rates of prostate and respiratory cancer than white workers.

Evidence from other industries shows that blacks also are assigned disproportionately to jobs using caustic chemicals in the electronics industry, to foundry jobs in the auto industry, to stemming jobs with substantial arsenic exposure in the tobacco industry, to sandblasting jobs with silica dust exposure in shipyards, and to furnace jobs in the steel industry.[60]

When evidence of health differences between white and black workers emerges, the question of causation arises. As mentioned, contrasting health patterns may be due to work history, living environment, or diet on the one hand, or genetic constitution on the other. The distinction between "environmental" and "inborn" is a murky one at best. For example, sickle cell trait is concentrated among populations that have been exposed to malaria over generations, because it confers an advantage by protecting against the most severe forms of malaria. Thus what seems at first to be the clearest example of "genetic" variation turns out also to be, in a sense, an "environmental" difference between racial and ethnic groups. But whatever the cause, the policy dilemma remains: what to do when evidence of systematic variation by race appears.

An example of this problem can be seen in the smaller lung capacity of black workers relative to white workers. This observed difference by race has been taken into account in federal OSHA health standards and NIOSH recommendations.[61] The OSHA cotton dust standard, for example, included an adjustment for lung function among blacks. Government regulations instructed employers to multiply the lung function test results for blacks by 0.85 "to adjust for ethnic differences. Comparative studies in general show the vital capacity of black workers to be about 15 percent less than that of white workers."[62]

OSHA included this adjustment on the advice of NIOSH, which had concluded that blacks intrinsically have smaller thoraxes relative to total body weight, aside from previous occupational and environmental conditions. NIOSH officials believed that without such an adjustment, employers might find limited lung capacity among blacks and not hire them. However, others criticized OSHA for adopting this adjustment. They argued that the data on race differences were insufficient and that the standard might foster discrimination by calling attention to the possibility that blacks may have limited lung capacity.[63]

Thus, both opponents and supporters of a race adjustment in medical testing at work expected that blacks as a group would suffer no matter which testing policy was adopted. In the case of lung function tests, blacks could be penalized for their health whether or not employers and government officials made an adjustment for smaller lung capacity. This case points to the fact that the social response to health differences by race reflects deep-seated patterns of differential working and living conditions among racial and ethnic groups and a long history of racial discrimination in employment.

Sickle cell testing

Sickle cell trait is different from sickle cell anemia, which is a disorder found in about 1 in 500 blacks who inherit the sickle cell gene from both parents. Sickle cell anemia reduces life expectancy and often entails debilitating symptoms. In contrast, sickle cell trait is fairly common, affecting about 1 in 11 black Americans who are heterozygous carriers of the sickle cell gene they inherit from one parent. Unlike sickle cell anemia, sickle cell trait may not make individuals more vulnerable to industrial chemicals. Whether the trait produces any symptoms or disability in carriers is controversial.[64] While some scientists believe that individuals with sickle cell trait might have sickle cell anemia crises if deprived of oxygen or exposed to specific chemicals, others disagree.[65] In fact, they argue, carriers may suffer no worse health than those who do not have the trait.

When OSHA officials evaluated possible risks associated with sickle cell trait among divers, they rejected including special provisions for those with sickle cell trait in their commercial diving standard. NIOSH had recommended to OSHA that divers with the trait not dive below certain depths. They based their recommendation on evidence suggesting that divers with sickle cell trait may suffer adverse effects, including hemoglobin crystallization and osteonecrosis, a bone ailment, from deep underwater work. OSHA did not adopt this recommendation, however. Both OSHA and NIOSH generally have taken the position that sickle cell trait is not a health risk for workers.[66]

The studies tentatively linking sickle cell trait to disease among blacks have received tremendous attention, even though numerous other studies refute this link and maintain that sickle cell trait poses no health hazard to carriers.[67] Despite major differences in perspective within the scientific community, blacks have been excluded from jobs. Employers who test workers for sickle cell trait, particularly in airline companies, chemical firms, and the military, have tested and excluded only blacks.

The Air Force Academy, for example, began rejecting all black pilot trainees with sickle cell trait in 1972, in the belief that lack of oxygen at high altitudes would be very dangerous for blacks with the trait. In 1979, the Academy dismissed six young black men with sickle cell trait. The U.S. Army, Navy, and Marines also have barred individuals with sickle cell trait from aviation and flight crew training. In addition, beginning in the early 1970s, major airlines have tested their black flight attendants for sickle cell trait, and have grounded or fired all those found to have the trait.[68]

Genetic screening for sickle cell trait in the industrial context raises some issues similar to those that public sickle cell screening has raised. Public sickle cell testing programs have screened newborns, schoolchildren, marriage license applicants, prison inmates, and state mental hospital patients. These public programs for genetic screening have proliferated since the 1970s. Some of them have been compulsory. Such programs have expanded because of improved diagnostic techniques, considerable publicity, the infusion of money, political concern with showing support for blacks, and charges of previous neglect.[69]

Public sickle cell testing programs have suffered from major problems that industrial programs have shared, including widespread confusion between sickle cell anemia and sickle cell trait,[70] nonexistent or inadequate counseling of those with positive test results, stigmatization of those with sickle cell trait, lack of confidentiality of medical records, and the lack of medical treatment for sickle cell anemia. Individuals have been denied employment when they have learned through public screening programs that they have sickle cell trait and have reported it on job application medical forms.[71] In addition, many insurance companies have raised rates for those with sickle cell trait.[72] Sickle cell testing in industry has led to problems similar to those that arise in public screening, sometimes magnified by the more coercive context of medical testing in the workplace – a situation that will be examined in Chapter 5.

As with blacks and sickle cell trait, virtually every ethnic

93

and racial group has a higher prevalence of at least one genetic trait that may predispose its members to disease.
Group members with the trait may then be considered to be
at special risk. Scandinavians and others with northern and
central European ancestry, for example, are the most likely
individuals to be deficient in serum alpha$_1$-antitrypsin (SAT).
This enzyme deficiency may make them more vulnerable to
emphysema or chronic bronchitis after exposure to industrial
chemicals. If employers screen for SAT, beta thalassemia,
G-6-PD, or other genetic characteristics, persons who are
Greek, Italian, Ashkenasi Jewish, Chinese, Filipino – to
name only a few of the ethnic groups involved – may also
have their genes deemed inappropriate for certain jobs.
However, individuals who have been excluded by susceptibility policies so far have come disproportionately from
groups that have traditionally been victims of discrimination
based on sex, race, or ethnicity.[73] The treatment of the group
that is considered high risk tends to reflect the group's position in the work force and in society generally.

WORK FORCE STRATIFICATION BY SEX AND RACE: CONCLUSIONS

Social stratification by race and sex exerts a powerful impact
on occupational health practices. It contributes to a misplaced emphasis on the susceptibility of female and minority
workers. These workers are more likely to be identified as
high risk and excluded. Exclusionary policies are not necessarily protective, however. Avoiding workers who may be at
increased health risk does not solve problems of reproductive and other occupational hazards. Nevertheless, the notion of high-risk workers contributes to a false view of most
workers as safe, as discussed in Chapter 3. Thus, white men
(or any other group) can be thought capable of withstanding
toxic chemical exposures normally and safely in higher paying positions. They can therefore be considered the biolog-
ically appropriate work force for those jobs.

An important additional reason that women and minorities can be considered risky workers in jobs they have newly entered, while other workers are considered safe, goes beyond their health. They may indeed be "high-risk workers" for companies to employ because of the threat of lawsuits for employment discrimination. However, this would not be the case if workers who remain in the jobs begin to sue employers, charging that they unfairly are being selected for exposure to particular toxins on the job.

The use of technologies for differentiating high-risk from low-risk workers has functioned to deepen divisions in the work force both by race and by sex. These policies reinforce the division of labor as well as widen the wage gap between men and women and by race and ethnicity. Genetic susceptibility policies can be, in effect, forms of sexual, racial, or ethnic discrimination that bolster social stratification. This perspective contrasts sharply with the stance of corporate managers – that their genetic screening and fetal exclusion policies benefit workers, employers, and the public and thereby advance the social good. As we have seen, however, susceptibility policies do not have to be designed to impede women and ethnic and racial minority groups for them to have that effect.

The new technologies, along with the new heightened awareness of reproductive hazards and other workplace risks, can indeed serve useful ends in improving public health. But certainly genetic screening and fetal protection policies in industry can be discriminatory and undermine health, too. These problems arise when companies respond to reproductive and other chemical hazards by compelling workers to choose between their jobs and their health, by resolving that dilemma through imposing exclusionary policies without employment protection or compensation, by failing to protect workers who remain, or by in effect pitting men against women and blacks against whites in a contest for jobs.

Alternative practices can circumvent the adverse effects of fetal exclusion and genetic screening policies. These alternatives include temporary exclusion and wage protection for those who are removed, more evidence on reproductive and other health risks to women and men, and engineering controls to limit the exposure of all workers to chemical hazards.[74] Even though in the areas of employment and occupational health the interests of women and men, and blacks and whites, are not identical, and though women's interests are not always going to be the same as the interests of their children or future children, such policy provisions would further some common interests.

The problem of occupational and reproductive hazards should be reframed so that it is conceptualized more broadly. Reproductive damage does not occur only in women in certain industrial production jobs, and occupational hazards do not confront only certain individuals with predisposing genetic traits. Instead, all reproductive and health hazards to both men and women in a wide range of jobs should be considered the problem of occupational risk. This would advance reproductive health and increase real protection in the workplace. The fact that chemical hazards have not been reconceptualized in this way has much to do with the industrial context of power and control in which work hazards exist. It is to these issues that we next turn our attention.

Chapter 5

Power and control in industrial medicine

The [susceptibility] tests do not deny employment; they
merely orient job placement to the advantage of both the
employer and the employed.

H. E. Stokinger and L. D. Scheel
(NIOSH scientists)

Normal "marketplace" corporate policies would discard
human beings (correctly or incorrectly from a biological
perspective) on a scrap heap for the impoverished.

Howard Samuel
(President, AFL-CIO Industrial Union Department)

GENETIC screening to test newborns and potential carriers for genetic abnormalities has been employed for years in public programs and private medical practice.[1] Genetic testing in the workplace is similar in some respects, but the social framework of industrial medicine makes it different in several important ways – most notably in the effects of control structures, in the doctor–patient relationship, in the limitations on choices of those screened, and in the confidentiality of test information. In the workplace, for example, the dynamics of gaining information and giving consent are very different. When supporters of genetic screening and fetal exclusion policies assert that susceptibility tests are useful means of enabling workers to have jobs with working conditions that suit them, they fail to recognize such important differences, particularly those that limit workers' ability to know or to choose. In this chapter, I will examine major characteristics of the work environment that affect both the flow of information and the control over decisions.

CONTROL OF INFORMATION

Employers retain major control over information regarding chemical health hazards and medical surveillance of employees. The use of risk information is almost entirely management's prerogative. Workers lack information that could be important to their decisions about employment, medical care, and reproductive life.

Limited employee access to information

Employers require about 48 percent of all employees and 62 percent of all manufacturing employees to take a preplacement medical examination. Approximately 34 percent of all employees and 37 percent of manufacturing workers also are given periodic medical examinations. In large manufacturing firms, the figures are particularly high.[2]

Workers and labor officials confront many obstacles in trying to learn what tests are conducted, what the results are, and how employers use them in making job placement decisions. For information regarding a company's medical tests and employment policies, employees and anyone outside the company must depend largely on what the employer is willing to provide them. For example, when a company official states that certain tests are not being conducted or that nobody is denied a job on the basis of test results, it may or may not be true, but it is difficult to obtain the information to make that determination.

In the case of preemployment screening, job candidates who are denied a job usually do not know what the tests revealed or the reason they were not hired. When an employer conducts blood and urine tests, for instance, job applicants are seldom told what the samples are tested for. They could be checked for anemia, inherited genetic traits, early pregnancy, chromosome damage, drug use, or even the risk of a heart attack.[3]

In the case of ongoing medical surveillance, too, currently employed workers have considerable trouble obtaining information on test results and actions based on them. Sometimes the data they do get are distorted. Control of chemical exposure information also is retained by the company.[4] As a national health and safety official with the AFL-CIO said in an interview: "Employers regard their testing and other medical information as extremely proprietary."

Thus, although medical tests in the workplace are ostensibly designed to benefit employees as well as industry, employers do not necessarily provide test results, explain their significance to workers, or describe exposure hazards that may be producing symptoms. Based on its review of documents and testimony at government hearings by labor, management, and scientists, OSHA concluded: "Denial of direct, unrestricted access to exposure and medical information is commonplace, if not the universal practice of industry."[5]

At the state level, employers' control over medical information is constrained somewhat by laws requiring that employees be informed of chemical hazards and medical test results. For example, employers in Massachusetts who require workers to take a medical exam must give them a copy of the medical report. In at least thirty states, right-to-know laws require employers to make information on toxic substances used at work available to employees.[6]

At the national level, employees received limited rights of access to their own medical records with the passage of the OSHA access-to-medical-records standard in 1987.[7] This measure requires employers to give workers certain medical records upon request, but it does not require them to disclose information about tests or medical examinations to workers who do not ask for it. It also does not give workers rights to correct invalid information. Job applicants are not covered at all under the standard. Employers generally have not been compelled to disclose the purpose and nature of medical procedures or reveal how the results are used.

Several cases from large manufacturing companies reveal problems that have arisen from management's control of information regarding health effects and chemical hazards.

Benzidine exposure. In New York, over 50 percent of the dye workers in a large chemical plant developed bladder tumors, with 22 percent (17 workers) contracting bladder cancer. The workers with bladder cancer were exposed to benzidine but were not informed of the nature of their illness or exposure by either the company or the university staff assisting in the medical examinations.[8]

Pesticide poisoning. In Texas, employees suffering early symptoms of pesticide poisoning were given medication that temporarily masked the symptoms, then sent back to work. In numerous cases, nonmedical company officials administered the antidote, although it is a prescription drug.[9]

Asbestos exposure. In New Jersey, workers exposed to asbestos were not informed of the hazards or treated properly for medical effects; information obtained later indicated that management knew of the health risks and medical problems long before employees learned of them. Workers and labor officials claimed that even after government investigation and legal action, they were still unable to obtain adequate information on the testing program and health risks.[10]

When issues of genetic testing arise, employees and union officials cite examples such as these to justify their skeptical stance. They usually state that it is very difficult to find out what genetic screening tests are conducted, what exposure hazards exist, and on what basis hiring, firing, and transfer decisions are made. Since screening tests are typically performed before hiring, employees have a hard time citing details regarding the exclusion of workers from jobs because of test results. The unions' ability to find out about medical testing used in hiring is limited. Further, their access to data on periodic testing of current employees is narrowly circumscribed. As an occupational health specialist for the Oil, Chemical, and Atomic Workers International Union has said: "Most of the companies employing our members have sophisticated medical surveillance programs set up. However, we don't know what those medical surveillance programs are set up to detect."[11]

In general, it is difficult to determine why an employee is not hired, or fired, or transferred – whether it is on the basis of abnormal test results, prior compensation claims, or general lack of qualifications for the job, unrelated to health. In this context, the potential for unfair treatment of workers who are excluded through susceptibility policies is magnified.

Employer use and abuse of information

Information problems also surround the confidentiality of medical records. Company officials may state that their genetic testing program does not affect job placement and is only for workers' information or for diagnostic, research, or other medical purposes. But genetic information entered into a worker's medical file may not be restricted to medical personnel. It could be submitted to management or to insurance companies, posing a threat to the worker's economic security.[12] As OSHA has concluded, "workers have little genuine expectations of true confidentiality as to employment medical records."[13] Records may be given to management for them to determine whether a particular illness should be considered occupational in origin. Moreover, legal restrictions do not prohibit employee medical records from being circulated within a company.[14]

In one chemical corporation, company directives have required managers to participate in deciding whether an illness is caused by work exposure. According to its rules, site managers must approve the medical specialists who evaluate evidence in order to establish disease causality. When the medical department notes disease symptoms in an employee, "the cases are [to be] reviewed by a management body which comprises the plant manager, assistant plant manager, and the medical director. Other management officials may join depending on the necessity of their input."[15]

Employers seeking to reduce work force costs can hire computer search firms to alert them to job applicants who have had medical problems in previous jobs.[16] One search company, for example, investigates the employment history, workers' compensation claims, and other records of job applicants in order to provide companies with a profile of potentially expensive workers. Evidence of genetic traits or other possible susceptibility could be entered into those files. Already, genetic information has affected the employment of workers through its inclusion in insurance company files.[17] Workers may be denied jobs because of insurance records of their genes.

When medical information indicating sickle cell trait has traveled beyond the industrial medical department, carriers of the trait have suffered job discrimination, been forced to pay higher insurance premiums, or have been barred from the armed forces.[18] Current laws have not prevented such medical information from entering into personnel and insurance files.[19]

Another important feature of industry's control of information pertains to their use of evidence on damage from exposure to toxic chemicals. Only certain studies are conveyed to workers or the public.[20] For example, DuPont has given national publicity to evidence that suggests that their workers are safer than the general population, but it has withheld other evidence showing negative effects from their particular industrial hazards.[21]

The fact that industry funds genetic research and research labs has important implications for the flow of information as well as for secrecy in the development of genetic technology. Corporations sometimes fund research under proprietary agreements that restrict publication of the findings. Industrial funding also can affect the types of questions chosen for research, the findings themselves, and the way in which the findings are disseminated.[22]

Industry trade associations such as the American Industrial Health Council and the Chemical Manufacturers Association, along with many individual companies, have opposed not only expanded employee access to medical records, but also chemical labeling and other right-to-know provisions. In fact, U.S. industry's recorded testimony on worker health data has been overwhelmingly against broader employee access.[23] Dow Chemical, for example, in its testimony against the OSHA access-to-medical-records standard, has argued that granting employees and unions greater access to records would give companies an incentive not to include information in workers' medical files.[24] This is an acknowledgment of the divergent interests that labor and management have had in information access.

Employers say that existing industrial procedures and government standards are adequate for ensuring that all the information employees need is provided to them. They explain that although cases in which companies have misused information are rare, government regulators, the unions, and the media have seized upon them to distort industrial practices. Managers say they cooperate with all "reasonable" requests for medical information. They emphasize the considerable resources they expend complying with government reporting requirements, conducting educational programs, circulating findings from company studies, and collaborating with outside research projects.

Employers exhibit a wide spectrum of cooperation in

providing data on exposures, testing programs, or medical conditions. While many are generally cooperative, many others give inadequate or inaccurate responses to those who seek information. Some refuse to provide medical findings, citing their concern with releasing data that could be misinterpreted or that could reveal company secrets. Others are relatively quick to initiate legal action to try to prevent unions, OSHA, NIOSH, or other government agencies from gaining access to health information.

Employers express concern with being forced to let out trade secrets, such as chemical components or industrial processes, that could benefit competitors. Broader access to industry data could also reveal information that might lead to troublesome and costly lawsuits: In some cases, employers are more vulnerable to legal action if it can be shown that they had prior knowledge of hazards. In regulatory proceedings, congressional hearings, and in the press, employers argue that their own practices do not pose the greatest threat to the confidentiality of medical and exposure records. That threat, they claim, comes from the government and the unions, who make excessive demands on industry for this information.[25] Extending access any further beyond the control of management, they maintain, would be to impose a substantial hardship on them.

The burden of proof

Workers bear the burden of proof as well as the risks of chemical exposure and the consequences of uncertain data. Many employers withhold information that would reveal incriminating working conditions. For example, industry officials have submitted misleading scientific evidence to government agencies such as OSHA or have refused to provide data. They have then criticized government data for its gaps or inaccuracies.[26]

One of the reasons workers do not understand the risks they face is that companies limit access to information about effects of toxic chemicals. Obviously, it is often not in management's interest to provide full job-risk information to workers or the government, given its concerns with liability, workers' compensation, insurance costs, trade secrets, and negative publicity. But there are other reasons as well. A worker's level of education, popular mystification of scientific information on carcinogenic chemical effects, and distorted publicity about product safety can be real impediments to knowledge. Workers often mistrust the information about risk provided by management. They may also lack confidence in their ability to obtain accurate chemical hazard data and interpret its practical significance for their own health.[27]

Despite these handicaps, it is employees who have the burden of proving that disease is work-related. An official with the Oil, Chemical, and Atomic Workers Union refers to the process of discovering chemical hazards as the "body-in-the-morgue" method because it deduces hazards from dead or injured workers.[28] Widely used epidemiological methods of assessing the distribution of disease in specific populations rely on counting injured or ill workers. Employees who notice a large proportion of birth defects or lung cancer within the work force have to press for an investigation.

Employees also have the burden of showing the occupational origin of their illness when company personnel claim that their disease stems from causes outside the work environment. In workers' compensation hearings, for example, the typical scenario in large manufacturing companies is that the company physician testifies on the extent to which industrial chemicals contributed to the worker's ailment and the extent to which other exposures or dangerous personal habits caused the problem. The possibility of bias is obvious, since the doctor's professional expertise cannot be kept entirely separate from the fact of corporate employment. Nevertheless, workers who disagree with the company physician's assessment must produce compelling evidence of work hazards and link it persuasively to their own disease.[29]

Individuals who undergo preemployment tests of blood and urine typically do not have the opportunity to prove their employability. When they obtain information that they have been screened out of a job for medical reasons, they must still confront the fact that employers have wide discretion in determining medical fitness.

Under fetal exclusion policies, female employees have been presumed to be high-risk workers by virtue of their reproductive capacity. In many companies where such policies are in force, women have sought to demonstrate their suitability for specific jobs by offering proof of surgical sterilization.

In addition, workers are often faced with assessing an employer's claim that tighter regulation of chemical hazards, or even the existing regulation, will drive the firm out of business. If they accept the claim as true and oppose further regulation, they risk preserving their jobs at the cost of their health. If they decide it is false and support further regulation, they risk protecting their health at the cost of losing their jobs. How should they balance these risks, when much of the information needed to judge the veracity of industry claims is proprietary, closely guarded by employers?[30]

CORPORATE PREROGATIVES

Proponents of susceptibility policies often emphasize their potential for allowing more informed decisions. If we could identify genetic predispositions to environmental hazards, they claim, people could be told of their increased susceptibility and take action to avoid exposure to hazardous chemicals in their jobs. In this view, genetic technologies simply offer a means of expanding choice, for the benefit of individual employees, management, and society as a whole.

Within the workplace, however, it is management – not the employees or society – that makes most decisions regarding job placement, medical testing, and information to be given to workers. Employees do not control industrial health and employment practices. Nor do they usually have the power to choose alternative means of protection. Instead, industrial workers are frequently asked to choose between their health and their jobs, a choice so heavily constrained by economic pressures that it is not a real choice at all.

Job placement decisions

A corporate scientist and physician has said that the purpose of susceptibility tests "should be the enhancement of proper placement."[31] Few would dispute this statement. There is disagreement, however, over the definition of "proper placement." Conceptions vary as to what is proper job placement for those identified as high-risk workers.

Occasionally, employers claim that they conduct genetic tests only in order to safeguard workers' health, and that they never use test information for firing, demoting, or not hiring individual workers.[32] More typically, they emphasize their desire to place workers at risk in suitable jobs.[33] They stress work alternatives for those displaced by screening programs, but vary in their expectations as to what jobs high-risk workers would be able to have. Managers and scientists sometimes explain that another job in the firm would be made available to susceptible workers that would be safe even for those judged to be high risk. While providing safe jobs for everyone in the company is the ideal, most managers feel pressure to minimize their costs by avoiding high-risk workers altogether. The real result of much medical screening in the workplace has been exclusion.

With the new genetic technology and susceptibility policies, high-risk groups may be identified and either consigned to lower paying jobs or barred from employment. Workers who are fired or not hired for medical reasons may have a hard time obtaining similar types of work. They may find jobs in companies that do not require exposure to the same substances or in firms that do not attempt to differentiate susceptible workers. As mentioned in Chapter 4, the jobs from which workers deemed susceptible are screened tend to be relatively high-paying ones. Jobs that workers turn to after having been screened out are generally lower paying

ones, often in smaller companies – which are also less likely
to have extensive occupational health protections or to be
unionized.[34] The corporate medical director of Manville Corporation, a large minerals firm, has acknowledged this trend:

> The ability to screen workers . . . probably has some correla-
> tion with the size of the employer and the extent and scope of
> his medical program; so that a person who would be denied
> employment might very well go to a "small business" . . .
> [The small company] may be no less honest, no less ethically
> motivated than the big business, but the tools at hand for
> identifying the susceptible worker or the tools at hand for
> maintaining a maximally protective environment are probably
> less in scope and effectiveness.[35]

Genetic tests are often evaluated in purely technical terms,
as if scientific predictiveness were the only standard relevant
to their use. Yet the industrial context in which they are used
can create problems of job security and employment discrimination for those who are tested. Workers who are identified
as susceptible to particular industrial substances may lose
their jobs, find their chances for promotion reduced, have
their insurance rates raised, or see their prospects for moving to a better job in another firm diminished.

Companies may systematically screen out workers perceived to be vulnerable, either because of a specific genetic
trait or for early symptoms of illness. Screening job applicants for indicators of increased risk is widespread. Employers can identify a broad range of predisposing health
factors through a physical exam, medical history, and specialized diagnostic tests. Genetic screening differs from other
types of workplace testing in two respects. It has the allure of
an exciting new technology, and it appeals to corporate officials and others whose values and economic interests predispose them to link illness to inborn frailties rather than to
working conditions. Despite its distinctive features, genetic
screening shares with other types of industrial screening the
goal of targeting individuals who are more likely to become
sick on the job. It also reveals dynamics of managerial power

in job placement similar to those found in other widely used company medical procedures. Employers "weed out" workers perceived to be at high risk for disease, even when the abnormality is not genetic in character. Major examples include exclusion based on tests that indicate increased risk of lower back trouble, pulmonary malfunction, or liver disease.

Back X-rays. Companies in the railroad industry and others have routinely given preemployment X-rays of the lower back to screen out job applicants who appear to be at increased risk for back injury. Such injuries are common in railroad work. They are a serious health problem for employees and a costly burden for both workers and employers. Proponents of genetic susceptibility policies often refer to railroad industry screening as a model that displays important benefits of medical screening.

A medical director of a railroad company emphasizes the high cost of legal claims, medical bills, and lost workdays caused by back injuries. He states that in 1980–81, the average company cost of settling a case of a ruptured intervertebral disc was in the realm of $125,000 to $150,000, and that 20 to 25 percent of all personal injury claims paid by the company were for back injuries.[36]

X-ray screening disqualifies approximately 10 percent of potential employees in the railroad industry. One railroad company in 1973 rejected about 40 percent of the 20,000 job applicants tested with back X-rays.[37] Company officials estimated that this high-risk group would have six to ten times the rate of back injuries as the group with "normal" test results. As many as one million job applicants undergo low-back X-ray examinations each year.[38] Hundreds of thousands of workers have been denied employment on the basis of these exams.

Railway officials assume that the developmental abnormalities that X-rays detect accurately indicate high risk of low-back injury. But estimates of the predictive accuracy of X-rays in detecting susceptibility to back pain or injury range from only 4 percent to 60 percent.[39] The X-ray tests have also been criticized for the risk of radiation exposure that they impose on job applicants. Nevertheless, railroad managers find back X-ray testing appealing in part because it locates risk in individuals rather than in workplace conditions. In addition, they maintain that such screening is cost-effective because what they save in compensation and disability claims is far more than the cost of X-ray testing programs. This is true despite the fact that back X-rays misclassify a high proportion of job applicants as high-risk workers, thereby misleading employers into rejecting valuable potential employees.

Pulmonary function tests. In the textile, chemical, mining, and electronics industries, testing programs for job applicants and employees have enabled companies to exclude workers with early signs of pulmonary problems. In one case, company officials posted a list of workers who had low scores on a breathing test, alerting them that they would be given a second chance to pass the test; failure would result in their losing their jobs.[40]

Liver function tests. In the oil and chemical industries, workers with low scores on liver function tests have been denied employment.[41] These tests indicate that the liver is not functioning properly, but they do not indicate why. Nor do they predict disease. Furthermore, they do not indicate which chemicals would be particularly hazardous.

Workers have been excluded on the basis of many types of test results. Employees and union officials base their doubts about genetic screening on extensive experience with medical surveillance programs. According to one national official with the United Steelworkers Union, "Workers' being transferred or fired as a result of medical surveillance is a constant issue." The president of the AFL-CIO Industrial Union Department expresses labor's reservations:

> Genetic screening has a potential for unjust application and short-sighted social policy. The probability of overreaction

that would unfairly reduce employment opportunities for thousands – perhaps millions – of men and women is established by past performance.[42]

Ample precedent exists for workers' exclusion based on medical tests to make union officials and employees especially skeptical about susceptibility policies.

Labor strength

The power of organized labor is frequently overestimated. Scientists and managers who support the existence of unions often point out that unions help establish company medical and employment practices and set up grievance procedures for employees who object to managerial actions. They argue that because unions offer employees many opportunities for effective participation in setting workplace policy, abuses of power by corporate management are not a serious problem. This argument ignores the fact that fewer than one in seven workers is a union member, and that since 1970 union membership has fallen in the chemical, oil, steel, auto, textile, and rubber and plastics industries (see Tables 9 and 10).

Of course, a union's effectiveness in the area of occupational health is only partly a function of size. A few industrial unions have developed a stronger voice in occupational health issues even as they have shrunk in membership. Initiative from national and local union officials has led to more labor pressure in the health arena than one would have predicted from the weight of the numbers alone. Unions that have actively addressed occupational health hazards in the 1970s and 1980s include the United Steelworkers, the United Auto Workers, the Oil, Chemical, and Atomic Workers, the International Chemical Workers, and the Amalgamated Clothing and Textile Workers. Each of these unions has conducted educational campaigns on toxics for their membership and the public. They have hired physicians, toxicologists, and others to develop their health programs. They have bargained with management over health issues and

Table 9. *Union membership within U.S. labor force, 1970–1989*

| Year | Union membership[a] | | Total labor force[b] |
	Percent of total labor force[b]	Number of members (in thousands)	
1970	25.7%	21,248	82,771
1971	25.3	21,327	84,382
1972	24.9	21,657	87,034
1973	24.9	22,276	89,429
1974	24.8	22,809	91,949
1975	23.8	22,361	93,775
1976	23.6	22,662	96,158
1977	22.7	22,456	99,009
1978	22.3	22,757	102,251
1979	21.5	22,579	104,962
1980	20.9	22,366	106,940
1981	—[c]	—[c]	108,670
1982	17.9	19,763	110,204
1983	15.9	17,717	111,550
1984	15.3	17,340	113,544
1985	14.7	16,996	115,461
1986	14.4	16,975	117,834
1987	14.1	16,913	119,865
1988	14.0	17,002	121,669
1989	13.7	16,960	123,869

[a]Includes active members reported by unions and employee associations, excluding Canadian members and members of single-firm labor organizations.
[b]Civilian labor force.
[c]Comparable data for 1981 are not available.
Sources: Bureau of Labor Statistics (1990, 1985), Bureau of the Census (1990), and Bureau of National Affairs (1984b, 1982).

lobbied for government regulation.[43] In some cases, small union locals also have developed a major interest in health and safety. In contrast, several large unions have virtually ignored workplace testing and other occupational health is-

Table 10. *Union membership in selected manufacturing industries, 1970 and 1980*

Industry	Percent and number union members of total employees[a] (in thousands)	
	1970[b]	1980[c]
Chemicals and allied products	34.4% 361	25.8% 320
Total	1,049	1,240
Rubber and plastics	46.9% 272	29.6% 205
Total	580	692
Steel and other primary metals	62.5% 788	58.3% 686
Total	1,260	1,176
Autos, aircraft, and other transportation equipment	59.8% 1,109	51.1% 1,038
Total	1,853	2,031
Textiles	19.6% 191	14.9% 117
Total	975	786
Petroleum	41.9% 80	34.1% 75
Total	191	220

[a] Includes all wage and salary employees.
[b] Includes active members reported by unions and employee associations, *including* Canadian members.
[c] Includes active members reported by unions and employee associations, *excluding* Canadian members.
Sources: Bureau of National Affairs (1982, Table 9), Bureau of Labor Statistics (1972, Table 16), and Bureau of the Census (1983, Table 707).

sues. Large manufacturing companies, where genetic testing is most common, are more heavily unionized than smaller manufacturers and firms in other industries.[44] Labor's responses to health hazards has varied widely in these firms.

Collective bargaining agreements between management and labor often include provisions regarding company medical practices. Approximately 80 percent of union contracts contain occupational safety and health clauses.[45] Some of these agreements provide wage and job security if workers show damage from industrial chemicals, or provide joint labor–management health committees.[46] In manufacturing, 62 percent of collective bargaining agreements mandated joint labor–management health and safety committees at union worksites in 1987.[47] However, collective bargaining agreements seldom address preemployment medical examinations or employers' hiring decisions.[48] Those that do constrain managerial initiative very little.

Despite inroads that unions have made in occupational health policy, many union locals – even those affiliated with large international unions – have had only limited influence over workplace practices such as medical testing and placement at specific plants. Unions have been no match for employers in bargaining over health surveillance programs, gaining access to chemical exposure information, and changing workplace policies.

Occupational medicine and company physicians

Large companies, as well as many small and medium-sized firms, routinely give preemployment and periodic physical examinations. Besides testing for such basic functions as hearing, vision, blood pressure, and lung capacity, they also test worker capacities to cope with conditions encountered in a particular workplace. Increasingly, employers check blood and urine for evidence of drug use.[49] These many tests are designed to see whether workers have health problems that would hinder their job performance or increase company medical costs. In addition, preemployment tests give base-line data to compare with subsequent exams.

The diagnosis of an occupational or genetic disease is not entirely a medical decision. Targeting high-risk workers through screening, and identifying an illness as an occupational disease instead of giving a genetic or life-style explanation, are not purely scientific processes. Despite technical similarities between much of worksite medicine and private practice, health care is different in industry. In such matters as getting professional advice, full risk information, and confidential treatment, the experience of workers differs from that of private patients. In a confidential interview, a physician with a large chemical firm listed some of the nonmedical concerns raised by identifying health hazards and linking them to working conditions:

> The legal staff worries about liability; the marketing staff worries about the sale of the product; the public relations staff is concerned with findings of possible hazards. Everyone is worried about costs and unfavorable publicity about working conditions and the safety of the products. Physicians understand this.

A physician with another major chemical corporation described to me a typical constraint placed on him by management:

> Company physicians are hamstrung by the companies they work for, such as in my case. I was allowed to monitor the workers and argue for its value. But as soon as we found problems, the work was stopped. We found abnormalities in some of the work force, which seriously threatened company products.

Although occupational physicians usually work directly for the company, employers often insist that they respect the confidentiality of the doctor–patient relationship. For example, in resisting proposals to allow workers and others broader access to industrial health information, they frequently argue that such access could undermine workers' faith in the private nature of meetings with the company's occupational physicians.[50]

The ethical code of the American Occupational Medical Association proclaims that physicians should "accord highest priority to the health and safety of the individual in the workplace," should "avoid allowing their medical judgement to be influenced by any conflict of interest," and should "treat as confidential whatever is learned about individuals served."[51] This code attempts to circumvent a real tension built into the work of physicians employed by industry. Employers expect company physicians to conduct medical screening in order to assist in hiring and firing, to testify at compensation hearings, to speak to the public regarding health issues on behalf of the employer, and to perform other tasks that make the confidentiality and patient-loyalty standards of private practice appear misplaced. The code implies that a physician's pursuit of many goals of the employer can constitute individual ethical misconduct that the upstanding physician should be able to avoid. Nevertheless, as part of their job, company physicians may convey to management not only test results but also diagnoses and other specific assessments of the medical condition of employees.

Legal provisions confirm the differences between a physician's responsibility to patients within and outside industry, with stronger patient-rights rules for private practice. For example, current statutes do not restrict the distribution of employee medical information within companies.[52] The law also deters employees from suing company physicians, in part because the "fellow servant" bar defines doctors as fellow employees, who are therefore shielded from suits against company management. This situation may change, however, so that occupational physicians and other company personnel will bear greater liability for workplace hazards.[53] The AFL-CIO Industrial Union Department president has deplored managerial control of occupational medicine in these terms:

Acceptable patient–physician relationships cannot usually be developed and maintained in a setting in which confidentiality and trust between the doctor and the worker is secondary to the interests of the corporation. Confidentiality, access to records for research, treatment and compensation, physician independence must be guaranteed.

Industrial genetic screening should only take place in a society that has created a system of screening within neutral community structures that protect the individual and his family during the counseling process. It must not take place in the coercive milieu of the typical industrial setting.[54]

In general, workers have limited influence over their job placement, the chemicals to which they are exposed, and the medical tests they are given. In the case of medical exams, an industrial worker told me:

We get a whole battery of tests: blood tests, breathing tests, X-rays. Workers don't have informed consent on the tests. They aren't told what the tests are for, and they aren't given the chance to refuse any test. If they tried, it would be a mistake, because then they are not cooperating with the medical department, which can threaten any subsequent claims.

Control over medical decisions in the workplace has different repercussions than it has in private medical practice. As an attorney with the United Steelworkers Union of America has said: "It is one thing to tell an individual you can't eat, or you can't have saccharin in your coffee. It is quite another thing to tell him you can't work in a particular kind of plant. I think we can get along without saccharin, or at least most of us can, but it is difficult to eat without a job."[55] Generally it has been labor, not management, that emphasizes employer control over medical risk and treatment in industrial settings. But a health and safety official at Eastman Kodak has admitted: "I am making the distinction between voluntary exposure versus industrial exposure. You have the choice to broil your steak or boil it. On the other hand, in the industrial environment, the responsibility for exposure, for controlling exposure, is not totally in the hands of the worker."[56]

In private medicine or in public genetic screening programs, the person who is diagnosed for an illness or predisposing trait is offered information or a counseling program. In industry, the same person can be denied employment. If an employee were found to be deficient in G-6-PD or SAT, it would be the rare company indeed that would give the employee the information and an opportunity to discuss its significance, and then offer the option of continuing in the present job or taking another position without loss of pay, seniority, and other benefits. Even when workers do obtain presumably valuable information concerning their genetic makeup from employers, they are not really in a position to choose jobs.

RISK BY CHOICE? THE ISSUE OF HAZARD PAY

Issues of choice are central to an understanding of occupational hazards and the policies developed in response to them. Implicit in the dispute over risk at work are conflicting assumptions about the extent to which workers voluntarily choose risk. Key questions include: Do workers choose the risks they face on the job? How do health hazards figure into their decisions? How effectively do current business practices and government regulation enhance choice or limit risk?

Proponents of susceptibility testing often describe a worker's on-the-job exposure to chemical hazards as little more than another aspect of an individual's choice of life-style, similar to smoking and eating habits. They draw parallels between workplace decisions and those made in outside life. In the process, they obscure important features of the industrial workplace that shape both medical screening and decisions about risk.

The dominant economic model for explaining the nature and extent of choice in the workplace has been put forth most forcefully in the past ten years by the economist W. Kip Viscusi in two books – *Risk by Choice* (1983) and *Employment Hazards* (1979) – and numerous articles. While Viscusi is the principal voice of the "risk-by-choice" view of work hazards, his perspective is shared by many others in universities, government, and industry, who use econometric studies to argue that workers who encounter risk receive additional compensation for it, and that the choices presented to them are adequate and fair.[57]

Viscusi's publications and the work of like-minded economists and other analysts have had a major influence on federal policy toward occupational health, particularly in the Reagan and Bush administrations of the 1980s and early 1990s. Creating financial incentives for business, not setting standards and enforcing them, has been in favor. Proponents of deregulation within and outside government have been emboldened by the notion that market forces enable workers to select risk and to benefit from their choices.[58]

The "risk-by-choice" approach has a natural appeal to employers. They claim they have done their fair share by using various tools to limit risk, including medical screening, hiring strategies, engineering controls, and personal protective equipment. Still, they argue, some workplace risk from toxic chemicals must remain, because of limitations in existing technology, the prohibitive cost of further reducing chemical exposure, the carelessness of certain workers, and the relatively hazardous working conditions that marginal companies offer. Employers and economists differ in their conceptions of how extensive this residual risk is. Economists are more likely to identify substantial work hazards, whereas employers are more inclined to argue that today's workplace is essentially safe. Nevertheless, both tend to agree that the risks remaining after employers carry out their placement and medical screening programs do not pose a significant problem. More stringent government regulation is unnecessary, they argue, because allowing some risk and permitting only employers to intervene in workers' choice of hazards is an important social good. Employers should be able to screen workers out of jobs, but the government should not restrict workers' choice of risks any further.

Examining Viscusi's widely shared perspective on choice

and risk will help clarify the major impact that the industrial context of power, control, and conflicting interests has on medical testing and on conceptions of risk. Viscusi portrays hazards as acceptable, chosen, and even socially useful. Yet his argument rests on some questionable assumptions about market forces, knowledge, work alternatives, compensation, government regulation, and consent in the workplace.

The hazard-pay model of choice through market forces

As the title of his book *Risk by Choice* announces, Viscusi believes that workers freely choose risky work. Just as individuals choose to smoke or use a power lawnmower, they are willing to confront danger at work in return for some offsetting advantage. "Occupational hazards are not unique," he argues, "either in terms of their severity or in terms of the nature of the choice to face the risk" (p. 38). He contends that individuals who select dangerous jobs receive substantial compensation, sometimes in the form of favorable hours and fringe benefits, but most importantly in the form of higher pay. By his calculations, on the average, employers pay workers a $925 annual "hazard pay" premium for dangerous work.[59]

Viscusi asserts that workers generally know enough about risks to be able to choose work suitable to their preferences and to gain adequate risk compensation from their employers. Those who seek less risk can find safer jobs, though they may have to forgo higher pay. Although Viscusi recognizes that this "quit factor" does not work well in the case of debilitating injury or death, he maintains that the ability of workers to learn of hazards on the job and to quit is otherwise an effective method of enhancing choice.

The risk-by-choice perspective favors market control of job risks. In this view, workers' ability to choose even life-threatening work should be encouraged. Government regulators should not prevent employers from acting in their own interest, nor should they hamper workers' ability to follow their own "risk preferences." Others should not interfere unless what they offer is information or more money for illness. Despite the claims of advocates of risk regulation, workers do not have a right to a safe work environment. Instead, they should have the right to choose hazardous work, and they should be able to decide to remain in a job they know is dangerous.

Viscusi argues that current OSHA standards and other risk regulations are not only too costly and inefficient but are detrimental to worker health and the national economy. He contends that the financial incentives for risk reduction generated by existing market forces have effects that are "several thousand times larger than OSHA" in reducing hazards (1983, pp. 44 and 162). Stringent OSHA regulation hurts poorer workers most because it impedes their opportunity to "boost their earnings through risk" (1983, p. 83). There is no major health problem, since risks were declining even before OSHA was created. Increased oversight from the White House could curtail regulatory costs and prevent new restrictive standards from being implemented.

Viscusi admits that some market imperfections can lead workers to choose overly risky jobs, and that employers may withhold data or provide deliberately misleading information; he sees that companies inform workers of major hazards only at a high price. Despite this, his preoccupation with economic efficiency and business freedom leads him to make some amazing recommendations: The government should give employers risk information for them to sell to employees, and companies should be allowed to establish their own penalty amounts they would have to pay if they disobeyed the law.

Viscusi argues that companies will not reduce risks or comply with government regulation unless it is in their own interest to do so. He believes that this is a good thing. Employers should be able to weigh the cost of abating hazards against the cost of government penalties and the cost of higher pay for employees who perform more dangerous work.

Knowledge, power, and alternatives

The risk-by-choice model severely discounts the effects of workers' lack of knowledge about risks and their lack of power to gain compensation or change their working conditions. Employees typically do not know enough about risks to make truly informed choices. We already have examined the limitations of scientific evidence and the difficulty of establishing causality for chronic health problems, especially in cases of exposure to many different chemicals. Chemicals that workers confront are generally unfamiliar and difficult to detect. Technologies for controlling emissions change, and so do exposure levels, often with significant medical effects. A worker may manage to obtain accurate information only to find that changes in the chemical mix, exposure levels, and control technologies have made the information obsolete. These barriers to knowledge exacerbate problems of employee illness, anxiety, alienation, and inaction in the face of chemical hazards.[60]

Even in cases where workers are aware of risks they face at work, a choice between employment and health is not much of a choice.[61] Viscusi's assumption that occupational hazards are like dangerous leisure activities obfuscates the workplace dynamics that constrain choice. Exposure to asbestos or benzene in the chemical industry is *not* like smoking or listening to a high-volume stereo, as Viscusi claims (1983, p. 38). Smokers and high-decibel addicts may indeed lack accurate information on risks.[62] Workers, while they may also lack such information, face the additional problems of financial need, restricted employment opportunities, family obligations, economic uncertainty, and minimal power to influence management. These and other social structural constraints that place fundamental limits on choice are what make workers all too willing to endure danger to keep a job.[63] Yet high unemployment rates for employees with specific skills or, more generally, the difficulties of finding alternatives to dangerous work do not figure into Viscusi's argument. He simply assumes that those out of work have ample leverage to choose among jobs that suit their "risk preferences."

For Viscusi, the best level of safety is whatever level workers choose to accept when informed about risks. Unlike many contributors to the risk literature, he portrays workers as rational actors.[64] Yet in one respect he agrees with those who argue that health and safety problems stem from workers' own irrational actions – smoking, carelessness at work, or attitudes that lead to the misapprehension of risk. The point of agreement is simple: If workers who are aware of hazards become sick or injured on the job, they have only themselves to blame for the trade-offs they have chosen.

Using econometric methods common in studies of risk, Viscusi infers worker motivation solely from economic models of their behavior. The perceptions and values of workers themselves should be of major concern in seeking to comprehend workplace risks and set social policy. Yet the overwhelming weight of economic risk literature discusses worker preferences and motivation without ever consulting workers.[65]

Studies based on in-depth interviews and survey research challenge Viscusi's assumptions. They also cast doubt on his conclusion that workers accept health risks by choice. Nelkin and Brown (1984), for example, draw on interviews with workers exposed to chemical health hazards in diverse occupations in order to understand the meaning and social context of workers' behavior. They find that relatively high wages do help persuade a few workers to keep their job despite health hazards. But accepting risk as worthwhile, often because it brings the enjoyment of more interesting work, is only one way workers adapt to hazards, and it is most common among professionals. Production workers more typically say that they "have no choice" but to accept dangerous work (p. 180). Some resign themselves to hazards, while others become involved in trying to change working conditions. My own interviews with industrial production workers support the Nelkin and Brown findings. I heard many examples of how barriers to accurate information, limited job alternatives, and fear of employer reprisal for complaints to management sharply undercut the ability of workers to choose. These interviews pointed to the ways in which power relations and other social factors shape workers' attitudes toward risk and influence their behavior in the face of occupational hazards.

Evidence from other research also calls into question two of Viscusi's major claims: that workers can reasonably choose to avoid hazardous work through quitting, and that they are fairly compensated for facing danger. Viscusi argues that workers learn about risks while on the job, if not before they are hired, making them more likely to quit if a job appears dangerous. Higher turnover in these jobs, he believes, gives employers a strong incentive to improve working conditions and to increase the pay of workers in those jobs. However, data from the Quality of Employment Survey, National Longitudinal Survey, Bureau of Labor Statistics, and the Panel Study of Income Dynamics indicate that quit rates are generally *lower* in hazardous jobs, though they may be higher in jobs that carry a risk of cancer. These data offer no consistent support for Viscusi's argument that workers respond to new information on work hazards by quitting.[66]

An important reason why workers are less likely to quit hazardous jobs is that those jobs are much more heavily unionized than safer ones.[67] Workers in unions leave their jobs far less often than nonunion workers, not only because of higher wages, but because of the pension benefits, seniority rights, and the grievance and arbitration process that unions provide as means of resolving disputes.[68]

Employers do not necessarily pay more to workers in positions with significant health hazards. Overall, safer jobs are better paid and dangerous jobs require lower skill levels, offer lower pay, and are less secure. Viscusi (1983), Robinson (1988a), and others have shown this. Their argument that workers receive better pay for hazardous jobs is based on evidence that if jobs with the *same skill requirements* are compared, hazardous jobs may pay better than safe ones. In other words, hazard and wage rates are positively correlated only when measures of skill – such as education, age, and job tenure – are controlled. Robinson (1986a), for example, finds that blue-collar workers in jobs they perceive to have significant injury or illness risks receive from 1 to 7 percent more in pay than workers in blue-collar jobs perceived to be safe.[69] Even this finding of a small positive association between wage rates and hazards is convincing only when the risk is injury, because reliable data on the occupational risk of chronic illness is particularly difficult to obtain.[70] Welders doing repetitive tasks all day, for instance, are in a much better position to assess their risk of injury than chemical production workers are to assess their risk of long-term illness from exposure to a changing mix of chemicals.

The hazard-pay model assumes that workers demand or bargain for greater compensation because they are informed of the risks they face. Even within the bounds of the hazard-pay argument, then, employers do not have an incentive to pay higher wages to workers who are unaware of chronic health risks. In addition, the fact that health hazards are to a large extent social costs, borne neither by employers nor entirely by ailing workers, means that employers have even less of an incentive to pay more to people who do hazardous work.[71]

The hazard-pay argument also assumes that safer alternatives are available to workers who take dangerous jobs. But the evidence on worker skills, status, and employment patterns does not support that assumption. Employers are more likely to raise wage rates for workers who are aware of hazards and whose skills give them better job alternatives. Therefore, rather than pay more, employers have a financial incentive to reduce the levels of skill, education, and training required in hazardous work. By restructuring hazardous jobs so that workers with fewer skills and slimmer employment prospects can be hired, they can avoid having to pay skilled workers more in order to keep them from quitting. This makes hazardous jobs even less favorable for those who take them. A further method of reducing wages for jobs using dangerous technologies is to employ workers whose opportunities are limited by employment discrimination.

Employment data bear out these generalizations. The more hazardous positions are filled by a disproportionate number of workers who are black, less-educated, younger, and less skilled or experienced.[72] Employees in the secondary work force of relatively insecure employment and low income, which includes a large share of perilous jobs, are affected by different compensation mechanisms than those in the primary work force of relative job permanence and high wages. Workers in hazardous jobs and industries also experience higher rates of layoff and job loss because of plant closure.[73] They are therefore less likely to quit than the risk-by-choice perspective would predict, in part because their experience of greater insecurity makes them more desperate to hold onto their jobs. This fact further reduces the incentive for employers to pay more to workers in dangerous jobs in order to keep them from quitting. Employers also can restructure hazardous work so that they can subcontract it out or hire day laborers to perform it.[74] It is worth considering whether this situation has changed since the industrial revolution began. John Stuart Mill wrote in 1848:

> The really exhausting and the really repulsive labours, instead of being better paid than others, are almost invariably paid the worst of all, because performed by those who have no choice. . . . The more revolting the occupation, the more certain it is to receive the minimum of remuneration, because it devolves on the most helpless and degraded, on those who from squalid poverty, or from want of skill and education, are rejected from all other employments.

The fact that union workplaces may formally provide hazard pay does not substantially support risk-by-choice arguments. Collective bargaining agreements, not market forces, set the wage rates for these hazardous jobs. Furthermore, injury risks rather than chronic disease hazards from chemical exposure are generally the focus of union-sponsored agreements.[75] These hazard-pay agreements are also atypical, because the workers they cover generally have greater power to influence management and more information about chemicals than is the case in nonunionized workplaces.[76]

Worker options within social constraints

Even higher wages for riskier work do not remove the other constraints on worker choice, such as restricted knowledge and power. Lower income workers, in particular, need regulatory protection to improve working conditions so that they do not risk their lives to keep their jobs. Government regulation has been insufficient for curbing occupational hazards, but not because of any inherent weaknesses. Its failings are due to insufficient funding, inadequate enforcement, and misplaced administrative priorities, all of which are rooted in the social and political context of risk regulation.[77] Contrary to Viscusi's argument, health hazards are a problem with profound human costs, and market forces have not protected workers' health adequately. Government risk regulation would be strengthened through more active standard setting, stricter enforcement, greater penalties for noncompliance, and enhanced worker-information provisions.

Viscusi sees the market as the ideal regulator of risk. The goal of regulatory oversight, legislative change, and other social policy, he believes, should be to improve the functioning of the market. He views economic analysis as an impartial, apolitical method of achieving social goals, a method that rises above the typically parochial, biased approach of regulatory officials. Economic myopia leads him to advocate "efficient" levels of health and safety. Yet production goals and the drive for profits can oppose workers' interest in a safe environment. Safety is a social and political question, shaped by conflicting interests and social values.

Viscusi supports the existing distribution of power between employers and workers. While his models focus on worker choice, the belief at the heart of his analysis is that employers should be able to select employees as they see fit and choose the level of risk they offer workers.[78] Workers, then, should be able to face the dilemma of losing their health or losing their livelihood. Viscusi sees this as an important freedom to be protected. His notion of worker choice could more properly be called "worker options," since "choice" implies the power to consider alternatives whereas "option" is more circumscribed, suggesting "the privilege of choosing as granted by a person or group in authority that normally exercises the power" (*New World Dictionary*, 1979). Employers create risky jobs and give employees the option of taking them or not.

Workers' views and decisions are important and should be understood. But the focus in addressing the problem of choice and risk should be on the social arrangements within which workers make decisions. In reframing the problem of occupational health risk and choice, the fundamental question should not be "How do workers choose risk at work and how could they make this choice more efficiently?" It should be "How can working conditions and institutional arrangements be changed so that workers do not have to make such a choice?"

SCREENING IN THE INDUSTRIAL CONTEXT: THE CASE OF SICKLE CELL TRAIT

Issues of choice and knowledge have arisen in private practice and public medical screening for phenylketonuria, sickle cell trait, Tay-Sachs, and other abnormalities.[79] Some proponents of susceptibility testing, in the belief that knowledge is valuable for those who undergo medical procedures, recommend "informed consent" provisions similar to the formal rules for public screening. They maintain that genetic tests help workers make informed choices about health care and whether to reduce their exposure to hazards. But public screening programs are not affected by the special features of the industrial context, which include economic incentives, liability pressures, different doctor–patient relationships, managerial decision making, and information controls. The special characteristics of the workplace provide many additional opportunities for abuse.

Preemployment genetic screening is usually mandatory – and always more coercive than it is in private practice or most public screening.[80] Employers who screen sometimes describe their programs as voluntary, designed to benefit workers by giving them valuable information and expanding their choices. But even in these cases, the work environment constrains the ability of employees to offer their informed consent to medical procedures.

When corporate officials discuss the voluntary approach to genetic screening, they most often refer to the highly publicized program run by DuPont, which began testing all black workers and job applicants for sickle cell disease and sickle cell trait in 1972. In the early 1980s, the extent to which the company's program was truly beneficial or in fact coercive and discriminatory was hotly debated in government hearings, professional conferences, and major news stories and editorials across the United States.[81] The evidence regarding DuPont's screening program mostly comes from this period. After that time, the threat of bad publicity and lawsuits made it very difficult to determine what testing programs throughout the company really entailed. Much of the controversy surrounds five related questions about choice:

Initiation of testing. Have workers in this or other programs actually requested screening for sickle cell trait, and have they been involved in planning the programs? DuPont's medical director, Bruce Karrh, explains that a group of black employees initially requested the screening program, though they were uninvolved in carrying out the program once it began. In community screening, populations at risk have often asked to be tested, and in many cases they have participated in creating screening programs. This has been the case in public genetic screening for Tay-Sachs disease among Ashkenasi Jews and for cystic fibrosis among those most affected, particularly whites of North European ancestry with a family history of the disease.[82] In workplace screening, however, management usually has initiated testing programs. Neither labor unions nor specific subgroups of workers at risk of chemical damage have often had a formal role in setting up programs.[83]

Informed consent. Have employers provided workers with information about the nature of the test and the test results, as well as an opportunity to refuse testing without punishment? In the early years of DuPont's screening, company physicians did not routinely tell black job applicants that sickle cell testing was underway. While the corporate medical director referred to the test as voluntary, he also stated that "at many sites, the physicians did not routinely tell the black applicant that sickle cell testing was being done."[84] The company later changed this policy so that workers would be informed of the test before they received it.

In general, job applicants are unaware of the nature of many tests they undergo and what their significance is for employment. Employees who do know about the tests may be afraid to reveal that they do not want to be tested. They usually have no opportunity to refuse tests, and those who are given a choice may jeopardize their employment by declining a test. Unlike the DuPont sickle cell screening program, which at least some company officials described as voluntary, the premise of much workplace screening is that it is required of job applicants and employees.

Counseling. Have companies that screen set up means of discussing test results with employees, usually through counseling services? DuPont had no policy for explaining sickle cell testing to its black employees. According to the corporate medical director, if the test indicated that black job applicants had sickle cell trait, applicants were given the test results in order to discuss them with their personal physician. Still, there was no companywide education program to inform people who were found to have the trait. Company policy was simply to tell workers that they carry the sickle cell trait and suggest that they consult their own doctors.[85]

In private medicine and public testing, genetic counseling has become an integral component of screening programs. The dominant view of counseling goals holds that counseled individuals should be regarded as autonomous decision makers who should receive clearly presented information and have an opportunity to discuss its implications for their own lives.[86] The prospects for nondirective counseling within industry are slim, however, in view of employers' economic interest in their work force.

Job placement. Have test results influenced job placement decisions, and if so, how? Have workers found to have abnormalities been able to retain their wages, benefits, and seniority? Has job placement been racially discriminatory? DuPont's medical director has maintained that no job placement decisions have ever resulted from sickle cell screening and that DuPont's program was designed strictly to inform black employees about their health – solely for the "education and edification" of the individuals involved.[87]

But the director of DuPont's Haskell Laboratory, a physician who was instrumental in starting DuPont's screening program, has published a journal article in which he states, "We generally employ individuals with sickle-cell trait who appear otherwise able to fill job requirements," adding that employees with sickle cell trait who also have a low hemoglobin count "are restricted from work involving the handling of nitro and amino compounds."[88] In addition, the president of the DuPont Chemical Workers Association has stated that DuPont's sickle cell screening affected employment, referring to at least one case in which a worker was transferred because of screening test results. The full extent to which DuPont's genetic screening has affected job placement is unknown.[89]

Unfavorable publicity on company screening left DuPont officials embattled. They put forward a barely plausible argument that they did not conduct other genetic screening tests because workers had not requested them. They also claimed that like other employers, they conducted preemployment screening only to comply with the requests of job applicants, who wanted the information for their own personal use.[90]

DuPont's screening program is an atypical case, because in most industries, corporate officials agree that job placement is a major reason for workplace testing. Individuals who lose jobs as a result of such screening seldom receive wage protection. In addition, the impact of screening programs has fallen most heavily on racial minorities. Sometimes genetic screening presents an indirect threat to employment, because employers may obtain information from workers' previous genetic tests through insurance records or medical questionnaires.[91]

Confidentiality. Have adequate protections been established to guard the confidentiality of test results? At DuPont, test results were entered into the employee's medical file. Company physicians, nurses, and clerical workers had access to these files, and the corporate medical director could see sickle cell test results.[92] In other companies, both medical and nonmedical officials have had access to results from sickle cell screening. The confidential doctor–patient relationship of private medicine does not exist in industry, where employers have a financial stake in test results and where screening can have direct and indirect effects on employment.

Similar questions pertain to DuPont's experience testing for G-6-PD and SAT. Company medical personnel conducted SAT testing at one plant and G-6-PD at two plants in order to determine if either test could predict whether individuals would be at increased risk due to workplace exposures. In neither case were employees told the purpose of the test before they were tested. At least four employees were removed from jobs with potential exposure to amino compounds as a result of positive G-6-PD tests.[93] Company officials explain that workers whose G-6-PD or SAT tests were positive were informed of this, and the test results were filed in the medical record. No educational or counseling programs existed for those with SAT or G-6-PD deficiency.

Numerous other companies' testing programs raise similar issues of choice. In general, industrial genetic screening does not provide for informed consent, counseling, confidentiality, and job protections. Such provisions are far less developed than in private medicine and public screening. In addition, workers seldom participate in planning and executing corporate testing programs. Safeguards designed for public screening programs cannot easily be transplanted into the workplace.[94] They give too little attention to the relatively coercive work environment, which presents additional impediments to testing programs that are voluntary, informative, confidential, and without adverse employment consequences. Whether or not employers describe their programs as voluntary, workplace screening reflects the industrial context of power and interest conflict, in which the ability of workers to make employment decisions and control medical treatment is severely limited.

POWER, CONSENT, AND JOB SECURITY

Corporate officials determine almost entirely the nature of preemployment tests, periodic monitoring, and the medical criteria used for job placement. Virtually everyone agrees that management is more powerful than labor in matters of medical testing and hiring. What is in dispute is whether the problems that arise from this distribution of power are cause for serious concern.

Employers often cite the strength of their medical policies, the value of the information they provide, and their active encouragement of worker participation in decisions through educational material, consent forms, health committees, and cooperation with OSHA rules regarding access to medical records. They stress their need to exercise judgment and to control resources, and thus generally oppose increased government intervention in company screening programs. They say that while many companies have a commitment to provide health care and education, a private corporation cannot be expected to offer the information, the choices, and the specialized services that might be more justifiably demanded of public screening. Managers who acknowledge the potential dangers of susceptibility policies tend to believe that the benefits of their programs and their own good intentions outweigh the risks.[95]

The treatment of workers thought to be more vulnerable to disease can be inequitable nonetheless. Few safeguards protect workers who are denied jobs or transferred to other jobs because of health factors. As we will see in Chapter 6, government officials have only limited jurisdiction over testing and job placement. In addition, labor has not had substantial influence over who employers can judge to be high risk. Genetic screening programs in industry do not ensure that employers will provide testing information, exposure abatement, and job security. Without formal protections, labor has to rely on the assurances and benevolence of employers to provide tests and employment that do not harm workers.

There are ways to improve the situation, however. Safeguards can be built into medical programs to protect individuals who have abnormal test results or reveal early signs of disease. Legislative and regulatory initiatives can help provide workers more information about risks and enhance their power to affect working conditions. Collective bargaining provisions also can facilitate the participation of employees in occupational health and otherwise protect their interests. If it can be demonstrated that workers are at greater risk because of past exposures or individual health problems, certain criteria for testing could be established. Provisions for information access, formal policymaking roles, job security, wage protection, and equal employment could help compensate for the general lack of power that employees have over industrial medical practices.

Workers' lack of bargaining power sharply limits their ability to gain information from employers. Ideally, from labor's point of view, they should be able to obtain full information on exposure hazards, medical effects, and tests that are conducted. Two OSHA standards – the "hazard communication" and "access-to-medical-records" standards – give workers rights to some of this information.[96] If passed, the "High-Risk Worker Notification Act," generally opposed by industry and favored by labor, would greatly expand worker access to information on hazards.[97]

Employment protection also can be incorporated into medical tests. In the absence of full employment, job security should be established through "medical removal" provisions, which protect workers against dismissal for job-related health problems, and through "rate retention" provisions, which protect wages and benefits in cases of job transfer for medical reasons. People should not be penalized because they become sick from exposure on the job. Surveillance programs could identify workers who show early signs of damage or whose continued exposure to workplace chemicals would exacerbate a prior health condition. These workers then could be transferred to other jobs without loss of pay, seniority, and benefits.

The OSHA lead standard includes some of these protective measures. It requires employers to monitor lead in the blood and remove workers from jobs that entail exposure to lead when their blood lead surpasses a set level. The standard also provides for maintaining the seniority and benefits of workers who are removed from such jobs and transferred to others. With new government regulation in the future, such safeguards could be extended to cover other workers whom employers suspect to be at risk for disease.[98]

Medical removal provisions have additional health and cost effects. Screening programs that offer job security enable workers to be more forthcoming in describing illnesses and to undergo diagnostic tests more readily. A physician with OSHA told me: "Medical removal is an important provision in terms of worker health. Having employment protections built into the testing program can encourage people to participate. As it is, workers do not have an incentive to cooperate fully when they know their jobs are on the line." And former OSHA director Eula Bingham asserted: "Medical removal protection is essential; without it, the major cost of health hazards falls directly on the worker and the worker's family in the form of illness, death, or lost wages."[99]

Medical removal for workers at risk, however, has been a subject of hot dispute between management and labor. Employers have opposed medical removal protection as a potentially expensive measure that would encroach upon their ability to screen, hire, and fire workers. Their opposition has been effective: Government regulators, legislators, and unions have been unsuccessful in pushing its wider use. During the Reagan administration, its adoption in industry was systematically delayed and its typical provisions reviewed for modification – usually in the direction of slower or narrower implementation.[100] As of 1991 its widespread incorporation into genetic screening and industrial medical surveillance programs remains unlikely, as does its extension into other federal exposure standards in the near future.

In contrast to management's opposition, employees and labor officials have strongly supported medical removal protection in federal standards and workplace screening. A national official with the AFL-CIO Workers' Institute for Safety and Health has said:

> Although the lead standard requires only temporary removal of the workers and may not necessarily apply to permanent displacement, it clearly signals a new direction for the protection of worker rights. It represents a means of last resort to protect individual workers where the established permitted level of exposure to risks is inadequate.[101]

And a health official with the United Steelworkers, linking medical removal to labor's misgivings about industrial screening, has said: "To what extent is a company willing to guarantee a job to people removed by screening programs – a job with the same rate of pay, the same seniority, and the same benefits? Is the company willing to guarantee jobs and earnings protection to those workers? If not, it seems to me our fears are completely legitimate."[102]

But workers and union officials, recognizing their limited power relative to management, realize that screening may continue whether they favor it or not. Since they do not control workplace policy, their stance toward medical removal and rate retention must be largely reactive. They have therefore focused their attention on identifying conditions in which screening takes place and proposing safeguards that would limit the adverse effects of the medical practices that management sets up. Since medical removal, along with rate retention and information-access rules, could clearly enhance workers' leverage in matters of medical surveillance, labor has favored provisions covering workers displaced by screening while at the same time opposing screening programs themselves.

Labor's opposition to susceptibility practices derives largely from the industrial context in which screening takes place. Thus a health official with the Oil, Chemical, and Atomic Workers Union explains that labor does not judge screening and monitoring procedures on their inherent properties alone: "It's not the test itself, but we ask: What are the consequences of the test in the context of the worker–employer relationship? We have the same position with reference to any medical screening test that is offered. You cannot consider these tests in isolation from the realities of the workplace." Specifically, labor's concerns with job security, discriminatory placement, unreliable tests, and information barriers prevent them from assessing susceptibility practices more favorably. These same issues related to power and control, however, contribute to their support for genetic monitoring (as opposed to screening). In most of the chromosomal testing programs of which they are aware, labor representatives have had access to the protocols and test results and have been considered in the planning process. Also, the potential problems of discrimination by race or sex that concern them with genetic screening tests have not emerged from the genetic monitoring projects they have examined. Further, problems of job security have not arisen yet; so far as they know, workers whom employers have found to have relatively high levels of chromosome abnormalities have not lost their jobs.

In any case, medical removal protection is only a partial remedy. Though useful in protecting displaced workers, it leaves unchanged the pervasive conception of work hazards as a problem of individuals at risk, and it can do little to mitigate preemployment screening practices. More broadly, it cannot transform basic power differences in the workplace that affect exclusionary practices. Nevertheless, medical removal protection, rate retention, information access, and other measures analyzed here can change the conditions in which employees are expected to "consent" to risk. Further, they can shift the balance of power between management and labor, even if only slightly.

The conflict over susceptibility policies will not be resolved scientifically. To achieve acceptance of such policies, it will not be enough to give workers evidence of the effectiveness of genetic tests. Supplying workers with information on screening programs will be insufficient, as will providing company medical departments with a list of ethical guidelines for hiring. The environment of medical screening in the workplace is highly charged, with clashing interests, apparent mistrust, and conflicting conceptions of risk and its remedies.

While specific genetic technologies are new, the fact that control of medical information and job placement decisions is firmly in the hands of management is old and familiar. One cannot assume that genetic testing information will be made available to workers, or that those identified as susceptible will be protected, or that employers will take action to guard workers' health. It is clear that tests are usually considered without an adequate grasp of the industrial environment in which they would be used. Many scientists and others outside the workplace believe that issues of power, information control, and conflicting interests have little to do with susceptibility policies. But that view reflects either ideological bias or ignorance of the realities of industrial medicine. The social context is crucial to all judgments about the value of genetic testing.

Chapter 6

Who bears the burden?

*The legal and economic context of
occupational disease*

When a worker is healthy, that's cheap; when he dies,
that doesn't cost the company much. But what is expensive is when a worker wheezes through life.

> Health Policy Official,
> U.S. Department of Labor

I don't think that we can talk about the screening of
workers without talking about discrimination.

> Peggy Seminario
> (Industrial Hygienist, AFL-CIO)

The law is a mandate and a mirror; it both commands
and reflects.

> Aubrey Milunsky and George J. Annas,
> *Genetics and the Law II* (1980:ix)

THE debate over identifying workers at risk emerges at a time when costs and liability for occupational disease are expanding rapidly. As I have indicated, the promise of susceptibility practices is bolstered ideologically. But it also is strengthened by legal and regulatory pressures on industry. These external pressures both shape and reflect the conflict over who is to bear the burden of occupational disease. Conflict over work hazards has influenced the law, which in turn has affected conceptions of risk, hiring practices, and medical testing.

Here I will analyze this legal and economic context of testing and exclusionary practices in the workplace. First, we will examine conflict over responsibility for the costs of occupational disease, such as the expense of supporting workers at risk. Second, we will consider the effect of major legal developments on genetic testing and exclusion, including laws covering medical screening, employment discrimination, fetal damage, and workers' compensation. Liability trends have shifted as government regulation has continued to pressure industry. Meanwhile, ideals and practices of "protection" have had a significant impact on the law and on industry. Finally, we will identify ways in which corporate concerns and the broader political environment have affected the development of workplace policies.

Throughout this analysis, we will see that the legal and regulatory environment shapes not only policies toward risk but also the perspective from which those policies are viewed. It encourages an industrial production worker, a government regulator, and an industrial manager, for example, to take different views of work hazards, and to form different opinions as to whether the cost of occupational disease should be distributed to the society at large or placed squarely on the individuals with the problem. It also helps determine whether they perceive exclusion as valuable protection or unnecessary discrimination.

WHEEZING THROUGH LIFE: COSTS AND LIABILITY FOR OCCUPATIONAL DISEASE

The expense of occupational disease and the conflict over who will pay for it has contributed to the pervasive genetic paradigm in occupational health. Economic pressures, such as rising employee health costs, may lead industrial managers to exclude workers who may be at only slightly greater risk of developing a disease or suffering reproductive damage. As noted in Chapter 3, it is often to industry's advantage to shift the focus away from the chemicals and industrial practices that cause occupational illness and toward groups of workers who become ill or are inherently at risk. Quite naturally, the identification of high-risk workers has very different significance for employees, particularly those who are excluded from jobs by this process.

Rising company costs

Industry officials generally argue that it would be unrealistic to try to limit workplace exposures so that every worker, including the few who are susceptible, would be safe. That degree of protection, they say, is either currently unattainable through engineering controls, or prohibitively expensive, or more costly than a medical testing and job placement solution. They would like to decrease time lost from work, avoid workers' compensation claims, and cut health insurance premiums. The understanding that economic incentives encourage industry to remove workers who may present a special risk for disease is widely shared. Thus the following comments:

A scientist at the Harvard Medical School: "It is so much cheaper for industry to screen out and not reduce toxins, that that is going to be the preferred approach."[1] An occupational health analyst in the Department of Labor: "Industry looks at everything in terms of economics. When companies talk about testing programs, there's a lot of talk about mom and apple pie: Save life, protect health, offer choices, but it comes down to economics." And most comprehensively, Albert Gore, speaking as chair of the House Subcommittee on Investigations and Oversight at government hearings on genetic screening:

> The increasing costs of making improvements in the workplace environment and the financial burdens posed by workers' compensation and similar statutes have provided many industries with a strong economic incentive to engage in preemployment screening. . . . By selecting employees in a manner which minimizes the number of these so-called "hypersusceptible" workers, companies hope to decrease the incidence of occupational illness and thereby decrease the associated costs of compensation.[2]

Among the incentives for employer screening are six major costs associated with occupational disease:

1. Costs stemming from OSHA rules, including new required engineering controls, some tightening government regulation in the area of occupational disease, and threats of more stringent rules in the future.[3]

2. Lost work time, absenteeism, and training and turnover costs related to illness.[4] Occupational illness rates have been rising since 1970, with a substantial upward trend in acute illnesses. The Bureau of Labor Statistics calculated that in 1989, occupational disease resulted in over 3,418,800 lost workdays stemming from an estimated 283,700 newly recognized cases of work-related illnesses.[5] These figures understate time lost from diseases that are chronic or have long latency periods, owing to problems of detecting them and linking them positively to work hazards.[6]

3. Rising medical costs and health insurance payments. Insurance companies contribute to the pressure on employers to screen workers and reduce medical bills. Firms that are self-insured or carry experience-rated health insurance coverage have a special interest in avoiding medical costs stemming from worker disease.[7]

4. Trends in workers' compensation. Workers' compensation was never designed to cover diseases. Less than 1 per-

cent of workers' compensation cases are for occupationally induced disease, and only 1 to 5 percent of job-related diseases are covered under current workers' compensation programs. According to the Department of Labor, only 3 percent of the 700,000 people severely disabled by occupational disease ever receive workers' compensation benefits. But recent changes widen its coverage to include more occupational disease and raise benefit levels.[8]

5. Disability and unemployment payments.[9]

6. Lawsuits stemming from toxic chemicals and disease. Company liability for chemical hazards is rising, and litigation by employees and the public is increasingly common. Employers' fear of lawsuits stemming either from health hazards or from their hiring policies is strong. An industry scientist has said:

> The inability of the scientists, the physicians, the employees or the employee representatives, and the industry itself, to really address this issue [of genetic screening] in the most beneficial fashion to everyone – that is, taking advantage of all the science that we know of – has the overriding problem of fear of or concern for *litigation*. And without the litigation fact, I think we could accomplish a whole lot more in terms of using this information for everyone's benefit. But I am afraid that that is something that is probably not going to happen.[10]

Developments in the area of willful negligence are the most ominous to managers. In some states, case law is developing that lifts the usual shielding of companies from liability other than workers' compensation when employers commit willful acts of negligence or intentionally inflict harm. If workers that the company knows are more likely to become sick are retained in hazardous jobs, the potential for company liability is heightened.[11] This concern with lawsuits resulting from knowingly employing high-risk workers surfaces in many industries.[12]

The prospect of increased liability is a major reason why employers oppose genetic monitoring. If employers conduct genetic monitoring, become aware through test results of exposure hazards, and fail to warn employees of the dangers of continued employment, the usual workers' compensation provisions protecting employers from worker lawsuits would no longer apply. Employers could be sued for breach of their common law duties, charged with negligence, and held liable for health damage to employees.[13]

As in the chemical, steel, and textile industries, fear of employee lawsuits is an important incentive for railroad companies to screen workers for evidence of susceptibility in back X-rays. Thus the medical director of the Southern Railway Company has stated:

> It behooves the railroad industry to ensure through its medical department[s] that its employees are in top-notch physical condition and, also, that the medical departments provide the railroad industry with applicants who are as near perfect physical specimens as is possible for us to find. . . . In the face of staggering claims and settlements, we feel we must do everything possible to exclude the potentially serious back injury.[14]

Such worries about liability are increased by the fact that railroad workers are not covered by state workers' compensation statutes, which restrict employer liability, but by the Federal Employers' Liability Act (FELA), which allows much greater employee recovery.

The increase in third-party suits is another legal trend propelling employers toward susceptibility policies. These third-party suits are of several types. A worker might sue the supplier of a product or a company physician. Perhaps most seriously, the employer may be sued on behalf of a damaged fetus or child. While workers' compensation statutes generally insulate companies from employee suits, awards for damaged fetuses could be unlimited. Although the evidence about birth defects is inconclusive, the potentially enormous costs and legal problems posed by lawsuits for fetal damage have led many employers to exclude women from employ-

147

ment. Thus in a personal interview, a physician for a large chemical company told me:

> Industry doesn't worry much about workers' compensation, because those awards are so pitifully small. The lawsuits that frighten them are those that don't have the protection of workers' compensation. There is the possibility that future generations may bring lawsuits against the company, which would have no workers' compensation protection against maximum awards. Or workers exposed to company products in another industry might sue.

Excluding workers who may be more likely to become disabled can benefit employers financially, whether the potential savings are the result of new screening programs or represent only an attractive by-product of routine preventive health programs.

Social rationality and the distribution of costs

Within an employer's framework of costs and benefits, hiring or retaining vulnerable or sicker workers often costs more than screening them out. For example, it might indeed cost companies more to reduce chemical exposures than to exclude particular employees they consider high risk, whether they be fertile women or people with $alpha_1$-antitrypsin deficiency. But we can look at susceptibility practices from another perspective: The social costs of work-related disease and continued exposure to toxic chemicals can be enormous. The burden of these costs rests almost entirely on individual workers, their families, and the public in the form of government programs.

According to a Department of Labor report, the major source of assistance for individuals severely disabled by occupational disease is the Social Security Disability Insurance Program. In addition to the 44 percent of the workers disabled by occupational disease who receive these Social Security benefits, 22 percent receive welfare benefits. However, many workers disabled by occupational disease receive no payments at all because they cannot meet the eligibility requirements for government benefits. Even workers who receive government benefits seldom receive full income maintenance.[15] The president of the AFL-CIO Industrial Union Department has said:

> Viewed as a renewable resource, a mere commodity in the workplace, workers and their families have always been the first to subsidize new industrial processes with their health and even their lives, and the last to benefit materially. Witness silicosis in King Solomon's mines, lead and mercury poisoning among potters and hatters at the beginning of the industrial era, and even today, cancer among dye workers in the prior and in this generation, and the widespread human devastation seen today in pesticides and plastics manufacture.[16]

The costs of occupational disease that workers and the public pay tend to be hidden, however. Considered "externalities," or social costs, they are routinely left out of the calculations that risk assessors in government and universities make. They are also generally absent from industry calculations of costs and benefits.

For risk analysts as well as employers, social rationality is no more than economic rationality. Viscusi, for example, in considering socially optimal levels of risk, estimates an "efficient allocation of society's resources" according to "society's valuations" of life at between $0.5 and $4.0 million (1983, pp. 93, 101, and 109). Yet the costs and benefits of various policies are not shared equally: employers usually control and often gain from the risks, and employees bear the costs and consequences of illness. For example, in narrow economic terms, reducing chemical exposure in certain cases may not appear economically rational to employers. For the rest of society, however, controlling such health hazards is eminently rational.[17]

Business perspectives on regulation

Employers seek to reduce business costs and expand the realm of externalities. They want government and the public to bear more of the burden of occupational risk. Individual companies and industry trade associations have also been vocal opponents of government regulation of toxic chemicals. Yet they have often supported government intervention in the workplace to help them redistribute the costs of dealing with chemical hazards and resulting disease. Under what conditions do companies favor or oppose government regulation, and what has been the impact of such regulation on susceptibility policies?

Industry officials often complain that they are ruled by regulation in setting medical and employment policies. For twenty years they have directed their antagonism toward the health and safety regulations issued by such government agencies as OSHA and EPA, in response to pressures from the public, labor, and consumer groups.[18] But employers do not refer to all government intervention as intrusive "regulation." In the arena of industrial chemicals, for example, they have advocated the following types of government support.

1. Subsidies for developing new information systems for chemical data, employee information, and health records.

2. Government intervention through Chapter 11 of the Bankruptcy Act. For example, bankruptcy provisions enabled the Manville Corporation to reduce its own payments to employees for diseases related to asbestos.[19]

3. The shifting of environmental and occupational health costs onto the public, through Social Security, Disability, welfare, and government workers' compensation provisions. As we have noted, these programs enable companies to limit their payments for occupational illness and avoid employee suits.[20]

4. Funding by state and local government agencies to clean up chemical spills, along with federal funding to detoxify polluted areas. Examples include government contributions to the EPA Superfund to clean up hazardous waste disposal sites, and $4 million to filter asbestos from city water. Companies do not protest when government assumes the costs of industry mishaps, miscalculations, and poor investments.

The chemical, oil, and nuclear industries provide many such examples.[21]

In the area of industrial chemicals, other examples of government involvement that business has generally favored include: infrastructure payments for roads and other facilities, funds for investigating new technologies and for other research and development subsidies, foreign aid from which U.S. chemical companies and other businesses benefit directly, federal money for nonproduction and for products that cannot be sold because of regulation, and contracts and tax measures that confer benefits on business.[22]

Throughout the business world, individual companies or entire industries find many reasons to favor certain types of regulation:

They will welcome regulations that allow them to gain a competitive advantage over other companies less able to conform to them.

They can happily support measures that promise to facilitate planning and rationalize costs, such as federal regulation to avoid state and local rules. For example, many companies have come to endorse standardized federal labeling instead of varying state rules. At other times, they support state regulation to avoid more restrictive local controls.[23] In general, companies will endorse moderate rules in order to avoid or defuse support for more stringent regulations.

They often favor standard penalties that put a ceiling on liability and costs in their industry. Examples include the use of bankruptcy proceedings for shielding employers from disease liability, and workers' compensation rules that limit awards to injured employees.

They may decide, in times of popular pressure for tighter controls (as in the case of toxic chemicals), that there is a public relations benefit in appearing to welcome regulatory reform.

Finally, companies will favor or oppose specific types of health rules, just as they vary in their support of screening programs, in part because of structural features, such as their size and degree of integration locally, nationally, or internationally, and ideological features, such as their public orientation toward corporate social responsibility. Some companies display fairly straightforward opposition to most forms of regulation, allowing themselves to be publicly recalcitrant. Others emphasize their interest in stability and their long-range vision that gains for labor and environmentalists are advantageous.

Management's relations with labor also have a major effect on their orientation toward government intervention. Labor–management conflict over the social and economic costs of occupational disease is played out in the arena of the regulatory and legal system. In the areas of occupational health and employment, management tends to oppose the sort of formal government measures that labor generally favors. These measures include provisions for information access, chemical labeling, access to medical records, and medical removal.[24] Part of the reason that business has opposed and labor has favored these measures is that they shift expenses, along with the burden of proving safe working conditions, onto employers but give them less control.

In general, industry tends to oppose government intervention in business that they believe is too costly to them and represents a threat – either immediate or long-term – to their own control. Their calculation of short-term costs typically is an important factor in their opposition. But in many cases their perceptions of how regulation will affect their power and initiative is more important. Corporations oppose much of the regulation by OSHA and other agencies regulating health hazards and the environment in part because corporate influence on regulation is relatively weak in these areas. Labor, environmentalist, consumer, and public interest organizations have often been able to use legal channels to shape regulation in their own interest and advance their own goals.[25] Government intervention can constrict corporate power and lead to major long-range costs. Still, employers' opposition to such costs does not undercut their substantial support for government involvement in business. Thus, they continue to advocate many types of government intervention in workplace policies, even as they condemn government regulation in general for limiting the ability of managers to set their own health and employment practices. Employers' impact on government regulation helps determine who pays the costs associated with genetic damage or predisposition, and who bears the burden of occupational disease.

EXCLUSION: PROTECTION OR DISCRIMINATION?

At what point does screening according to innate characteristics constitute invidious discrimination?[26]

It is true that increasing costs and liability for occupational disease have considerable influence on the medical surveillance and employment practices of industry. But management often overstates legal pressures to protect workers and fetuses from hazards and to avoid discriminating against the sick and vulnerable. As we shall see, rules that affect susceptibility policies are few, and most of them are narrow in application. Nevertheless, the legal context of industrial policies has had significant effects on genetic testing and exclusionary practices in the workplace. These legal effects depend in part on the distribution of power in society. The social organization of power helps determine whether excluding individuals at risk is seen to be a valuable method of protecting employers and vulnerable workers or an unnecessary, pernicious form of discrimination.

Employer perceptions of conflicting pressures

Company officials, while sometimes claiming that they favor susceptibility practices because they are good from a preventive medicine standpoint, argue that government regulations require them to adopt such policies but statutes and case law require them not to discriminate by excluding high-risk workers. In other words, they complain that because of the irrationality and conflicting demands of the law, they are required to identify and exclude susceptible workers, and are then penalized for doing so. They frequently refer to pressures that subject them to complaints and claims no matter what policy they establish. In this way, industry officials frame policy questions about screening for genetic predisposition and reproductive hazards in terms of a conflict between legal demands to provide occupational health protection and to avoid discrimination. As one official put it, "Companies are in a catch-22 bind, hemmed in between an obligation to make the workplace as safe as possible, and not to discriminate." Many industry officials describe this conflict as putting them "between a rock and a hard place."

Corporate personnel perceive this conflict between pressures to screen and not to screen, and between protection and discrimination, to be sharpest in the area of fetal hazards. Excluding women of childbearing capacity from exposure to certain chemicals may make a company more vulnerable to charges of sex discrimination. But employers believe that fetal exclusion policies have the greater advantage of guarding the fetus from harm and thereby insulating companies from third-party litigation for fetal damage due to a woman's work.

Industry officials often point out that the conflict between discrimination and occupational health protection becomes sharper when a genetic screening program uncovers risk factors found disproportionately in a particular ethnic or racial group. For example, not hiring workers because they have G-6-PD or sickle cell trait may be similar to excluding them for being black. Further, job placement policies depend on the types of workers identified as high risk. Minority workers might be either more or less likely to be excluded than white workers on the basis of their genetic constitution.

In cases of susceptibility policies, whether the focus is on fertile women or on workers with specific inherent genetic traits, the pressures to screen can overwhelm the pressures not to screen. As an occupational health official in a major industry trade association told me: "Companies will really have no choice but to screen for high-risk workers. Like it or not, companies are going to be dragged, kicking and screaming, into genetic testing. They will be forced to do it, and if they don't, insurance companies will force them."

Although virtually everyone acknowledges that legal and economic pressures affect industrial medicine, managers do not always emphasize the legal and financial reasons for screening. Some argue that regulators and other lawmakers tend to exaggerate the influence of government action on company health surveillance programs. They acknowledge that within a large corporation the toxicology, epidemiology, legal, marketing, public relations, and corporate medical departments may all participate in particular health matters. But they maintain that decisions concerning whether to test workers and which tests to use are made solely on the basis of medical evidence. One company official, for example, told me: "It's very gratifying to know that the company doesn't let the regulatory or legal situation influence our decisions in the health field." Other industry officials sometimes emphasize corporate altruism: "Our concern is whether we are doing the right thing for our employees and their offspring and for society."[27] But such statements are the exception, and usually reflect a "company line" developed by the public relations department. Even those officials who highlight major corporate commitment to the welfare of workers will discuss frankly on occasion the economic and legal incentives that affect company medical practices.

Government involvement in workplace practices

Employers do experience powerful pressures both to conduct and not to carry out susceptibility practices, as we have seen. Their fears of increased liability stem in part from the formal requirements of existing statutory and case law. The general regulatory framework of industry policy has a major impact on employers' treatment of workers at risk. Susceptibility policies should be understood in the context of this occupational health law and employers' response to it.

Company practices have been influenced by the medical surveillance requirements in the Occupational Safety and Health Administration (OSHA), the equal opportunity provisions of Title VII that the Equal Employment Opportunity Commission (EEOC) administers, and the disability stipulations in the Rehabilitation Act.[28] In addition to the actual laws and their enforcement, government officials have affected industry policies by publicly evaluating genetic testing and by describing employment practices they believe are appropriate for protecting high-risk workers.

OSHA

The general approach of OSHA is that exposure levels should be reduced to protect every worker. That is, no employee should suffer an adverse health effect, and any employee found to be affected or particularly vulnerable should not be penalized. The principle is that the most susceptible worker should be protected whenever possible. The Occupational Safety and Health Act requires OSHA, in promulgating standards, to assure that employers maintain a safe workplace "free from recognized hazards." It says OSHA should "set the standard which most adequately assures, to the extent feasible, on the basis of the best available evidence, that *no employee* will suffer material impairment of health or functional capacity even if such employee has regular exposure to the hazard dealt with by such standard for the period of his working life" (emphasis added).[29] It promises *"every working man and woman* in the Nation safe and healthful working conditions" (emphasis added).[30]

In general, OSHA regulations lack an enforcement mechanism for placement. While OSHA has broad authority to regulate chemical exposure hazards and some authority over employer medical procedures related to significant risks to worker health, it does not have similar authority over general rights or conditions of employment per se. Further, OSHA does not protect job applicants from discrimination.

New York Times publicity of OSHA screening policies. In February 1980, the *New York Times* journalist Richard Severo, in a front-page series on industrial genetic testing, reported that corporate officials believe that OSHA requires them to conduct genetic tests, such as those for sickle cell trait and G-6-PD deficiency.[31] He wrote: "A regulation, well known to industry, exists in rules promulgated by the Occupational Safety and Health Administration. To industry, the regulation is a mandate for genetic screening. But key people in OSHA were either unaware of its existence or unable to explain it."[32] In implying that there is an OSHA clause that requires genetic screening, and that industry officials are aware of it but OSHA officials are not, Severo may have overstated his case.

OSHA regulations specify only that employers must offer a medical surveillance program within which the physician shall obtain a medical history that includes "family and occupational background, including genetic and environmental factors."[33] This vague clause quickly became subject to widely varying interpretations.

The director of OSHA, Eula Bingham, responded to the news coverage by issuing a public statement clarifying the rule and insisting that OSHA regulations should not be interpreted as a mandate to screen.[34] She explained that obtaining such a medical history is a routine part of standard medical practice designed to identify factors important to the worker's general health status. In a directive to OSHA enforcement officers, she stated that the responsibility of employers is to reduce exposure problems to protect high-risk workers, but not to remove workers whose genetic structure may put them at higher risk. She stressed that the Agency neither requires nor advocates the exclusion of otherwise qualified workers from jobs on the basis of genetic testing. In a public Agency statement published as a letter to the editor in the *New York Times* a few weeks after Severo's series appeared, she stated:

> Exclusion of workers as a result of genetic testing runs counter
> to the spirit and intent of the Occupational Safety and Health
> Act of 1970. It wrongly puts the burden of controlling toxic
> substances on the worker who is denied employment because
> of a supposed sensitivity. Employers should make the work-
> place safe for all workers, rather than deprive some workers of
> their livelihood in the name of safety.[35]

These comments opposing genetic susceptibility policies by
the OSHA director under the Carter administration have been
the most publicized views on genetic testing on the part of
Agency officials. More important in influencing business practices, however, have been the specific OSHA provisions regarding medical surveillance, chemical hazards, and their control.

OSHA medical surveillance rules. OSHA regulations identify
high-risk workers in terms of their exposure risks, but they
have had only limited impact on genetic testing and the protection of high-risk workers. Few of the OSHA standards
require preplacement and periodic medical tests. Most
OSHA standards were adopted en masse in 1971 from the
threshold limit values set by the American Conference of
Governmental Industrial Hygienists.[36] These standards establish permissible exposure limits for each substance but do
not include specific requirements for health surveillance.

Each of the standards that OSHA developed after 1971,
however, does contain medical surveillance requirements.
These include tests for establishing a diagnosis, for detecting
increased susceptibility, and for providing baseline data on
employees prior to working with hazardous substances. In
addition to a medical history and a general physical examination, they require tests such as chest X-ray, pulmonary function, sputum cytology, blood count and blood chemistry
analyses, liver function, urinalysis, and blood lead levels
(see Table 11). None of the standards, however, specifies
what medical tests employers may not conduct.

Table 11. *Medical surveillance requirements in OSHA
health standards*

Substance	Medical procedure required
Acrylonitrile	1. Complete medical history and exam 2. Chest X-ray 3. Fecal occult blood screening for workers age 40 and over
Inorganic arsenic	1. Complete medical history and exam 2. Chest X-ray 3. Sputum cytology
Asbestos	1. Complete medical history and exam 2. Pulmonary function tests 3. Chest X-rays
Benzene	1. Complete medical history and exam 2. Detailed blood studies 3. Pulmonary function tests for respirator wearers
13 Carcinogens[a]	1. Complete medical history, including genetic and environmental factors 2. Consideration of reduced immunological competence of employees undergoing treatment with steroids or cytotoxic agents, pregnancy, and smoking
Coke oven emissions	1. Complete history 2. Chest X-ray 3. Pulmonary function tests 4. Sputum cytology 5. Urine cytology
Cotton dust	1. Complete medical history 2. Standardized respiratory questionnaire 3. Pulmonary function tests
DBCP[b]	1. Complete medical and reproductive history 2. Examination of genitourinary tract 3. Serum specimen for radioimmuno assay
Ethylene oxide	1. Complete medical history and exam 2. Blood studies
Formaldehyde	1. Complete medical history 2. Pulmonary function tests for respirator wearers

Table 11. (*cont.*)

Substance	Medical procedure required
Lead	1. Complete medical history and exam
	2. Detailed blood studies
Vinyl chloride	1. Complete medical history and physical exam
	2. Liver studies

[a]The thirteen carcinogens include: 4-nitrobiphenyl; alpha-napthylamine; methyl chloromethyl ether; 3,3'-dichlorobenzidine (and its salts); bis-chloromethyl ether; beta-napthylamine; benzidine; 4-aminodiphenyl; ethyleneimine; beta-propiolactone; 2-acetylaminofluorene; 4-dimethylaminoazobenzene; and n-nitrosodimethylamine.
[b]DBCP is 1,2-dibromo-3-chloropropane.
Sources: 29 *Code of Federal Regulations* Sections 1910.1001–1101 (1990), and Rothstein (1984).

While the OSHA standards promulgated since 1971 specify medical surveillance procedures, only a few establish protections for individuals who may be at highest risk. The most comprehensive standard is for lead, which includes a medical removal provision that sets out procedures that must be taken if employees are shown to be at increased risk, as measured by their blood lead levels.[37] Under the lead standard, workers may be removed from their regular jobs on the basis of an examining physician's medical opinion or when the measured level of lead in their blood is high enough to indicate a "material impairment to health or functional capacity." Employees removed under this provision are to receive compensation for up to eighteen months in the form of maintained earnings, seniority, and other benefits, whether or not another job is available for them.

The OSHA standard for benzene also provides for medical removal protection and rate retention. There are weaker and less inclusive medical transfer provisions in the vinyl chloride and asbestos standards.[38] The medical transfer provision in the cotton dust standard requires that a worker be transferred to another job only if another job was available.

None of these other standards, however, provides for workers who have abnormal test results and are shown to be at higher risk of disease due to their genetic predisposition or employment history.

Thus in the vast majority of OSHA standards, no specific requirements indicate how workers found to be affected by toxic chemicals or viewed as at high risk must be protected. Very few government rules apply either to the identification of high-risk workers through industrial testing or to their protection. While OSHA can mandate that certain tests be conducted, no provisions require the employer to take any particular action based on a positive test result. Further, since OSHA regulations have no enforcement mechanism for placement of high-risk workers beyond the lead and cotton dust standards, they do not protect employees who are transferred or fired because of their health.[39] OSHA has virtually no authority over the medical criteria an employer establishes for job applicants or employees. It gives companies almost free rein to test workers for whatever they want and to use the resulting medical information as they wish. Though influential, formal OSHA regulations have not significantly reduced the enormous latitude employers have in using medical information to help them make job placement decisions. Employers can define high-risk workers in nearly any terms they choose. As two OSHA medical officers told me in personal interviews:

> If an employer wants to hire supermen – only the healthiest of specimens, we have no jurisdiction to say that's unreasonable or unacceptable. And as long as it's not based on sex or race or another class covered by Title VII, employers can establish any criteria they want to screen workers, whether it is a back condition, a prior cancer history, or diabetes, or some genetic trait, or extensive chromosome breakage.

> Under OSHA, with the exception of the medical removal protection provision in the lead standard, an employee does not have a right to a job because he or she is sick or has some abnormality. An employer can fire employees because of their particular illness.

If a firm's exposure levels exceed the OSHA standards and the company excludes a worker or a particular group from working with the substance, OSHA can cite the company for exceeding the exposure limits and pursue compliance mechanisms. Even then, OSHA officials do not have the authority to require that high-risk employees be retained in jobs or reinstated after having been dismissed. OSHA does, however, have authority over job placement where it can be shown that a worker was fired after exercising his or her rights under the law, such as when a worker is fired after filing a complaint or calling for an inspection. In a few cases, OSHA has cited companies for what they judged to be inadequate medical surveillance programs, but none of these cases concerned genetic testing or treatment of workers viewed as susceptible.

In the case of fetal exclusion policies, OSHA has claimed that American Cyanamid's policy of excluding fertile women resulted in the women becoming sterilized in order to keep their jobs. Agency lawyers argued unsuccessfully before the OSHA Review Commission that the company's policy constituted a "hazard" and impaired the workers' "functional capacity," which is protected under the General Duty Clause, Section 5(a)(1) of the OSHA Act. This case was appealed unsuccessfully by the Oil, Chemical, and Atomic Workers International Union.[40]

NIOSH recommendations to OSHA. The National Institute for Occupational Safety and Health (NIOSH) is an agency that conducts research and advises OSHA, though without rule-making or enforcement powers. Its research and funding strategies, the advisory documents it prepares, its orientation toward chemical hazards, and the perspectives of its specific officials have influenced OSHA policy. NIOSH has also influenced workplace health practices by advising employers and employees.

NIOSH has not pursued any significant research into the detection of predisposing genetic factors. The NIOSH staff responsible for industrial health studies contends that identi-

fying high-risk workers through genetic markers is a relatively unimportant and less useful tool than genetic monitoring. A NIOSH scientist articulated this evaluation of genetic
screening:

> In any human population, people vary in their susceptibility
> to any disease or agent that you might consider. Despite that,
> it's our basic belief, which stems from the language of the
> OSHA law, that the goal of the Act is to create a safe and
> healthful workplace for every working man and woman, and
> that it is counter to the spirit of the Act to get involved in
> identifying certain categories of workers so that they can be
> excluded from the workplace on the basis of their susceptibili-
> ty. The workplace ought to be made safe not by excluding a
> fraction of the work force but by using safer materials, putting
> in proper ventilation, etc., so that the work force will be pro-
> tected.[41]

NIOSH has located high-risk workers by identifying high-
risk workplaces and exposure problems, for which they have
used two methods. Major risks are either discovered in the
laboratory, or they are first suggested through observation in
the field by workers or health professionals or through more
formal epidemiological studies.[42] NIOSH has studied
groups who are believed to be at high risk based on laboratory and epidemiological information that leads them to suspect a major exposure problem exists. Another NIOSH official explains the agency's orientation toward high-risk
workers this way:

> We'd rather consider a whole group of workers to be at high
> risk. For example, we're sure that rubber workers have in-
> creased leukemia, because they're exposed to benzene. We
> would argue you shouldn't waste your time looking for those
> people who are particularly susceptible to leukemia so that
> you can remove them from the workplace.

In contrast, NIOSH officials have judged genetic monitoring studies favorably, in the belief that they are valuable in
assessing exposure risks. They have undertaken major ge-

netic monitoring studies, including a study of workers exposed to ethylene oxide at a plant in Texas, and a study of workers exposed to nuclear radiation at the Naval shipyard in Portsmouth, New Hampshire. They have also conducted sperm studies of DBCP, Ordram, and carbon disulfide.[43]

NIOSH researchers have maintained that chromosomal monitoring for environmental exposures provides useful information. While admitting that genetic monitoring tests yield no definite conclusions about an individual's health risk, they say that the findings can be used to help determine guidelines for safe exposure levels. They have documented suggestive associations between chronic occupational exposures and both chromosomal alterations and increased cancer risk. Further testing of industrial populations can substantiate these relationships.[44]

NIOSH has also pursued genetic monitoring and epidemiological studies to see whether chromosomal changes are associated with cancer or other clinical health effects. Although this second use of genetic monitoring is more difficult, in part because of the latency periods involved, NIOSH scientists have expressed confidence that it will eventually be more significant for preventive health. As one NIOSH official explained to me, "Our cytogenetic research does not result from a focus on the susceptible workers, but from our long-standing interest in the prevention of cancer and reproductive impairment."

As was the case at OSHA, the official who was most outspoken on genetic testing and susceptibility policies – the NIOSH director – was replaced soon after President Reagan was inaugurated. Individual OSHA and NIOSH officials, including former directors, have maintained that industry susceptibility practices should not replace engineering and other exposure controls. They have argued that no group should be excluded systematically. Since the time of the public statements on susceptibility policies by the directors of OSHA and NIOSH under the Carter administration, however, no administrator in either agency has taken a formal position on genetic testing and exclusionary practices.

Title VII and EEOC

Title VII makes it unlawful for an employer, because of a person's sex or race, or other protected class, "to fail or refuse to hire or to discharge any individual or otherwise to discriminate against any individual with respect to his compensation, terms, conditions or privileges of employment."[45] Title VII also makes it illegal for employers, based on sex or race, "to limit, segregate or classify his employees . . . in any way which would tend to deprive any individual of employment opportunities or otherwise adversely affect his status as an employee."[46]

As with OSHA, the Equal Employment Opportunity Commission's coverage of high-risk workers is narrowly circumscribed. EEOC officials have conceived of high-risk workers as people whose placement is affected by an employer's determination – medical or otherwise – that they are at greater risk on the job. But the EEOC can do very little concerning the hiring, firing, or transferring of workers because of their health, or because they are judged to be at high risk, unless the screening program in question disproportionately affects a class protected under Title VII.

The EEOC does not have jurisdiction over screening practices unless one of two conditions is met: (1) the employment screening device treats people of different sexes or races differently, or (2) the test is neutral on its face but has an adverse impact on a protected group. An example of the first condition would be testing only women, or only blacks. An example of the second would be testing all workers for genetic markers and then excluding workers with sickle cell trait, who will be disproportionately black.

When either of these conditions exists, the screening is prohibited under Title VII unless employers can justify it by presenting a recognized employer defense. One of these is the "BFOQ" defense: under Title VII, policies that explicitly discriminate against protected classes may be permitted "on the basis of bona fide occupational qualifications reasonably necessary to the normal operation of that particular business or enterprise."[47] Another defense, this one for neutral policies that have a discriminatory impact, is "business necessity." To make this claim, employers must prove two things: that the medical or scientific tests on which they base their exclusionary practices are scientifically valid and reasonably applied; and that "business necessity" prevents them from adopting alternative policies that would avoid the discriminatory exclusion. These alternatives could include product substitution, engineering controls, job rotation, and personal protection equipment.[48]

If employers meet these qualifications for demonstrating the "BFOQ" or "business necessity" justifications, they can exclude individuals on the basis of any medical condition, even if their policies treat a group differently or disproportionately affect a protected class, as defined by Title VII. However, the EEOC and the courts have interpreted the broad language of these two defenses fairly narrowly, limiting their usefulness to employers.

Susceptibility policies might be found to be discriminatory along the lines of race, sex, or ethnicity under Title VII, since genetic traits often are found disproportionately among a particular racial or ethnic group, and fetal exclusion policies explicitly treat women differently. But the EEOC so far has seen few charges of discrimination by workers who have been judged to be at high risk for a genetic trait or medical condition and fired, not hired, or transferred as a result.

Title VII cases involving the exclusion of fertile women from jobs considered to be at highest risk to the fetus have dealt with issues of business necessity and the "BFOQ" defense. Employers have attempted to use these defenses in order to justify their policies. They have been largely unsuccessful in doing so.[49]

Under Title VII and the EEOC, the issue of discrimination by race arises when statistical evidence shows that a disease affects one group disproportionately, as with PSB, sickle cell anemia, sickle cell trait, and hypertension. Only two EEOC court cases have considered the business necessity defense for exclusionary policies based on race-related medical conditions. Both concerned PSB, a health problem pertaining to ingrown facial hair that is more common among blacks.[50] In addition, one published Commission decision on sickle cell anemia concerned a worker refused a position as a telephone operator because she had sickle cell anemia. The employer's policy of rejecting all applicants with sickle cell anemia was held to violate Title VII.[51] Under the race discrimination provision of Title VII, at least two cases involved sickle cell anemia. At least two charges have been brought by workers who were denied jobs because they had sickle cell trait.[52] The EEOC also has considered charges of employer discrimination based on hypertension, a health condition that disproportionately affects blacks as a group. It has drafted a Commission decision on hypertension and a section of the EEOC Compliance Manual on race-related medical conditions that discusses sickle cell screening in industry as well. These four criteria – PSB, sickle cell anemia, sickle cell trait, and hypertension – are the major areas in which workers considered high risk because of a disease or trait have brought charges before the EEOC.[53] The EEOC has not seen any discrimination charges stemming from other diseases known to affect a particular group disproportionately, nor have they determined that other diseases do not affect a protected class.

Rehabilitation act provisions

The federal Rehabilitation Act of 1973, Sections 503 and 504, prohibits employers who are government contractors or recipients of federal assistance from discriminating against otherwise qualified handicapped persons.[54] "Handicapped" individuals are defined broadly, as persons with physical or mental impairments that substantially limit one or more of their major life activities. The definition includes those who have a record of such an impairment and those who are regarded as having such an impairment. However, the Rehabilitation Act covers only select groups of employees in the private sector. Also, the legal remedies available to employees under the Act are narrow. Workers have limited rights to sue an employer.[55]

State laws provide handicapped people with other protections, which are usually broader. Forty-seven states have employment discrimination statutes that include the handicapped as a protected group, three of which specifically refer to genetic traits. No suits or complaints involving genetic deficiencies have been filed yet in these three states, however. The types of employers covered and the enforcement mechanisms available in state employment discrimination statutes vary widely.[56]

These federal and state handicap laws offer potential protection for genetically susceptible individuals, but certain major issues are unresolved. These include whether increased susceptibility to occupational illness is a handicap, and whether a person who is currently fully capable but at increased risk of illness in the future is qualified for work.

Limited government protection

Regulation affects industrial medicine by requiring that certain tests be performed, information collected, toxic exposure hazards curtailed, and placement procedures followed. Specific requirements such as these influence susceptibility practices as well. Companies screen partly in response to regulatory pressures for stricter occupational health standards and compensation for affected workers. Both of these make protecting workers more costly. Industry officials believe that by screening out high-risk individuals, susceptibility practices will protect both workers and company interests. The legal context also affects employers' opposition to genetic monitoring, which may leave them more vulnerable to adverse legal consequences. Monitoring may uncover ambiguous potential health hazards that mean employers could be sued or suffer regulatory penalties for knowingly endangering the work force.

But government agencies such as OSHA and EEOC directly affect the use of susceptibility policies only within quite limited parameters, as we have seen. No government requirement compels industry to conduct genetic testing. Government officials in OSHA, EEOC, and NIOSH have evaluated the industrial application of screening tests in interviews and press releases, yet few regulations are designed to shape such testing when a corporation elects to do it. Legal limits do not substantially constrain the ability of employers to hire and fire according to their own assessments of health risk. A legal expert in the area of genetic testing has emphasized the weakness of the law in protecting workers whom employers consider to be high risk. According to common law, he has written, "employers had virtually unfettered control in selecting their employees. The employer could hire or refuse to hire any person for any reason or no reason at all, including the employer's opinion about the medical fitness of the applicant or employee. To a large extent, this is still the current state of the law."[57]

With these weak regulatory protections for high-risk workers in view, critics' concern about the application of genetic screening and fetal exclusion is especially cogent. The regulatory environment affects the prospects for genetic testing being used to protect workers' health. Stronger regulatory constraints might make susceptibility policies less threatening to workers by assuring greater employment protection for workers considered high risk and by further limiting chemical exposures. Requiring improved working conditions would also lessen the appeal of screening workers instead of reducing workplace hazards.

THE POLITICAL ENVIRONMENT OF GENETIC TESTING

The general political environment has a major impact both on government regulation and on industrial screening programs. Employers may want to exclude fertile women or workers with sickle cell trait or G-6-PD deficiency from certain jobs, partly because of their assessment of the medical evidence. Whether they do so, however, typically depends on their assessment of equal employment and occupational health stipulations and, more generally, on the current political, legal, and labor environment.

During the 1980s, enforcement of OSHA regulations and equal employment laws declined.[58] Advisory regulation was favored. Legislative and regulatory initiatives attempting to tighten workplace safeguards were few. With broad cutbacks in regulatory staff, lighter enforcement, and less pressure for stricter standards, incentives to conduct screening programs also diminished. The effect of the curtailed apparatus of regulatory rule making and enforcement has been important in deflating pressures to screen workers. Despite this effect of reduced regulation in recent years, major incentives to screen workers remain, such as those provided by continued high rates of cancer and other occupational diseases, trends in legal liability, and prospects of rising health insurance costs.

The current regulatory environment makes critics of susceptibility policies condemn genetic screening and fetal exclusion practices with even more vehemence. This is because less government and corporate support for occupational health regulation weakens provisions that protect all workers, not only those who may be most vulnerable. The weakened provisions include those for access to medical information, labeling of hazards, tighter engineering controls, and enforcement of exposure standards.

Legislative initiatives have highlighted limitations of the genetic technologies and prospects for abuse. A few state legislatures have addressed the impact of susceptibility policies with laws designed to guard against discriminatory effects of medical tests and related employment practices.

Several states have legislated restraints on firing or other employment actions based on the genetic traits or reproductive capacities of workers. For example, New Jersey has amended its state employment discrimination law to prohibit employers from firing, refusing to hire, or otherwise discriminating against people who have an "atypical hereditary cellular or blood trait."[59] North Carolina, Louisiana, and Florida also prohibit employment discrimination based on sickle cell trait.[60] In Connecticut, employers must notify workers who confront reproductive hazards and must make an alternative job available to pregnant women who are exposed to these hazards.[61]

Several other legislative measures have proposed controls on genetic screening but have not been enacted into law. For example, a bill introduced in the New York Assembly in 1980, titled the Genetic Testing and Employment Act, was designed to prevent employers from requiring that employees or job applicants undergo genetic testing, or from using the test results for job placement except when requested by the employee or authorized in a labor contract. The bill also provided for voluntary testing, confidentiality, and civil penalties for noncompliant employers. It would also have barred employers from giving the results of a genetic test to anyone not approved by the employee.[62]

The most influential government activity relating to susceptibility policies at the federal level has been the congressional hearings held in Washington, D.C., in 1981 and 1982. These hearings on "Genetic Screening and the Handling of High-Risk Groups in the Workplace" were called by the U.S. House Science and Technology Committee's Investigations and Oversight Subcommittee, which was chaired by Albert Gore, Jr., of Tennessee. The hearings examined genetic testing and fetal exclusion programs as part of their investigations into health-related employment practices. Corporate, government, and labor officials were among the many expert witnesses called before the congressional subcommittee, and their testimony brought greater national attention to susceptibility policies.

The most extensive media coverage of susceptibility policies prior to the hearings had been published two years before. The series of front-page articles by journalist Richard Severo, titled "The Genetic Barrier: Job Benefit or Job Bias," had appeared in the *New York Times* February 3–6, 1980. Employers regarded these articles as unfavorable publicity because they raised questions about the uncertain scientific basis and possible discriminatory impact of susceptibility policies. The *New York Times* articles, and later the congressional investigation, led to prolonged news coverage, editorial comment, and debate. This ranged from front-page stories in the *Wall Street Journal* to debate on the MacNeil–Lehrer news program and letters to the editors of local newspapers.

This widespread publicity brought the new genetic technologies to the attention of even more employers. Despite the critical tone of some of the coverage, the publicity aroused more avid interest at meetings of scientists and policymakers in examining them. Wide public support for drug and AIDS screening has further intensified the focus on testing for individual vulnerability. Overall, increased public awareness has led many employers to adopt susceptibility policies, even as it has inhibited others from adopting more broad-scaled use of these policies.

CORPORATE CONCERNS AND FUTURE WORKPLACE POLICY

Controversy in government hearings, stockholder meetings, and in the press has made industrial managers more restrained in carrying out genetic screening and exclusionary policies. The prospect of highly publicized discrimination suits has made them more careful to emphasize that their exclusion of women or minority workers is a neutral policy and therefore nondiscriminatory. Proponents of genetic screening, in particular, have become considerably more sensitive to the legal dimension of screening over the past few years.

Company officials, who usually describe their own employment practices as an expression of their concern for worker health and public service, say that much of the recent publicity has, out of misunderstanding or malevolence, cast their medical programs in an unfavorable light. They are most worried about charges of racial and sexual discrimination in testing and job placement, accusations of bias in conducting studies and in circulating findings among workers and the public, and publicity of legal action resulting from testing programs.

Many corporate officials view labor, government, scientific, and media critics of genetic testing programs as unduly ideological actors who have seized upon limitations of specific screening tests. They protest that hysteria over exclusionary employment practices has whipped up anticorporate sentiment and exacerbated labor–management conflict.

Industry officials complain that companies in the forefront of health research and medical surveillance have been the most heavily criticized. Therefore, they say, perhaps it does not pay to be innovative or allocate much of their resources to these medical programs. A corporate official who had been an enthusiastic proponent of susceptibility policies told me after attending a major industry trade association meeting, where he heard arguments about genetic testing and exclusionary practices, that "Congressional investigation has companies running scared." According to an auto industry official, "The companies that have tried this testing have been burned, and the other companies are watching."[63]

Thus, proponents of screening for genetic markers have become more cautious. This is partly as a result of employer concerns with the effectiveness of the tests in identifying high-risk workers, as well as with the discrimination, publicity, liability, and regulatory problems. They have become more reluctant to discuss details of their programs. They consult industry lawyers about company medical practices more readily. Even corporate physicians and executives who were once outspoken advocates of genetic screening for its preventive health potential are now quick to add caveats to their recommendations. Some in industry approach genetic screening with the concerns they once reserved for genetic monitoring. Fearful of being singled out for criticism, many companies stress that they rely only on conventional, widely accepted clinical procedures. The corporate medical director of a large chemical company told me: "We are using only the standard physiological tests to determine if employees have a condition that would predispose them to specific health effects or would make them more vulnerable to substances we use in the workplace. We rely on only those tests for which the value is known." Similarly, the vice president of a major oil company in charge of the corporation's medical policies said: "Our company has taken an extremely conservative position on anything that varies from what is generally considered sound medical practice nationwide."

Yet even employers who adopt a cautious "wait-and-see" approach to their current business practices retain their overall optimism about susceptibility policies. Fear, caution, and legal sensitivity coincide with strong belief in the technologies and with major economic and legal incentives for susceptibility policies. In fact, these incentives to screen can overshadow worries about publicity, lawsuits, and congressional action. Employers' awareness that their companies' medical surveillance practices seldom become public knowledge is important in counteracting their trepidation about legal tangles and other repercussions from publicity. Further, companies can institute measures to diminish the likelihood of trouble. They can guard against negative press coverage and take steps so that employees, and not employers, assume more of the risks of industrial policies.

Corporate officials and scientists continue to believe that genetic screening in industry is a new field with considerable potential. Most of the circumstances described here that have made some company officials more cautious about susceptibility policies are short-term conditions of publicity, legal activity, and regulation. As the adverse publicity subsides, the genetic techniques are developed further, and the medical evidence is established more conclusively, we can expect that policies for locating genetic susceptibility to disease will be adopted even more widely in medical surveillance programs.

Chapter 7

The social construction of workplace hazards

Conclusions and policy implications

It is not inconceivable that through screening, industry will become the modern counterpart of Diogenes as it searches for a perfect worker.

Zsolt Harsanyi and Richard Hutton,
Genetic Prophecy: Beyond the Double Helix (1981:89)

THE prevailing notion of risk in the workplace is shifting from a conception that locates risk in hazardous working conditions to one that locates risk in workers themselves. Over the past two decades, the problem of occupational risk, once considered a problem of chemical hazards, has increasingly come to be seen as a problem of the work force and of individual or genetic susceptibility. This shift reflects not only scientific and technical developments, but also, and more fundamentally, a transformation that is socially constructed.

While everyone agrees that biological variation exists in response to occupational exposures, the focus on certain workers as susceptible is another matter. There is considerable disagreement over the value of genetic tests for differentiating low-risk and high-risk workers and for contributing to the health of the work force. With genetic screening, monitoring, and fetal exclusion, views differ sharply as to which company practices are in the best interest of employees.

The responses to susceptibility policies are socially patterned. This study has emphasized the social meaning of the divergent perspectives, which goes beyond fairly narrow questions of technical prediction into those of belief in genetic technology, conceptions of safety, stratification by race and sex, power, and the legal context of conflict over occupational disease costs.

Complex social factors affect the rise and differential appeal of susceptibility policies. This study has identified major factors that contribute to this change in conceptions of risk at work and to the divergent responses it has invoked.

The ascendance of the genetic paradigm in industrial medicine reflects advances in genetic technologies and the resurgence of biological explanations for social phenomena. As we saw in Chapter 2, general enthusiasm for developments in genetic technology and greater attention to biological explanations for behavior lend credence to susceptibility practices. What could have been sensitivity to normal human variation in responses to chemical exposure instead is an overarching perspective focusing on high-risk workers. This perspective has flourished despite the limited effectiveness of many tests. Scientists' and managers' enthusiasm – even faith – in genetics leads them to underestimate the weaknesses of current susceptibility policies.

The power that stems from scientists' expertise and social position reinforces the credibility of their views. It also overshadows the fact that many know very little about the industrial context in which genetic tests are carried out. Susceptibility proponents doubt the comprehension and motivation of those who do not share their advocacy of these practices. They subscribe to a new orthodoxy that pays lip service to the health effects of environmental and social influences but in fact focuses narrowly on genetic characteristics intrinsic to those who are deemed susceptible.

This conceptual shift toward susceptibility policies exemplifies a larger dynamic that pertains to the risks of many other new technologies in industry and in medicine.[1] Too often, fascination with the power of the technologies blinds people to the fact that genetic susceptibility and occupational risk are not purely technical problems. Advocates of susceptibility testing have become so enamored with the technologies that the social issues and political dimensions of workplace practices become obscured.

Conflicting ideological orientations toward the locus of risk on the job have played an important role in the rise of the susceptibility thesis and in its selective appeal. Chapter 3 examined the ways in which conceptions of safety shape industrial genetics. Management's argument that risks from chemical exposures at work are minimal lends support to the susceptibility perspective, just as screening out workers at risk reinforces management's claim that the workplace is safe for all but a few. Genetic screening and fetal exclusion practices reflect employers' interest in finding the cause of occupational health problems in employees' genes or somewhere else in the constitution of workers themselves, not in industrial working conditions.

This helps explain labor–management conflict over susceptibility policies, since management tends to locate risk in the unusual biological vulnerability of certain workers, whereas labor locates it in industrial poisons to which employees in general are exposed. Therefore, labor favors monitoring for evidence of chemical hazards to the entire work force and management favors screening out workers who may present risks from genetic traits or fetal exposure. The different conceptualizations of risk and safety can be seen in conflicts over the extent of occupational cancer hazards and the meaning of disease clusters that are discovered at work.

Advocates of susceptibility policies see them as neutral applications of medical technology – as embodying an approach to risks to the individual worker that presumably would protect everyone equally. The search for types of workers at risk, however, often results in the identification of gross biological categories, giving "susceptibility" a racial or sexual component. As we saw in Chapter 4, stratification of the work force by race and sex has strongly influenced the rise of susceptibility policies and the divergent perspectives that have risen in response to them.

The fact that many genetic traits or reproductive hazards are found disproportionately among certain racial or sexual groups contributes to the different treatment these groups receive in the workplace, but it does not entirely explain it. Employment patterns and cultural views are also salient factors in determining which workers come to be seen as high risk. Those who are identified as susceptible tend to be persons in relatively high-paying positions whose sexual or racial group has only recently come to hold those jobs. The practices of fetal exclusion and sickle cell testing illustrate how groups that are socially at risk come to be identified as the source of a medical problem. The two cases reveal both similarities and differences that stem from the social positions and histories of the two affected groups.

Employers have framed the problem of reproductive risk and other health hazards in a way that reinforces, and in fact deepens, the division of labor by sex, race, and ethnicity.

Susceptibility policies also widen the wage gap between men and women and between blacks and whites. Policies intended to be preventive medicine may actually penalize workers without protecting them at all.

Although genetic testing is carried out in private medicine and in public screening programs, Chapter 5 explained the ways in which power structures in the workplace exert a major influence over medical practices and on the ways in which labor and management view them. Identifying certain workers as at risk and excluding them from jobs are exercises of corporate power and control. To be sure, this corporate control of industrial health policy is not complete; specific labor initiatives have influenced corporate policy. Nevertheless, unions in general are weak and labor remains relatively powerless compared with management. Employers continue to make most decisions regarding job placement, medical surveillance, testing information, and chemical exposure levels. This power imbalance limits workers' ability to become informed and to make meaningful choices.

New government regulation, such as that exercised by OSHA, has the potential for limiting management prerogatives. Indeed, industrial managers complain that they suffer conflicting legal pressures to clean up the workplace but not to exclude anyone. Yet as we saw in Chapter 6, while the law does influence managerial decisions regarding genetic testing, it does not do so primarily through the direct impact of formal rules concerning occupational health and equal employment. In reality, the combination of government regulations, shifting company costs, and legal liability trends can encourage susceptibility policies by making it cheaper to harm or exclude particular individuals than to reduce exposure levels, or by leading industrial managers to believe that this is the case.

The interest in identifying high-risk, genetically susceptible workers has intensified in an era when the problems of employer costs and liability for occupational disease have been expanding rapidly. Developments such as increased obligation to provide workers' compensation benefits, greater corporate liability for injurious products, expanding threats of third-party suits, and rising medical insurance expenses have raised the business costs of occupational disease. The promise of susceptibility policies as cost-cutting tools is strengthened by legal pressures on companies to bear a greater share of the burden of occupational disease.

SOCIAL INTERESTS, POWER, AND CONFLICT

The problem of workers at risk should be reframed so that it takes into account the impact of social stratification, power relations, and divergent interests. The need to emphasize conflicting interests may at first seem to be a sociological truism, but it is seldom acknowledged in the literatures on risk, new technologies, or occupational health. It is thus important to ask: Whose interests are served by specific workplace practices and orientations toward risk? What are the risks of these practices and who experiences them? What is the relative power distribution among groups that affects industrial policy and supports the divergent views toward risk?

I have shown how each paradigm for risk at work is related to major aspects of social life, such as scientific expertise, law, ethnicity, and sex. I also have highlighted the different social interests that contribute to the conflict over genetic testing and exclusionary practices in the workplace. By analyzing these interests, we can see that each paradigm, by locating risk either in the work force or in the workplace, has an inherent appeal to specific groups. Indeed, positions on technologies and industrial practices reflect perspectives that derive from social location. Those whose interests are served by a particular paradigm take part in the social conflict through the legal system, in occupational health conferences and journals, in press releases, and in legislative hearings.

It is not the technology itself, but rather the way in which it is used, that determines whether industrial practices will focus on workers or on workplaces as high-risk. Genetic monitoring tests, for example, can be used either to deny employment to individuals with high rates of chromosome aberrations or to discover a need to reduce toxic chemical exposure levels for all workers. Evidence of reproductive risks derived from genetic tests can be used to justify either tighter engineering controls or exclusionary employment practices. In favoring certain tests, most of those attracted by susceptibility policies have misunderstood, or underestimated, or tried to obscure the significance of this distinction between scientific technique and industrial application. Nevertheless, workplace groups have usually recognized the reasons behind current applications of genetic testing. Labor has therefore favored monitoring because of its focus on reducing employer-controlled chemical hazards, and it has opposed screening because of its focus on inherent worker abnormalities. Management has taken the opposite positions.

Partly by design, managers have distorted the social issues and interests involved here. It is in their interest to claim that industrial practices are scientific, technical matters that they are best equipped to control. This claim, of course, tends to obscure their conflict with labor. They explain that when they reject industrial medical practices, they do so largely on the basis of technical limitations; and that when they accept them it is because of their technical effectiveness in differentiating high-risk workers, which furthers scientific progress and preventive medicine. Thus, while industry managers control the implementation of technology, they make their decisions regarding the use of genetic testing and exclusionary employment practices seem to be a function of science and technological capability. Labor, on the other hand, finds it in its own interest to recognize issues of power and describe them as such. Many labor leaders see that in order to increase their own relative power, and to reverse the paradigm shift away from the high-risk workplace and toward the risky worker, they must speak to the realities of power, control, and divergent interests.

POLICY IMPLICATIONS

This focus on conflicting interests and power in analyzing the shifting conceptions of occupational hazards has certain implications for recasting the problem of workers at risk. Alternative policies could be implemented that could advance occupational health without further limiting employees' access to jobs, information, and levers of power and control.

First, instead of excluding high-risk groups, occupational health policy could focus on making the workplace safe for everyone. Are companies excluding workers instead of reducing exposure risks? Are they in compliance with OSHA rules, or are they illegally exposing people to toxic chemicals? When hazards are known and it is technologically and economically feasible to prevent them, reducing them has the added benefit of eliminating the competitive advantage that less vigilant employers gain.[2] In many cases, the cost of abating hazards also declines, due to the economy of scale produced when many employers pursue new emission control technologies. Cleaning up chemical hazards can cost less than originally estimated, and in some instances managers even can save money. By installing engineering controls on vinyl chloride, for example, industry was able to profit through capturing gases that previously escaped into the atmosphere to affect workers and the public.[3] We should not imagine that this is the typical case, however. It can be very costly to employers to reduce exposures. Yet it can be even more costly to society *not* to curtail toxic exposures of the work force.

Second, the scientific evidence could be investigated more carefully. Linking disease risks to specific biological characteristics should have a sound scientific basis. What evidence do companies have to support their claim that an individual or a group is in danger and must be removed? In the case of reproductive hazards, the greater attention they have recently received is a positive development. But when scientists or managers identify risks to the fetus, the health hazard may not be confined to fetal damage, and the teratogenic risk may not be significantly greater than the effects of chemical exposure on adults. Reproductive and other effects through both men and women should be investigated. Companies should present their evidence for claiming there are special risks to which only women are subject. If they do not have it, the burden should be on them to investigate toxic effects on both men and women, including teratogenic, mutagenic, and carcinogenic damage. Further, medical tests should be truly predictive and should be related to relatively common ailments and exposures.

Third, workers and the public could be provided with more useful and complete information on occupational health hazards. Employees should be told of chemical risks and medical test results.[4] Recent policy measures expanding chemical labeling and access to medical records, though limited and long in coming, have extended rights to information and given more power to employees and to the public.[5] But workers also need independent evidence of health hazards, for otherwise they cannot evaluate employers' warnings of hazards or assurances of safety. Further, they need more protection than information alone can offer. They should not have to choose between their jobs and their health.

Fourth, measures could be instituted to limit the discriminatory impact of exclusionary policies. The impact of the social context of industrial medicine should be acknowledged. If we recognize that most jobs are fundamentally insecure and that current evidence on occupational health hazards is uncertain, we can see the value of protections for workers who are removed for reasons related to their health. There may in fact be cases in which certain workers *are* at special risk. They can be given other jobs if any are available. In any case, though, they should not lose their pay, benefits, or seniority. As we have seen, medical removal and rate retention provisions, such as those included in the OSHA lead standard, offer this protection.[6] Individuals who are considered high risk or damaged can be removed temporarily but have the right to retain their wage and seniority levels. Individuals planning to have children in the near future, for example, could be temporarily removed from reproductive hazards, but keep their wage rates and benefits.[7] Meanwhile, the company should be setting up engineering controls to reduce exposure and collecting scientific information on reproductive effects. Without medical removal protection and rate retention, any worker or group who is removed is heavily penalized.[8]

What should be done about health hazards in the workplace is not simply a question of policy. It is also largely a question of power. We must recognize that new policies – to mandate stronger controls on toxic chemicals and extend medical removal protection, for example – can be very difficult to bring about, requiring a complex process of legal challenges, government regulation, education, and collective bargaining. Since power, control, and money are at stake, the questions remain: How can employers or government officials be persuaded to change current policy, and who will pay the resulting costs of the change? Industry and government decisions as to which policies are chosen, and how they are carried out, depend only in part on the scientific evidence of risks. They are also shaped by the social and political terrain on which employment and medical decisions are made.

It is clear from this study that if we want to safeguard workers' health, then existing industrial practices should be changed so that labor's position in their conflict over health hazards is strengthened, medical and employment information is used more often in the interest of employees, and workers are empowered to make more meaningful choices on policy concerning health, employment, and the workplace.

PROSPECTS FOR THE FUTURE

Susceptibility policies are likely to become more pervasive because the concept and ideology of high-risk workers is already in place and the social conditions we have examined are generally favorable for their expansion. Also, while many current screening tests are unreliable predictors of disease under industrial conditions, technological improvements are likely to make tests more accurate within certain technical parameters, so that they will be accepted with even more enthusiasm.

From our examination of the social factors that have supported the use of genetic testing and exclusionary policies, we can predict that a long struggle lies ahead. Labor–management conflict in this arena will intensify and the public will become more involved as people gain awareness of the different interests involved and begin to recognize what is at stake in terms of health hazards, social costs, power relations, and public policy.

Whether the monitoring or the screening paradigm will prevail – whether the growing concern over occupational hazards will focus on high-risk workers or on the high-risk workplace – will depend in part on the relative power, influence, and control of social groups, particularly industrial labor and management.

Genetic techniques have considerable potential as preventive health measures, but susceptibility policies also have tremendous potential for abuse. By targeting those who may be at increased risk for disease, genetic screening and fetal exclusion practices may penalize individuals for occupational health hazards. Moreover, they may deepen social divisions and conflict.

For all these reasons, genetic screening, genetic monitoring, and fetal exclusion remain highly controversial. Any attempt to construct a consensus view of these practices would be seriously misguided. Instead, the divergent perspectives should be considered carefully, both in planning industrial programs and in setting government policy. The different social locations and interests that underlie alternative paradigms for risk in the workplace also must be understood. If they are not, genetic testing is likely to be used in ways that exacerbate social inequality. In considering the potential of any susceptibility policy, then, we should always ask whose interests would be served by its application. The central questions arising from genetic testing and exclusionary practices are not questions of science at all. They are questions of power and conflicting interests.

TOWARD A SOCIOLOGICAL UNDERSTANDING OF RISK, POWER, AND CONFLICTING INTERESTS IN THE WORKPLACE

Conceptions of risk, and of the proper use of technologies, are socially constructed. One major objective of this study has been to raise the veil of scientific expertise and progress that has allowed genetic testing practices to masquerade as technical questions.

The methods by which risk is defined and high-risk groups are identified have major consequences for individual workers as well as for the direction of occupational health as a whole. In spite of the accumulation of more and more genetic knowledge and the incorporation of increasingly sophisticated technologies in the field of occupational medicine, our social understanding of these practices has been inadequate.

Risk analysis is a critical arena of social policy, and it should be undertaken by those who are sociologically informed, rather then exclusively by economists, engineers, and systems analysts.[9] A proper understanding of occupational and environmental risk – one that takes careful account of social structures of power and conflict – is bound to make risk analysis a more effective tool of policymaking.

My approach toward the case of genetic susceptibility policies, and toward deconstructing the ideology that supports them, has something in common with Charles Perrow's notion of "normal accidents" (1984). Perrow argues, with a sense of alarm, that the high-risk technologies embodied in nuclear power, nuclear weapons, petrochemicals, recombinant DNA, and other advanced systems are so complex that accidents carrying grave consequences must now be considered not only inevitable but a "normal" feature of life in modern society.

What I have argued in this book is that when certain workers come to be seen as the "problem" – as they have been, increasingly, in industrial practice and public policy – most exposures to toxic chemicals can be considered "normal hazards" or *not hazards at all*. This development both reflects and reinforces structures of power in the workplace and in society as a whole.

The problem we face can perhaps be illuminated by an example from the history of the coal mines. Because canaries are especially vulnerable to noxious methane gas, they were once commonly taken into the mines, where their death would signal dangerous conditions for miners. Just as canaries were used to detect a deadly hazard to miners, evidence of damage to high-risk groups can be used as a warning signal of dangerous conditions for all workers. But reacting to the warning by removing those groups instead of reducing the exposure may actually magnify health hazards: Companies, and sometimes employees, may then presume that exposure is safe for the workers who remain. So far, the ways in which industry has used genetic susceptibility policies have *not* provided real protection for all workers by eliminating chemical hazards in the workplace.

Clearly, identifying workers at risk is more than a medical or scientific problem. It is a highly charged social and political dilemma. Unless the problem of occupational hazards is reconceptualized, it will continue to be seen largely in terms of individual susceptibility and inherently high-risk groups rather than for what it is: a set of health and environmental problems of far-reaching proportions, which are largely socially constructed and must ultimately be solved by social action.

Appendix

Research design

DATA, METHODS, AND RESEARCH FOCUS

The principal data and methods used in the research are fieldwork, which entailed 120 in-depth interviews and observation at conferences and workplaces; and an analysis of documentary, historical, and statistical materials (see Appendix Tables 1 and 2). The interviews and documentary sources yield varied and rich data that help explain the social context and significance of susceptibility policies in the workplace.

I have focused on the chemical industry, in which some of the largest genetic testing projects have been carried out and in which many of the most enthusiastic proponents of susceptibility policies have held official positions. The issues of health effects from hazardous chemicals and the identification of high-risk groups have also been most salient there. Further, the toxic exposure problems in the chemical industry are in many cases "upstream" and therefore magnified versions of exposure in the industries they supply, such as electronics, automobiles, and textiles. I therefore give secondary attention to the oil, auto, steel, and textile industries.

I have examined mainly large firms, for they are the ones that have the sophisticated technology, in-house medical programs, and greatest interest in genetic testing. However, a few smaller firms were also investigated for purposes of comparison. In addition, I developed case studies of two large chemical companies – Dow and DuPont – whose substantial experience with genetic testing has been widely publicized and discussed.

INTERVIEWS

I conducted in-depth interviews with 120 people I identified through a variety of resources, notably articles, legislative hearings, and conference proceedings. Interviewees were selected so as to ensure breadth of region, company position, type of organization, and perspective.

Those interviewed include: (1) Corporate managers and medical directors in companies that have used genetic testing and exclusionary practices, such as Allied Chemical, General Motors, Dow Chemical, Exxon, and DuPont, as well as trade association officials.[1] (2) Workers and labor representatives, with emphasis on the chemical, oil, auto, and steel industries, where genetic testing and fetal exclusion policies have been more pervasive. Unions include the Oil, Chemical, and Atomic Workers Union, the International Chemical Workers Union, and the United Steelworkers Union. (3) Biomedical scientists in universities, lawyers, and others outside industry and government who are familiar with occupational health and genetic technology issues. (4) Government officials concerned with occupational medicine, such as those in the Occupational Safety and Health Administration (OSHA) and the National Institute for Occupational Safety and Health (NIOSH) (see Appendix Table 1).

Many of the corporate, labor, academic, and government personnel selected for interviewing were key individuals concerned with workers at risk. These informants were prominent in their own fields and known for their expertise in occupational health. The majority of them were leaders rather than lower ranking members of their organizations. For example, those interviewed include directors of federal occupational health and safety agencies, labor officials responsible for health and safety in international unions, directors of university occupational medical clinics, legal scholars specializing in corporate professional liability and workplace

Table A1. *Interviews*

As part of this study of genetic testing and related employment practices, I interviewed 120 people, 30 each in the areas of industry, government, labor, and academia. A partial list of their occupations, agencies, and organizations follows.

Industry personnel:
Corporate medical directors
Occupational physicians
Industry lawyers
Toxicologists and hygienists
Industrial research laboratory staff
Trade association representatives, particularly from Chemical
    Manufacturers Association, Chemical Industry Institute of Toxicology,
    and American Industrial Health Council
Public relations and government affairs personnel

Government officials in agencies concerned with health, employment,
discrimination, and medical technology, in:
Occupational Safety and Health Administration
Equal Employment Opportunity Commission
Department of Labor
National Institute for Occupational Safety and Health
Investigations and Oversight Subcommittee, U.S. House Committee on
    Science and Technology
Environmental Protection Agency
Office of Technology Assessment, U.S. Congress

University scientists, lawyers, and others familiar with these issues
of occupational health, genetic technology, and industrial medicine:
National Academy of Sciences, Institute of Medicine
The Hastings Center
Council on Economic Priorities
Massachusetts Institute of Technology, Yale, Columbia, University of
    Illinois, Howard, Brookings, Berkeley, Lawrence Livermore
    Laboratory, University of Massachusetts, University of Texas, Mt.
    Sinai School of Medicine, etc.

Employees, labor union members and officials:
Employees in the chemical industry
Employees in auto, steel, textile, oil, and other industries
Local, regional, and national labor union officials in the Oil, Chemical,
    and Atomic Workers Union; International Chemical Workers Union;
    United Steelworkers; Amalgamated Clothing and Textile Workers;
    United Auto Workers; etc.
National labor officials in the AFL-CIO Health and Safety Division, Indus-
    trial Union Department, Workers' Institute for Safety and Health, etc.

health issues, the president of a national occupational medical association, and the environmental affairs director of a major chemical company.

Those interviewed were chosen to be generally typical of those in the same types of positions and organizations. The research decision to interview more leaders than lower ranking members reflects a desire to find particularly well-informed respondents – persons who were not only highly knowledgeable about occupational medicine and the conditions affecting it but also aware of the range of perspectives on it in their own and other organizations.

Initial and follow-up interviews were conducted between 1980 and 1990, most of them before 1987. I talked with persons from all regions of the country, but particularly at locations in the industrial Midwest, the Northeast, the Pacific Coast, and the Southwest. The interviews generally lasted from one-and-a-half to three hours, and many of them extended over more than one session.[2] They were conducted in an office or a home, as the interviewee preferred. I conducted follow-up interviews with many of these 120 individuals as well as supplemental interviews with others. Some of these were by phone, but most were carried out in person. In addition to formal interviews, I was able to observe and talk informally with many people at conferences and hearings on occupational risk and at a wide range of workplaces.

The interviews were focused and semistructured. They elucidated factors underlying the rise of susceptibility policies, divergent perspectives toward them, and the social meaning of their selective appeal. I asked questions in areas such as: (1) what they knew about the ways in which genetic tests have been applied in industry; (2) how they assessed the strengths and weaknesses of genetic tests and exclusionary practices; (3) how they identified workers at risk; and (4) how they viewed the broader arena of health and employment practices in industry, as a context for genetic testing.

I asked individuals about their general perspective and

their own experience. For example, I questioned corporate managers about their perspective on what should be done with workers at risk and about how management is and should be involved in decision making regarding new medical technologies. I also asked them about their own experience in deciding what should be done with workers at risk and how new medical technologies should be used.

The individuals I interviewed for this study were generally cooperative and willing to talk with me at length. Many, however, requested anonymity in order to speak frankly. These persons are therefore not quoted by name in the book. The position or affiliation of individuals who are quoted by name is generally the one they held at the time of the statement.

In general, I have quoted from publicly available sources whenever they convey essentially the same point as interview statements. Thus when I have been able to uncover a social pattern through extensive interviews, field research, and documents, I typically have quoted from a public source that expressed that social pattern succinctly. The advantage of this approach is that I could keep to a minimum the anonymous interviews I cite and instead quote public sources known to readers and readily available to them. The significant disadvantage, however, is that quoting from single public sources rather than from my own interviews tends to mask the value of the insight I gained from the 120 interviews I conducted. Despite this disadvantage, I tried to quote or cite publicly available sources to illustrate social phenomena I uncovered through my interviews and the broad range of other evidence on which this book is based.

OTHER DATA SOURCES

In addition to the interviews, data sources include government documents, conference proceedings, employment and health statistics, scientific and other publications, and unpublished documents. Historical and sociological materials regarding occupational health and protectionist policies, employment trends, regulatory developments, past use of medical screening, and explanations of testing programs are also major sources (see Appendix Table 2).

The scientific evidence includes books, articles, conference transcripts, monographs, and unpublished research reports on high-risk workers. Corporate and union documents include health and exposure information, employment records, policy statements, trade association reports, research reports, internal memoranda, press releases, and public policy statements. Statistical data include data on the health of workers and on the composition of the work force by sex and race in specific industries and jobs. Government documents include transcripts of legislative, administrative, and judicial hearings on disease liability, genetic testing, and employment discrimination; government regulatory standards; laws and proposed bills; health data; and reports on debates over genetic specifications in occupational health. Other materials include medical, legal, ethical, historical, and policy literatures on high-risk workers and genetic testing.

I drew from existing survey data on genetic testing, company policies, and risk perspectives for this study.[3] However, I concluded that carrying out my own intensive field research was essential for moving beyond limitations of existing knowledge and uncovering the true social patterns to the controversy over genetic testing in the workplace. In a hotly contested arena such as this, relying on a mailed questionnaire as my major source of data certainly seemed out of the question. In addition, I wanted to allow those I interviewed to describe and analyze cases of genetic testing and exclusion in detail without being limited to multiple-choice or otherwise brief, easily quantified responses. I had to commit myself to the labor-intensive enterprise of interviewing a broad range of people in person with a flexible interview guide, studying documents, and observing people functioning in their daily work in order to capture the complex reality of their social world.[4]

Table A2. *Other data sources*

Evidence of industry practices, positions taken by various parties to the controversy, and the social context are examined through the following data sources related to genetic testing and exclusionary policies.

Scientific and other evidence from literature on high-risk workers and genetic testing, including medical, legal, ethical, and policy sources

Government documents, particularly regulatory standards, health and employment data, laws, and proposed bills

Conference proceedings, including reports on debates over genetic specifications in occupational health

Policy position papers and other written material that gives evidence of the varying perspectives on industrial genetics

Transcripts of testimony at legislative, regulatory, and judicial hearings on liability for disease, genetic testing, and employment discrimination; and other data regarding important legal cases

Statistical data, particularly health data and employment data on the composition and division of labor in the work force by sex and race in specific industries and jobs

Industry documents, including employment records, policy statements, health information, trade association reports, public relations material, research reports, internal corporate memoranda, and press releases

Union and other labor organization documents, including position papers, employment and health information, research reports, public relations papers, correspondence, and employee records

General news periodicals, particularly *New York Times*, *Wall Street Journal*, and *Business Week*

Specific major periodicals, such as *Journal of Occupational Medicine, Environmental Health Perspectives, Chemical Week, Chemical and Engineering News, Occupational Safety and Health Reporter, BNA Chemical Regulation Reporter, BNA OSH Reporter, Toxic Substances Journal*, etc.

Historical and sociological materials regarding occupational health and employment policies, trends, regulatory developments, etc.

Notes

1 See Kurzman (1987), Levine (1982), and Meier and Winslow (1984).

2 Two pathbreaking articles featured in the *Journal of Occupational Medicine* herald this orientation toward susceptible workers that many companies have adopted. Written by a scientist at DuPont, "Chemical Hypersusceptibility" advocates greater attention to high-risk individuals (Reinhardt, 1978). The other article, "Progress in Detecting the Worker Hypersusceptible to Industrial Chemicals," by two government scientists, proclaims great potential for susceptibility testing (Stokinger and Mountain, 1967).

3 For discussion of technical research on predisposing traits, genetic abnormalities, and birth defects, see Office of Technology Assessment (1990, 1983), Holtzman (1989), Perera et al. (1986), Carrano (1986), Antonarakis (1989), Schulte (1986), Brandt-Rauf (1988), Calabrese (1984), Vaino et al. (1983), National Research Council (1983), Council on Environmental Quality (1981), Bloom (1981), and Bridges et al. (1982).

4 Calabrese (1986), Evans (1988), Lewy (1983), and Fraumeni (1975).

5 Evaluations of genetic testing and exclusionary practices include those by union officials and employees (Samuels, 1986; Itaya, 1982; Mazzocchi, 1980; Wright et al., 1979; and Ringen, 1980), industrial management (Guthier, 1986; LeClercq, 1983; Karrh and Dixon, in U.S. Congress, 1981; Kilian et al., 1975; Kotin, 1977; and Hathaway, 1978), and government (Carrano,

1986; Office of Technology Assessment, 1983; Bingham, 1980a,b; Meinhardt, 1981; Stokinger, 1981; and Plumlee et al., 1979).

6 Legal studies of genetic testing and exclusion in the workplace include Rothstein (1986, 1984), McElveen (1986), Field and Baram (1986), Ashford et al. (1990, 1984), Raines (1986), McGarity and Schroeder (1981), Shaw (1984), Goerth (1983a), Bassett-Stanford (1981), Stillman (1979), Warshaw (1979), and Williams (1981). Publications that examine ethical dimensions of genetic testing include Lappé (1988, 1983), Bayer (1986, 1982), Atherley et al. (1986), Murray (1985, 1983), Schneiderman (1982), Sheridan (1983), and Powledge (1976).

7 Omenn and Gelboin (1984) and Peto and Schneiderman (1981) offer examples and analysis of these technical-scientific models of risk as they are applied to occupational hazards.

8 See Stuller (1988), Greer (1985), Viscusi (1983, 1979), Zeckhauser and Nichol (1979), and Zeckhauser and Shephard (1976).

9 Douglas and Wildavsky maintain an overly relativistic stance toward the processes by which people assess risk. In chapters on "Scientists Disagree," "Assessment Is Biased," and in their introduction, Douglas and Wildavsky (1982) argue that we cannot know the risks we face now or in the future, so we need a cultural theory of risk perception to explain why people focus on particular risks and not others. Despite flaws in their argument, Douglas and Wildavsky do draw attention to cultural and social dimensions of technological hazards.

10 For example, see Don MacKinnon, "Chemophobia," *Chemical and Engineering News* (July 13, 1981). See also Passell (1989a, b), Hocking (1987), Guthier (1986), and Boxer (1985). Ames (1987) argues that regulators and the public reveal their chemophobia and create high costs to society when they focus on limiting synthetic pollutants in drinking water and pesticide residues in food. He maintains that few serious carcinogenic hazards exist beyond tobacco and saturated fat.

11 A few studies of related areas of risk do consider the impact of stratification and power structures on social policy and perspectives toward risk. They include studies by Perrow (1984), Nelkin and Brown (1984), and Levine (1982).

12 A major portion of my analysis lies within the tradition of the sociology of knowledge and science, as developed by writers

like Mannheim (1952, 1936), Berger and Luckmann (1966), and Merton (1979, 1973) and exemplified by Latour and Woolgar (1979). This perspective helps explain how industrial genetics is socially constructed and how different perspectives and interests stem from actors' divergent social locations.

13 I analyze industrial genetics by linking it to sociobiology and biological explanations for human behavior as well as to conflicting approaches to social structure, culture, and human variation, such as those found in Wilson and Herrnstein (1985), Lewontin et al. (1984), Wilson (1978, 1975), Jencks (1987), Duster and Garrett (1984), Rossi (1984), Keller (1984), Montagu (1980), Gould (1981), Barash (1977), Bock (1980), MacCormack and Strathern (1980), Sahlins (1977), and Dawkins (1976). See Chapters 2 and 3.

1. GENETIC TESTING AND EXCLUSIONARY PRACTICES IN THE WORKPLACE

1 In this study, G-6-PD refers to glucose-6-phosphate dehydrogenase, SAT refers to serum alpha$_1$-antitrypsin, and HLA refers to human leukocyte antigens. For virtually all of these traits listed in Table 1, the individuals who have them generally show absolutely no sign of disease. In fact, scientists vigorously dispute whether the individuals would suffer any special effects when exposed to particular toxic chemicals. See Office of Technology Assessment (1990, 1983), Calabrese (1984), and Omenn and Gelboin (1984).

2 *Journal of Occupational Medicine* (1986), U.S. Congress (1981), Holtzman (1989), Otten (1986), Harris (1983), Reinhardt (1978), Severo (1980a), Office of Technology Assessment (1990), and Chapters 3–5 discuss DuPont's testing programs.

3 The terminology for describing genetic tests varies somewhat in the scientific literature. Here, "genetic screening" refers to one-time, usually preemployment tests for identifying heritable genetic traits or diseases. The term "genetic monitoring" (or "chromosomal monitoring" or "cytogenetic monitoring") refers to repeated short-term testing of chromosomal material to detect possible genetic damage.

4 Rather than reduce chemical emissions when monitoring reveals evidence of health hazards, employers could decide to exclude individuals with high levels of abnormalities from par-

ticular jobs. Chapter 3 discusses this potential use of monitoring.

5 For a detailed and insightful study of Love Canal, including an analysis of the controversy over what chromosome changes signify, see Levine (1982).

6 *Journal of Occupational Medicine* (1986), Legator (1987, 1981), Office of Technology Assessment (1990), Otten (1986), Severo (1980a), Venable (1978), and Kilian et al. (1975). Chapters 3 and 5 examine this important case.

7 Technicians use laboratory tests to check chemicals for teratogenic effects. To some extent fetal exclusion policies are based on laboratory evidence indicating teratogenic risk from chemical exposure. Yet in many cases, very little or no evidence suggests that the substances from which women are excluded actually do harm the fetus, or that reproductive damage is limited to female employees' toxic exposures. Chapters 3 and 4 analyze these issues of reproductive risk, company policies, and evidence.

8 Greenhouse (1991), Lewin (1990), Savage (1990), Postol (1988), Randall (1987), McElveen (1986), Bertin (1983), Perrolle and Rustad (1984), Williams (1981), Bayer (1982), Draper (1991, 1984b), Randall and Short (1983), Office of Technology Assessment (1985), Severo (1980a), Rao and Schwetz (1981), U.S. Congress (1981), and Chapter 4 discuss these company policies.

9 Contract research firms that conduct genetic and other tests for companies include Litton Bionetics, Huntington Toxicol Laboratories, and Inveresk Research International.

10 The medical director of a fairly small utility company expressed this attitude: "We've wondered whether genetic screening would be useful to us. We're not one of the larger companies" (personal interview). Data from the NIOSH National Occupational Exposure Survey (1982) reveal that 22 percent of small manufacturing plants (employing fewer than 100 workers) require medical screening for prospective or new employees. In contrast, 57 percent of medium-sized (100 to 499 workers) and 78 percent of large (500 or more) manufacturing plants require medical screening for job applicants and new employees.

11 Office of Technology Assessment (1990:171–200, 1983:33–40). The rate of reported use of screening and monitoring tests is higher among companies for whom these technologies are

especially relevant, such as manufacturing companies in the chemical, oil, and pharmaceutical industries.

12 The veracity and meaning of these congressional Office of Technology Assessment surveys is difficult to interpret. However, it is likely that the OTA surveys understate the extent of testing practices, in part because of the problem of industry self-reporting in surveys tied to controversial congressional committees. At least some company officials, and probably many, felt threatened by the studies, believing that companies' positive responses to the survey questions would result in further onerous publicity, greater legislative activity, and more stringent regulation harmful to industry. U.S. Congress (1982a) provides evidence of employer resistance to the 1982 OTA survey, such as opposition by the American Industrial Health Council, a major corporate trade association. The 1982 survey further understated the extent of screening and monitoring by including a narrower set of questions than the 1989 survey (OTA, 1990:177).

13 Savage (1990), Kilborn (1990), Lewin (1988a, b), Williams (1981), and U.S. Congress (1981). A study of 198 large chemical and electronics companies in Massachusetts, conducted by the Massachusetts Department of Public Health and the University of Massachusetts Occupational Health Program, found that nearly one in five (37 companies) restrict women's work options on the ground of potential risk to their reproductive health. Many put some systematic restrictions on all women or on all women of childbearing age. All 37 put some limits on the work available to pregnant women. Most ignored the reproductive hazards faced by men (see Lewin, 1988a).

14 The more prominent corporate advocates of genetic testing in industry have included: Paul Kotin (former Johns-Manville medical director), Charles Reinhardt (as Director of Haskell Research Laboratory at DuPont), and Jack Kilian (as a medical director at Dow).

15 Omenn and Gelboin (1984), Vaino et al. (1983), ACGIH (1982), Picciano et al. (1977), and Stokinger and Scheel (1973).

16 Office of Technology Assessment (1990, 1983), Schulte (1987), Calabrese (1986), Khory et al. (1985), Antonarakis (1989), National Research Council (1983), and Omenn (1982).

17 Lappé (1988), Halperin et al. (1986), Samuels (1986), Omenn (1982), Last (1980), Knudson (1977), and Messite and Bond (1980).

18 *Environmental Health Perspectives* (1987a), Omenn and Gelboin (1984), Calabrese (1986, 1978), *Journal of Occupational Medicine* (1986), Fraumeni (1975), and Litwin (1978).

19 Severo (1982a, b; 1980a, b), Lewin (1988a, b), McAuliffe (1987), Murray (1985), Holden (1982), West (1982), and Bronson (1979a, 1978).

20 *Journal of Occupational Medicine* (1986), International Symposium (1986), U.S. Congress (1981, 1982a, b), Berlin et al. (1984), Omenn and Gelboin (1984), ACGIH (1982), National Academy of Sciences (1980), Calabrese (1979), and American Society of Law and Medicine (1983).

21 Three major public sources that reveal controversy over susceptibility policies are: the front-page series in the *New York Times* on workplace testing (Severo 1980a); the National Academy of Sciences, Institute of Medicine, Conference on Genetic Influences on Responses to the Environment (National Academy of Sciences, 1980); and the congressional hearings on genetic screening and high-risk groups held by the House Science and Technology Committee's Investigations and Oversight Subcommittee (U.S. Congress, 1982a,b, 1981).

22 See Calabrese (1986), Hunt (1986), Omenn (1982), Stokinger (1981), Leach et al. (1981), and Reinhardt (1978).

23 Samuels (1986), Ashford et al. (1984), Itaya (1982), and Wright et al. (1979).

24 See Office of Technology Assessment (1990), Holtzman (1989), Schulte (1987), Calabrese (1984), and Omenn and Gelboin (1984).

25 These differences can be seen in Samuels (1986), Otten (1986), U.S. Congress (1982a,b), National Academy of Sciences (1980), Utidjian et al. (1979), and Dabney (1981).

26 For articulation of this perspective, see Hunt (1986), Mazzocchi (1980), and Wright et al. (1979).

27 See, for example, Otten (1986), Samuels (1983), and Krekel (1981).

28 Howard Samuel (President, Industrial Union Department, AFL-CIO) in Testimony to U.S. Congress (1981:34).

29 Meinhardt (1981) and Landrigan (1982) discuss this study.

30 Guthier (1986), Hunt (1986), Leach et al. (1981), Reinhardt (1978), Paul Kotin in Wright et al. (1979), Cooper (1973), and Stokinger and Scheel (1973) provide statements of industrial managers and occupational physicians advocating genetic

screening. One corporate official, in comparing genetic screening with genetic monitoring, opposes genetic monitoring but finds screening to be a promising method of identifying individuals with a genetic disease or trait who may be susceptible, arguing that genetic screening is "far more precise and far more accurate" (William J. McCarville, as Director of Environmental Affairs for the American Industrial Health Council, a trade association, in U.S. Congress, 1982a:54 and 47).

31 See, for example, Otten (1986), Legator (1987), and Paul Kotin and D. Jack Kilian in Wright et al. (1979).

2. THE RISE OF THE GENETIC PARADIGM FOR OCCUPATIONAL RISK

Epigraphs: Motulsky, Presentation at the National Academy of Sciences Conference on Genetic Influences on Responses to the Environment (July 10, 1980); Kotin, quoted in Severo, *New York Times* (February 3, 1980).

1 Haldane (1938:179). Haldane goes on to link the focus on genetically high-risk potters to the search for accident prone workers, as articulated in the quote by Haldane introducing Chapter 1. He also recommends that some of the funds for pottery research be "spent on potters rather than on pots" (p. 179). Ironically, Haldane was a prominent Marxist, unlike more typical screening proponents who favored industrialists' search for the vulnerable worker. Haldane's concern with high-risk individuals, however, was combined with a more general orientation to eliminating chemical hazards in industry.

2 Starr (1982), Reiser (1978), and U.S. Congress (1981:249–250) examine the history of major approaches to combatting infectious disease.

3 See Tesh (1988), Nugent (1983), Starr (1982), and Reiser (1978).

4 Kolata (1989), Holtzman (1989), Office of Technology Assessment (1990, 1983), King et al. (1984), Bishop (1984), Calabrese (1984, 1978), *Journal of Occupational Medicine* (1986), Fraumeni (1975), National Academy of Sciences (1980), Harris (1980), Antonarakis (1989), and Omenn and Gelboin (1984) examine genetic factors that may increase risk of cancer or heart disease.

5 Major sources examining differential susceptibility to chemical hazards include Office of Technology Assessment (1990),

Omenn and Gelboin (1984), *Journal of Occupational Medicine* (1986), Calabrese (1984), and Fraumeni (1975).

6 Examples include Breiger (1963) and Jensen (1962).

7 See Office of Technology Assessment (1990), Calabrese (1986, 1984), Omenn and Gelboin (1984), *Environmental Health Perspectives* (1987a), Perera et al. (1986), Fabricant and Legator (1981), Bridges et al. (1982), National Research Council (1983), Berlin et al. (1984), Antonarakis (1989), and Vainio et al. (1983).

8 For example, the National Institutes of Health has supported projects on sickle cell testing and genetic screening at the University of California, Berkeley, and elsewhere. The NIH awarded grants of over $104 million in fiscal year 1990 to support 627 projects that directly or indirectly relate to genetic screening and monitoring (Office of Technology Assessment, 1990:210–11). The National Academy of Sciences Institute of Medicine sponsored a conference in 1980 that examined industrial and public genetic screening. The National Science Foundation has funded numerous projects on genetic testing and related employment practices, including projects at The Hastings Center on new technologies used in screening workers and in industrial medical surveillance, a study at Cornell University examining genetic screening as part of their study of workers' perceptions of risk, and many basic research projects indirectly related to genetic screening and monitoring. Holtzman (1989), Office of Technology Assessment (1990:209–212), *Journal of Occupational Medicine* (1986), Calabrese (1984), and Beutler (1984) provide evidence of major government spending for genetic susceptibility screening and research. Calabrese (1984) and Omenn (in Omenn and Gelboin, 1984) recommend that genetic susceptibility testing continue to be a high priority for research funding. See also Stephens et al. (1990) on human genome mapping.

9 One example is a National Cancer Institute research project designed to develop a simple test that could be used in the workplace to identify cancer-prone individuals (*Chemical Week*, 1982). The principal investigator of the project stated that the test could be as simple as "detecting VD." It could be used in companies where "workers are exposed to radiation or carcinogenic chemicals, allowing employers to screen out workers with a high susceptibility to cancer – perhaps 2–3 percent of the population."

10 Professional organizations that have held conferences on susceptibility to environmental chemicals include the American Conference of Governmental Industrial Hygienists (in Arizona, 1981), the American Occupational Medicine Association (in Colorado, 1978), and the American Society of Law and Medicine (in Washington, D.C., 1983).

11 See Holtzman (1989), Carey et al. (1990), Nichols (1988), President's Commission (1982), and Yoxen (1983).

12 For summaries of much of the scientific evidence on genetic screening, see Office of Technology Assessment (1990, 1983). These studies also review evidence concerning genetic monitoring. See also Brandt-Rauf (1988), *Journal of Occupational Medicine* (1986), Calabrese (1984), Holtzman (1989), Antonarakis (1989), and Omenn and Gelboin (1984).

13 Heterozygous carriers have been the focus of public genetic screening programs as well as workplace screening. Many public screening programs target reproductive decisions of heterozygous carriers, since carriers who produce children with similar carriers have a one-in-four chance of producing a homozygous disease state in their children. Before its application to the workplace, genetic markers research was oriented more strongly to the problem of children being born with abnormalities. Therefore, most public screening for heterozygous carriers sought to avoid marriages or pregnancies that could produce such children.

14 Nelkin (1987) shows ways in which news coverage makes genetic explanations and solutions for heart disease, diabetes, cancer, and other diseases appear imminent, even when the basis for such optimism is highly uncertain. See also Carey et al. (1990), McKusick (1988), Palca (1988), and Etzioni (1973).

15 Bernard D. Davis (Adele Lehman Professor of Bacterial Physiology, Harvard Medical School), Statement at the Conference on Genetic Influences on Responses to the Environment, organized by the National Academy of Sciences Institute of Medicine (conference subsequently referred to as National Academy of Sciences, 1980) (p. 232).

16 Gilbert S. Omenn (Professor in Departments of Medicine and Environmental Health; and Dean, School of Public Health and Community Medicine, University of Washington), personal interview.

17 Arno Motulsky (Professor of Medicine and Genetics, University of Washington School of Medicine, Seattle), National Academy of Sciences (1980:239).

18 W. Clark Cooper (Tabershaw-Cooper Associates, Berkeley) (1973:355–359).

19 H. E. Stokinger (Chief, Toxicology Branch of the Division of Laboratories and Criteria Development, National Institute for Occupational Safety and Health) and L. D. Scheel, (Toxicology Branch, NIOSH) (1973:564–573).

20 Stokinger and Scheel (1973:572).

21 Examples of criteria used to evaluate specific tests include King (1984) and Omenn (1982).

22 "Predictive value" refers to the likelihood that a person with a positive test result has the disease or that a person with a negative result does not have the disease. The term also refers to the likelihood that the index or marker predicts the occurrence of a disease. "Sensitivity" refers to the ability of a test to identify correctly those who have a disease. "Specificity" refers to the ability of a test to identify correctly those who do not have a trait or disease that is being tested.

23 Office of Technology Assessment (1990, 1983), Holtzman (1989), *Journal of Occupational Medicine* (1986), and Chapter 3 examine specific factors limiting the medical usefulness of screening tests. Chapter 4 analyzes tests and exclusionary policies designed to limit reproductive damage. For discussion of scientific evidence concerning genetic monitoring, see *Environmental Health Perspectives* (1987a), Carrano and Natarajan (1988), Evans (1988), Brandt-Rauf (1988), National Research Council (1983), Bridges et al. (1982), Office of Technology Assessment (1990, 1983), Bloom (1981), Fabricant and Legator (1981), and Chapter 5.

24 Howard Sloan (Professor of Pediatrics, Ohio State University) in Testimony at U.S. Congress (1982:64 and 75) offers an example of a tepid assessment of genetic screening tests and their applications. See also King (1984). Beutler (1984) analyzes the case of screening for G-6-PD. He points to screening errors stemming from limitations of available tests and ambiguous data on genetic predisposition to drugs.

25 In a parenthetic phrase in his table of fifty genetic factors, Calabrese makes slight reference to the shortage of evidence for genetic susceptibility the text discusses. He lists chemicals

as "Environmental Agent(s) to Which the Group is (May be) at Increased Risk." With no such caution, however, he refers to the fifty factors as identifying "high-risk groups."

26 Scientist Gilbert Omenn follows the same dynamic as Calabrese and other scientists in his work (Omenn and Gelboin, 1984; Omenn, 1982). He refers to problems of evidence but endorses the general approach of susceptibility testing. Salter (1988), Gilbert and Mulkay (1984), Gutting (1980), Knorr-Cetina and Mulkay (1983), Keller (1984), Collins (1981), Kuhn (1970), and Fleck (1979) discuss truth claims in scientific debates.

27 Chapters 3, 5, and 6 discuss reasons why corporate executives are far less likely to endorse genetic monitoring than genetic screening, despite the fact that both sets of techniques draw from the exciting new genetic discoveries. Compared with screening, data limitations in the case of monitoring more often call into question the entire approach of genetic monitoring. As we shall see, corporate executives in particular use evidence problems as reasons for rejecting genetic monitoring altogether.

28 James Q. Wilson and Richard J. Herrnstein (1985), for example, maintain that crime and delinquency are genetically based. In addition, Mednick et al. (1988, 1984), Rowe (1986), and Gordon (1987) attribute problems of crime and delinquency to genetic factors.

29 Sherrington et al. (1988), McGuffin and Sturt (1986), and Kety (1976) argue that faulty genes produce schizophrenia.

30 Bouchard et al. (1990), Gordon (1987), Herrnstein (1971), Eysenck (1973, 1971), and Jensen (1977, 1969) maintain that differences in intelligence have a genetic basis.

31 Most notable for its prominence in this vast literature has been the work of E. O. Wilson. Wilson, trained as an entomologist, applies his genetic theories to human as well as insect societies. He discusses implications of sociobiology for human behavior in his final chapter of *Sociobiology: The New Synthesis* (1975); his 1978 book, *On Human Nature*, for which he was awarded the Pulitzer Prize; and *Genes, Mind, and Culture* (Lumsden and Wilson, 1981), which puts forward a genetic theory of culture. His work has influenced the field of sociology and other social sciences. For example, see Rossi (1984, 1977) and Gutting (1980).

32 See, for example, Wilson and Herrnstein (1985), Mazur and Robertson (1972), and Kety (1976). For critical analysis of these theories, see Lewontin et al. (1984), Jencks (1987), Duster and Garrett (1984), Caplan (1978), Suzuki and Knudtson (1989), Montagu (1980), Sahlins (1977), Schiff and Lewontin (1986), Currie (1985), Warner (1987), Marsh and Katz (1985), and Bock (1980).

33 Lewontin et al. (1984), National Academy of Sciences (1980), and Gershon et al. (1980) examine genetic components in behavioral disorders, including the research methodologies used.

34 See, for example, Calabrese (1986), Hunt (1986), and Omenn (1982).

35 Gilbert S. Omenn (Professor in Departments of Medicine and Environmental Health; and Dean, School of Public Health and Community Medicine, University of Washington) in Omenn and Gelboin (1984:393).

36 Elliot Gershon (Chief, Pyschogenetics Section, Biological Psychiatry Branch, National Institutes of Health), National Academy of Sciences (1980:236).

37 Lappé (1988), Hunt (1986), and National Academy of Sciences (1980:268–281) discuss the effect of environmental and genetic factors on respiratory illness. Calabrese (1984) points to the major role of environmental factors in the etiology of lung disease.

38 Individuals with phenylketonuria (PKU) disease suffer a toxic response to high levels of phenylalanine that they are unable to metabolize. They are deficient in the enzyme phenylalanine hydroxylase.

39 Mulinare et al. (1988) and Lappé (1979) examine factors contributing to spina bifida defects. Duster (1990) analyzes the case of a small industrial town in Southern Wales that has the highest rate of spina bifida in the world.

40 See *Environmental Health Perspectives* (1987b), Rom (1983), and Levy and Wegman (1983).

41 King (1984) and King et al. (1984) discuss methodological problems involved in family history studies used to detect inherited susceptibility. Irving Selikoff (Physician and Research Director, Department of Community Medicine, Mount Sinai School of Medicine) (in Fraumeni, 1978:183–184) argues that rather than indicating genetic predisposition, cancer in young

employed individuals may be the earliest cases associated with a previously unsuspected environmental carcinogen. Calum Muir (International Agency for Research on Cancer) maintains that high cancer levels found in particular countries or in groups within countries "should be considered largely the result of environmental factors until proved otherwise" (1978:293).

42 One scientist, for example, reveals some of the assumptions scientists make about opponents of susceptibility policies: "It's anti-scientific and anti-medical to say that whatever happens to workers, we don't want to know. We want to answer the question, 'Why me, doc?' " Gilbert Omenn (Professor of Medicine and Dean of the School of Public Health, University of Washington, Seattle), quoted in Harris (1983:12). The controversy over the technical effectiveness and bias in evaluating genetic monitoring will be examined further in Chapter 3.

43 See, for example, Lappé (1983), President's Commission (1983a,b); Wertz and Fletcher (1989a); and Alexander Capron (Executive Director, President's Commission for the Study of Ethical Problems in Medicine and Biomedical and Behavioral Research), Testimony to U.S. Congress (1982b). An earlier example of this approach is the National Academy of Sciences National Research Council review of genetic screening programs (National Academy of Sciences, 1975b). In their report, scientists point to problems of insufficient counseling, confusion over medical issues, the misapplication of genetic tests, inadequate interpretation of findings, and lack of education programs.

44 Nicholas A. Ashford (Professor of Technology and Policy, Center for Technology, Policy, and Industrial Development, Massachusetts Institute of Technology), personal interview.

45 Samuel S. Epstein (Professor of Occupational and Environmental Medicine, University of Illinois School of Public Health, Chicago), personal interview.

46 Analyses of social and political dimensions of scientific judgment in related areas of new technologies include Salter (1988), Englehardt and Kaplan (1987), Lynn (1986), Perrow (1984), Levine (1982), Douglas and Wildavsky (1982), Ashford (1976), Kevles (1985), Bazelon (1979), Keller (1984), and Knorr-Cetina and Mulkay (1983).

47 On the linkage of scientific perspective and sociological factors, see also Yoxen (1983), U.S. House Subcommittee on Health and Safety (1987), Epstein (1979), and Brodeur (1985).

48 Peto (in Peto and Schneiderman, 1981:269 and 281) and Doll and Peto (1981). The authors of the Bridbord et al. (1978) report include scientists from the National Cancer Institute (NCI), National Institute of Environmental Health Sciences (NIEHS), and NIOSH. The report was submitted to the OSHA hearings on carcinogen identification and regulation and subsequently published in Peto and Schneiderman (1981). The authors of the Bridbord report responded to Doll and Peto's attack in Davis et al. (1983, 1981).

49 Doll and Peto (1981:1241). Chapter 3 analyzes the debate over the extent of occupational cancer hazards further.

50 Scientists sometimes refer to the widely publicized work of Douglas and Wildavsky as they bemoan what they perceive to be the technophobic and anti-industry bias of those who criticize new technologies. This work shares some of the same weaknesses as scientists' own views of bias.

51 This very faith that risks from workplace chemicals are minimal bolsters industrial managers' belief in a *genetic* basis for occupational disease. Chapter 3 develops this argument about industrial genetics.

52 For discussion of scientists' competing perspectives and bias on questions of new technologies, see Nelkin (1987), Fujimura (1988), Duster (1990), Epstein (1979), Robin and Markle (1987), Greenwood (1984), Englehardt and Kaplan (1987), and Kaye (1986).

3. COMPETING CONCEPTIONS OF SAFETY: HIGH-RISK WORKERS OR HIGH-RISK WORK?

Epigraphs: Bearn, Presentation at the National Academy of Sciences, Conference on Genetic Influences on Responses to the Environment (July 10, 1980); Mazzocchi (1980).

1 Jackall (1988), McCaffrey (1982), Kelman (1980), Mendeloff (1979), and Green and Waitzman (1981) discuss business opposition to regulation and provide evidence of managers' belief that health hazards have been overestimated. See also Chapter 6.

2 Employers typically claim that their own and similar workplaces are safe. However, they usually can point to employers they deem to be unusual who do not give enough attention to safety, allowing hazards to remain instead. Furthermore, in some cases employers publicly have defended their safety record while withholding or distorting information implicating chemicals in their workplaces, as discussed in U.S. House Subcommittee on Health and Safety (1987, 1981), Legator (1987), Brodeur (1985), Epstein (1980), and Chapter 5. Epstein (1979) offers a detailed analysis of industry efforts to show that a small proportion of cancer cases is due to industrial chemicals. See also Peto and Schneiderman (1981) and Ashford (1976).

3 A major component of this debate is asbestos. In the proceedings of a conference focusing on estimating occupational cancer (Peto and Schneiderman, 1981), estimates of the proportion of cancer due to asbestos exposure ranged from lows of 1 percent (Enterline) and 2–3 percent (Peto) to a high of 13–18 percent (Bridbord et al.).

4 Doll and Peto (1981). Davis et al. (1983:364) state, "Most investigators agree that it is difficult to estimate with accuracy what proportion of new cancers may be associated with industrial production, smoking, and living patterns."

5 *Journal of Occupational Medicine* (1986), Brodeur (1985), and Davis et al. (1981) discuss confounding effects involving smoking and occupation in the study of cancer causation.

6 Robinson (1987a, 1984), Davis and Rowland (1983), and Chapter 4 consider the concentration of blacks and other racial minorities employed in more hazardous jobs.

7 Doll and Peto (1981), for example, calculate cancer causation only on the basis of people age 65 and under. They argue that Medicare access, duplicative recordkeeping for individuals treated in multiple locations, diagnostic fads, and improved cancer diagnosis in the aged artificially make it appear that old people are dying of cancer much more frequently than in the past. Therefore, they argue, it is best to restrict attention to trends among younger people, since these are less subject to error. However, the weight of the factors Doll and Peto cite is reduced by the nearly thirty-year history of Medicare and the fact that problems of diagnosis and duplicate cancer records cross age groups.

8   Davis et al. (1981), Epstein and Swartz (1981), and Bridbord et al. (1978).

9   Davis et al. (1983) and Peto and Schneiderman (1981).

10 Labor organizations that have taken a stand on the proportion of cancer that is related to work have tended to favor higher estimates. For example, U.S. and British trade unions have joined the International Labor Organization and 17 U.S. federal agencies in endorsing the Bridbord et al. (1978) report by government scientists estimating occupation-related cases to be "up to 20 to 40 percent." Epstein and Swartz (1981), Davis (1981), and Doll and Peto (1981) discuss controversy over this report, along with more general issues of cancer and work exposure.

11 See Harris and Associates (1980). This survey was the most expensive that the Harris organization ever had carried out. It was conducted for the world's largest insurance company, Marsh and McLennan.

12 William Alexander Newman Dorland, *Illustrated Medical Dictionary*, 25th ed., pp. 744 and 1505, Philadelphia: W. B. Saunders; cited in Reinhardt (1978:319) as the classical medical definition of hypersusceptibility. "Susceptibility," "hypersusceptibility," and "high-risk" commonly are used interchangeably, as they are in this book. Each of these terms refers to a significant predisposition or special vulnerability to chemical agents. Levy and Wegman (1983:134–135) define hypersusceptibility as "an unusually high response to some dose of a substance." "Sensitivity" is one type of special risk that refers to immediate, short-term, acute responses to chemicals. They refer to sensitivity as one form of susceptibility "characterized by an acquired, immunologically mediated sensitization to a substance." Indications of sensitivity include rashes, asthma, and other symptoms more akin to allergies than the type of longer term and chronic potential disease effects stemming from inborn susceptibility that are the focus of this book.

13 Ernest Dixon (Tabershaw Associates, former corporate medical director of Celanese), statement prepared for delivery to Hearings on Genetic Screening and the Handling of High-Risk Groups in the Workplace, U.S. Congress (1981:12).

14 Bernard D. Davis (Adele Lehman Professor of Bacterial Physiology, Harvard Medical School), National Academy of Sciences (1980:233).

15 Other expressions of this approach include: Charles Reinhardt (Director, Haskell Laboratory for Toxicology and Industrial Medicine, E. I. duPont de Nemours and Company) (1978:319); H. E. Stokinger (Chief, Toxicology Branch, Laboratories and Criteria Development Department, NIOSH) and L. D. Scheel (Toxicology Branch, NIOSH) (1973:564); and Arno Motulsky (Professor of Medicine and Genetics, University of Washington School of Medicine, Seattle), National Academy of Sciences (1980:18).

16 H. E. Stokinger (Chief of the Toxicology Section, U.S. Public Health Service) and J. T. Mountain (Occupational Health Program, U.S. Public Health Service) (1967:538).

17 Stokinger and Mountain (1967:541).

18 The threshold limit values (TLVs) developed by the American Conference of Governmental Industrial Hygienists (ACGIH) are published in the ACGIH, *Documentation of the Threshold Limit Values*, 4th ed. (Cincinnati: ACGIH, 1980). In 1971, OSHA adopted 450 TLVs from the ACGIH as established federal standards. See Salter (1988) for insight into the heated debate over incorporation of ACGIH threshold limits in government standards.

19 Stokinger and Mountain (1967:537). See also Stokinger (1981).

20 Salter (1988), McCaffrey (1982), Englehardt and Kaplan (1987), Ashford (1976), Peto and Schneiderman (1981), Epstein (1979), and OSHA (1980b) discuss the controversy over safe exposure levels for carcinogens.

21 See Samuels (1983) for a similar statement opposing the threshold concept of safe carcinogen exposure.

22 In its guidelines, the Office of Science and Technology Policy (1985) rejected the threshold concept for carcinogen safety. Peto and Schneiderman (1981) provide evidence of declining support for the "threshold" concept of safe carcinogen exposure levels.

23 Guthier (1986), Ruttenberg and Powers (1986), Daniels (1985), and Boden (1986) discuss employer costs and the economic feasibility of protecting vulnerable workers.

24 Academic scientist, personal interview. Similar expressions of the genetic explanation for responses to environmental chemicals appear in Kouri et al. (1984) and Omenn and Gelboin (1984). See Alexander et al. (1980) for a report on studies of brain tumors among petrochemical workers to which the sci-

entist referred. Subsequent investigation uncovered a total of at least forty-nine brain tumor deaths in two Texas chemical plants (Dow and Union Carbide). Two industry reports of these brain tumor mortality studies are Austin and Schnatter (1983) and Bond et al. (1983).

25 Hillman (1981). Another textile industry official claims that "fewer than two percent of textile workers may be adversely affected by cotton dust" (Salmans, 1981).

26 Heterozygous means having different alleles (alternate forms of a gene) at a genetic locus. Homozygous refers to having the same alleles at a genetic locus. Sickle cell trait is an example of a heterozygous case and sickle cell anemia is an example of a homozygous case. Although exceptions exist, genetic screening typically identifies heterozygous carriers. These individuals appear normal but disease manifestation may be more likely than in "normal" individuals. Individuals who are homozygous for a particular abnormality usually are identified as individuals with a "disease" rather than carriers with a "trait" or "condition."

27 For example, other hemoglobins (D or G) can be mistaken for hemoglobin S, and other conditions (sickle beta thalassemia or hereditary persistence of fetal hemoglobin) can be mistaken for sickle cell anemia because of the presence of hemoglobin F.

28 Office of Technology Assessment (1983) offers details concerning the narrow applicability and limited predictiveness of current screening tests. The OTA report states "[T]he ability of the techniques to identify people who are predisposed to occupational illness has not been demonstrated" (p. 5) and "None of the genetic tests evaluated by OTA meets established scientific criteria for routine use in an occupational setting" (p. 9). Their critical assessment applies to both screening and monitoring. See also OTA (1990).

29 Hans Weill (Professor of Medicine, Tulane University), U.S. Congress (1981:24).

30 Ashford et al. (1984) considers disease risks that may stem from screening workers from jobs and replacing them with others.

31 For example, see Ruttenberg and Hudgins (1981).

32 Goffman's (1963) work offers insight into processes by which individuals become stigmatized. The process of casting occupational health problems in individual terms is akin to the

process of blaming victims of poverty rather than the social and economic forces creating inequality that Ryan (1971) examines.

33 U.S. Congress (1981:109–110) discusses one company (Southern Pacific Transportation Company) that includes this question in their preemployment medical history. Test results can disqualify workers from jobs in specific companies or from entire industries.

34 "Statement of the Chemical Manufacturers Association for the Health and Safety Subcommittee of the House Education and Labor Committee Hearing on the Withdrawal of the Department of Labor's Proposed Standard on Hazards Identification," May 27, 1981. See also Richard Lewis (Occupational Health Specialist, International Chemical Workers Union), Testimony before the Health and Safety Subcommittee of the House Committee on Education and Labor on the Worker's Right to Know and the Withdrawal of OSHA's Proposed Rule on Hazards Identification, Washington, D.C., July 14, 1981.

35 For discussion of employers' standards of evidence for proving and disproving chemical hazards, see Salter (1988), Englehardt and Kaplan (1987), Brodeur (1985), U.S. House Subcommittee on Health and Safety (1987), Field and Baram (1986), Epstein (1980, 1979), Nelkin (1979), McCaffrey (1982), and Rothstein (1984).

36 A good example of the company's argument about evidence of chemical safety is W. C. May (Manager, Labor Relations, Lederle Laboratories, American Cyanamid Company), letter to W. P. Siemers, Jr. (President, Local 143, International Chemical Workers Union), December 19, 1978. Chapter 4 discusses the ambiguous scientific data on which American Cyanamid's and other companies' fetal exclusion policies have been based.

37 Betty Dabney (biochemist and molecular geneticist, industry consultant) (1981:630–631).

38 A representative expression of this research-only view – and one that industrial monitoring advocates often cite to bolster their case – is Dabney (1981:630): "Clearly positive findings in an occupational group, confirmed by repeated samplings at more than one time, should be an indication for further clinical studies which might include formal reproductive epidemiology and prospective morbidity and mortality studies."

39   Jill D. Fabricant (Department of Preventive Medicine and Community Health, Division of Environmental Toxicology, University of Texas Medical School) and Marvin S. Legator (Director, Division of Environmental Toxicology, University of Texas Medical School) (1981:624). See also Legator (1987, 1982).

40   Anthony V. Carrano (Section Leader for Cell Biology and Mutagenesis, Biomedical Sciences Division, Lawrence Livermore National Laboratory) (1982:307). See also Carrano and Natarajan (1988) and Carrano (1986).

41   Theodore Meinhardt (Industrywide Studies Branch, Division of Surveillance, Hazard Evaluations, and Field Studies, NIOSH) (1981).

42   David Brusick (Director, Department of Genetics and Cell Biology, Litton Bionetics), in National Academy of Sciences (1980).

43   Samuels (1983), Otten (1986), Legator (1987), Dixon in U.S. Congress (1981), Venable (1978), Mazzocchi (1980), and U.S. Congress (1981).

44   Lynn (1986) offers evidence that scientists who work for industry tend to share employers' views on safety and regulation – and do so to a much greater extent than do scientists who work for universities or government. See also Englehardt and Kaplan (1987), Wertz and Fletcher (1989a), Dabney (1981), and U.S. Congress (1981, 1982a,b).

45   Workers exposed to benzene and epichlorohydrin showed high rates of chromosome breakage. Earlier cytogenetic studies of vinyl chloride had revealed no significant problem.

46   Dante J. Picciano (geneticist, Dow Chemical Company) in Severo (February 5, 1980).

47   Legator (1987, 1981), Dabney (1981), Office of Technology Assessment (1990), Otten (1986), Epstein (1980), Severo (1980a), and personal interviews with corporate officials, government officials, and academic scientists provide additional evidence regarding Dow's testing program. Both advocates and opponents of industrial monitoring refer to this case in their arguments for or against testing.

48   John Venable (Medical Director of Dow Chemical, Texas Division) (1978).

49   Michael Wright (industrial hygienist, United Steelworkers of America) (1979:143–153).

50   James English (Associate General Counsel, United Steelworkers of America), National Academy of Sciences (1980:386–387).

51 Omenn and Gelboin (1984), Lavine (1982), Plumlee (1979), an(Calabrese (1978) examine EPA's standard-setting history, in cluding their approach to specific groups at risk.

52 Where compelling evidence indicates working conditions pre sent a special problem for specific individuals, these indi viduals can be placed in other jobs and receive compensation Medical removal protection, rate retention, and other mea sures for protecting workers removed from health hazards are discussed in Chapter 5.

4. SEX, RACE, AND GENETIC PREDISPOSITION

Epigraph: Gore (as U.S. Representative and Subcommittee Chair), in introductory statement, U.S. Congress hearings (1981:172).

1 U.S. NIOSH identifies 65,000 chemicals that are used in U.S. worksites (Halperin et al., 1986:552).

2 See Kilborn (1991), Savage (1990), Lewin (1990, 1988a), Draper (1991), McElveen (1986), Office of Technology Assessment (1985), Bayer (1982), LeClercq (1983), Williams (1981), Bronson (1979b), Rao and Schwetz (1981), Shabecoff (1981), and U.S. Congress (1981).

3 Rothstein (1986:108) and U.S. Congress (1981).

4 See Randall (1987), McElveen (1986), and Williams (1981).

5 See Daniels et al. (1988), Lewin (1988a), Office of Technology Assessment (1985), Sheridan (1983), and Bronson (1979b). The EEOC estimate appears in the introduction to the "Proposed Interpretive Guidelines on Employment Discrimination and Reproductive Hazards" (1980:7514). The EEOC Guidelines subsequently were withdrawn: 46 *Federal Register* 391b (1981).

6 Chavkin (1984), Blakeslee (1991), and Society for Occupational and Environmental Health (1977) discuss methods of testing for reproductive damage.

7 Anthony Robbins (NIOSH Director in 1981), personal interview.

8 Bruce W. Karrh (Corporate Medical Director, E. I. duPont de Nemours and Co.), U.S. Congress (1981:263).

9 Blakeslee (1991), Rosenberg et al. (1987), Office of Technology Assessment (1985), Bertin (1983), Bayer (1982), Williams (1981), and Stellman (1977).

10 Dibromochloropropane (DBCP) and chlordecone (Kepone) cause male sterility and other severe effects on spermatogenesis, in addition to other health damage. See Rosenberg et al. (1987), Levine et al. (1983), Whorton (1983), and U.S. Department of Labor, *Protecting People at Work: A Reader in Occupational Safety and Health* (1980:296 and 306).

11 For evidence of reproductive damage through the exposure of male workers, see Blakeslee (1991), Daniels et al. (1988), Office of Technology Assessment (1985), Ashford (1987), Council on Environmental Quality (1981), Williams (1981), Messite and Bond (1980), and Bloom (1981).

12 See Ashford (1987:1084–1085), Blakeslee (1991:36), and Stellman and Henefin (1982:134).

13 This observation stems from findings of the United Nations Scientific Committee on the Effects of Atomic Radiation. See Vilma Hunt (Associate Professor of Environmental Health, Pennsylvania State University) in U.S. Congress (1981:236).

14 See Bellinger et al. (1987).

15 Vinyl chloride and benzene are carcinogenic; and carbon disulfide causes damage to the brain, liver, and kidneys. See Daniels et al. (1988) and Zenz (1984).

16 The company claims that they maintain exposure levels low enough to protect sperm but not low enough to prevent fetal damage through the mother. However, Daniels et al. (1988), Zenz (1984), Hunt (1982), and U.S. Congress (1981) discuss data deficiencies that call into question confident assumptions that fetuses are in danger while adult workers and male reproduction remain safe.

17 See Kilborn (1990), Sheridan (1983:73), Bayer (1982:15 and 17), and Williams (1981:661 and 666).

18 Chemical industry officials (American Cyanamid, October 19, 1979) in public statement cited in Sheridan (1983:73).

19 Johnson Controls company statement, quoted in Kilborn (1990).

20 Bruce Karrh (Corporate Medical Director, DuPont), quoted in Bayer (1982:17).

21 Corporate officials typically are convinced that by excluding fertile women they not only protect fetuses but also succeed in preventing fetal damage lawsuits. For discussion of the legal dimension of fetal exclusion policies, see Chapter 6 and the

section of this chapter entitled, "The Legal and Economic Framing of Reproductive Hazards."

22 The policies also do not consider other factors that affect whether a woman is likely to become pregnant, such as her contraceptive practices, sexual activity, marital status, or husband's fertility.

23 See Bureau of the Census (1988). Only 1 percent of all U.S. births in 1987 were to women age 40 and older. See also U.S. Congress (1981).

24 OSHA findings regarding fetal risk and lead exposure appear in the lead standard: 29 *Code of Federal Regulations* 1910.1025 (1990) and in 43 *Federal Register* 52959 (1978). See also Bellinger et al. (1987).

25 Milkman (1987), Reskin (1984), Kessler-Harris (1982), and Smith and Ward (1984) provide evidence for work force stratification by sex and supporting ideologies.

26 See, for example, Brodeur (1989), Daniels et al. (1988), Equal Employment Opportunity Commission (1980), Occupational Safety and Health Administration (1978), and U.S. Congress (1981). Further evidence for this point includes transcripts of government hearings and other documents on reproductive hazards and exclusionary policies related to health hazards; interviews with lawyers, equal employment opportunity government officials, union representatives, and corporate executives; studies of reproductive hazards; and other publications on corporate health and employment policies. All these data sources support the point that the question of excluding all fertile women does not arise in female-intensive jobs and occupations. Occasionally, all *pregnant* women are removed from female-intensive jobs. See Daniels et al. (1988:8–9) and *Wall Street Journal* (1987).

27 The proportion of women in production jobs in the textile industry has increased somewhat over the past several decades. From 1950 to 1980, women workers as a percentage of all production and related workers comprised 43.8% (1950), 45.3% (1960), 47.8% (1970), and 48.9% (1980), according to the Bureau of the Census (1954, 1963, 1972, and 1984).

28 See Whorton (1983), National Academy of Sciences (1980), and Occupational Safety and Health Reports Volume 7 (1977:529).

29 John H. Weisburger (Vice President for Research, American Health Foundation, New York), writing in *Chemtech*, the maga-

zine of the American Chemical Society, in 1977, quoted in Severo (February 6, 1980a).

30 U.S. Congress (1981:117). See also "Hiring handicapped, not easy," *Pittsburgh Post-Gazette* (September 18, 1980:16).

31 The Massachusetts Department of Public Health and the University of Massachusetts Occupational Health Program conducted the study. See Daniels et al. (1988) and Lewin (1988a).

32 For discussion of DBCP and Kepone cases, see Zenz (1984:40–41), McElveen (1986), Barnard (1982), and Joan E. Bertin (attorney, American Civil Liberties Union), "Prepared statement" in U.S. Congress (1981).

33 An attorney for DuPont explains, "We have an employment relationship between us and the men and women that are in our employ. There is no such relationship with the fetus. . . . We would be exposed to different kinds of liability under workers' compensation laws as opposed to not under workers' compensation laws." Gerald A. Hapka (attorney, Legal Department, E. I. duPont de Nemours and Co.) in U.S. Congress (October 15, 1981:275).

34 The suits that male veterans have brought for damage from exposure to the herbicide Agent Orange cite birth defects in their children, miscarriages, and serious illnesses in the men themselves. For discussion of Agent Orange and DBCP suits, see Whorton (1983), Rothstein (1984), and "Five makers of Agent Orange charge U.S. misused chemical in Viet Nam: Companies replying to suit say Federal negligence is responsible for any harm to veterans and kin," *New York Times* (January 7, 1980:14).

35 See Andrews (1987), McElveen (1986), Shaw (1984), Rothstein (1984), and Bassett-Stanford (1981:1196).

36 See Rosenberg et al. (1987), Bertin (1986), Zenz (1984), and Hunt (1982:40–41).

37 See Levine (1982), Randall and Short (1983), Severo (1980c), and U.S. Congress (1981).

38 "Title VII" refers to Title VII of the Civil Rights Act of 1964, 42 *United States Code* Section 2000e (1987 Supplement). The Pregnancy Discrimination Amendment of 1978 amended Title VII to cover discrimination based on pregnancy, childbirth, or related medical conditions (Public Law No. 95-555, Section 1, 92 Stat. 2076 (1978), codified at 42 *United States Code* Section 2000e (K) (1987 Supplement)).

39 See Kilborn (1991, 1990), Lewin (1990, 1988b), Postol (1988), McElveen (1986), Rothstein (1986, 1984), Shaw (1984), Bertin (1983), Barnard (1982), Williams (1981), Schlender (1980), Howard (1981), and Hinds and Moran (1983).

40 See Greenhouse (1991), Wermiel (1991), Hagar (1990), Lewin (1990), and Savage (1990). The U.S. Supreme Court agreed to hear the United Auto Workers union challenge to the Johnson Controls company policy in 1990, after the 7th Circuit Court of Appeals in Chicago had upheld the exclusionary policy. In the California case, the California Supreme Court rejected the company's challenge to the appellate decision against the Johnson Controls fetal exclusion policy that began in 1982. The company is the largest maker of automobile batteries and operates 16 auto battery plants throughout the United States.

41 See Coalition for Reproductive Rights of Workers (1980), Stone (1986:686–687), and Equal Employment Opportunity Commission (1980). Members of CRROW included women's groups, major unions in industries affected by fetal exclusion policies, civil rights organizations, and others.

42 This debate is most vigorous among feminist and labor lawyers – sometimes even among feminist labor lawyers. For example, Krieger and Cooney (1983) offer a "positive action" approach, and Bertin (1983) and Williams (1982, 1981) articulate "equal treatment" approaches to fetal exclusion policies.

43 See, for example, Kilborn (1990), Shaw (1984, 1980), National Academy of Sciences (1980), and OSHA (1978).

44 Luker (1984), Otten (1985), Shaw (1984, 1980), and Hubbard (1986, 1982b) discuss developments in the areas of fetal rights and "prenatal torts." Hubbard (1982a:32) has argued that focusing on fetal rights treats the pregnant woman "as though she were merely the container in which the real patient – the fetus – gets moved about."

45 Joan E. Bertin (attorney, American Civil Liberties Union), "Prepared statement" in U.S. Congress (1981:198–199).

46 Calabrese (1984), Rothstein (1984), Severo (1980a), U.S. Congress (1981, 1982a,b), and Reinhardt (1978) provide evidence of chemical companies testing blacks for sickle cell trait and G-6-PD deficiency.

47 Industry concerns with health risks, company liability, and medical costs in any case can supplant their interest in hiring a specific relatively low-wage subgroup of workers. If a numer-

ically dominant group in an occupation is replaced, it is more likely to be a racial or ethnic group rather than women who are replaced, due in part to the broad-ranging sex segregation and stratification of the work force. The fact that predominantly female jobs generally pay less than those of male workers, whether white or black, makes it highly unlikely that women employed in jobs that are virtually all women would be replaced (Bureau of the Census, 1984, and Treiman and Hartmann, 1981).

48 Schuman et al. (1985), Farley and Allen (1987), Lieberson (1980), Williamson (1984), Chase (1977), Jones (1981), and Gordon et al. (1982) discuss the history of hiring and eugenic policies that affect black workers.

49 Robinson (1987a, 1984), Davis (1980, 1977), Rowland (1980), and Bureau of National Affairs (1981) provide evidence of differential hiring patterns and treatment of black workers exposed to occupational hazards.

50 U.S. Bureau of the Census (1990). Table 103: Expectations of Life at Birth, 1960 to 1988, and Projections 1990 to 2010.

51 Farley and Allen (1987:47–52) identify three major factors that explain the racial difference in U.S. black–white infant mortality: the higher proportion of black births occurring to women at greater risk of infant loss, the lower birth weights of black infants, and the timing and extent of prenatal care of black mothers. Data from the National Center for Health Statistics (1984) reveal that the infant mortality rate is higher for U.S. blacks than for populations in nations such as Jamaica, Cuba, and Greece.

52 These data on life expectancy and disease rates appear in an eight-volume federal report on minority groups' health issued by the U.S. Department of Health and Human Services Task Force on Blacks and Minority Health in 1985. This report attributes much of the race differences in disease and death rates to education and to life-style. The study emphasizes homicide, smoking, alcohol, diet, and obesity as major public health problems affecting blacks. It gives little attention to the effects of poverty, government policies, or genetic factors. The study refers to the "persistent, distressing disparity" in death rates in the U.S. as a "tragic dilemma," but calls for no increases in government spending to address the problems (Davidson, 1985; *San Francisco Chronicle*, 1985). See also data provided by

the U.S. Bureau of the Census (1990) on life expectancy, disease, and death rates by race.

53 See Calabrese (1984) and National Academy of Sciences (1980:163).

54 Pseudofolliculitis barbae (PSB) is a medical condition of ingrown hairs that precludes shaving. This problem is found largely among black males and has been the focus of discrimination complaints under Title VII of the Civil Rights Act of 1964 (see Chapter 6). Calabrese (1984), Farley and Allen (1987), and Williams (1974) discuss diseases that appear more or less frequently among blacks than among other groups.

55 Wilson (1987), Syme and Berkman (1986), and Donovan (1984). An example of the mortality significance of housing patterns is the fact that for blacks the death rate from fires is three times that of whites, reflecting in part the concentration of blacks in older central city housing (Farley and Allen, 1987:55).

56 For discussion of the uncertain data on causation of disease patterns among blacks and whites, see Farley and Allen (1987), Levy (1991), and Williams (1974).

57 William Lloyd (epidemiologist, University of Pittsburgh and subsequently OSHA) headed a research team that studied the mortality of over 59,000 steelworkers in Allegheny County, Pennsylvania, from 1952 to 1962. Early findings indicated that black workers were at increased risk of lung cancer. However, later data from the study indicated that while black coke oven workers did indeed have an increased cancer risk, white coke oven workers also were at risk. The earlier study results indicating an effect only among blacks were partly due to the small number of white coke oven workers in the study sample. Also, 19 percent of all black coke oven workers were employed full-time at the more hazardous *topside* jobs on the ovens, compared with only 3 percent of white coke oven workers. Lloyd reported that many steel industry officials believed and sought further documentation that blacks are more susceptible to lung cancer. See Lloyd (1971, 1970) and Schulte (1987) for discussion of this case.

58 William Lloyd (epidemiologist, OSHA), personal interview.

59 Robinson draws on the U.S. Bureau of the Census Current Population Survey, the University of Michigan's Quality of Employment Survey, and Michigan's Panel Study of Income Dynamics. In an earlier study, Kotelchuck (1978) shows that

compared with whites, black workers have a 37 percent greater chance of suffering an occupational injury or illness and a 24 percent greater chance of dying from job-related injuries and illnesses. These figures are based on U.S. OSHA, EEOC, and Census Bureau data. Davis (1980) also provides evidence of blacks being employed in more hazardous jobs relative to whites.

60   For evidence of disproportionate placement of blacks and other racial minorities in hazardous jobs, and resulting higher disease and disability rates, see Robinson (1987a, 1984), American Public Health Association (1982), Davis and Rowland (1983), Equal Employment Opportunity Commission (1980), Reich (1981), Davis (1980, 1977), and Lloyd (1971, 1970).

61   OSHA refers to the Occupational Safety and Health Administration, the U.S. Department of Labor agency responsible for workplace safety and health regulation. NIOSH refers to the federal National Institute for Occupational Safety and Health, which conducts research and makes recommendations to OSHA, but does not have rule-making and enforcement authority. Chapter 6 examines these agencies as they affect industrial health surveillance and other employment practices concerning workers at risk.

62   43 *Federal Register* 27391 (June 23, 1978).

63   Government officials and academic scientists, personal interviews; and cotton dust standard. The lung function adjustment appears on pages 27391–27392 of the standard: "Occupational Exposure to Cotton Dust," 49 *Federal Register* (June 23, 1978). NIOSH had recommended this adjustment for black lung function in the "NIOSH Cotton Dust Criteria Document." For discussion of lung function differences by race, see Schulte (1987:884–885), Rothstein (1984:28), Corey et al. (1979), and Rossiter and Weill (1974).

64   However, it is widely accepted that sickle cell trait confers an important advantage by protecting against malaria. In some parts of Africa, as much as a third of the population are carriers (Edelstein, 1986, and Maugh, 1981).

65   See Calabrese (1984) and Sears (1978) for reviews of the literature on health effects from sickle cell trait. The President's Commission study of genetic screening (1983a:22) concluded that a carrier of sickle cell trait "very rarely, if ever, manifests any medically significant adverse effects."

66 Documents and personal interviews with government officials support this point. At least one diver with sickle cell trait has complained to OSHA and the EEOC that he was not hired because of the trait. NIOSH officials have advised companies to use special diving suits that adjust to different depths.

67 Kark (1987), Kevles (1985), Sears (1978), Calabrese (1984), Bristow (1974), and Holden (1981) discuss the evidence of health risks from sickle cell trait. Jones et al. (1970) attributed four deaths to sickle cell trait in army recruits undergoing basic combat training at an altitude of 4,000 feet. This article has been cited extensively as evidence of health hazards of sickle cell trait. Yet the overwhelming majority of individuals who have sickle cell trait in the United States have had no apparent problems associated with it (Office of Technology Assessment, 1983:91).

68 Sources that examine the testing and exclusion of blacks from airline companies, the military, chemical firms, and other jobs include Calabrese (1984), U.S. Congress (1981, 1982a,b), Wertz and Fletcher (1989), *New York Times* (1980a), Duster (1990), Rothstein (1984), Holden (1981), Bowman (1978, 1977), and Brodine and Uddin (1977).

69 President Nixon's focus on sickle cell disease in his February 1971 health message also brought more attention to sickle cell. He advocated large increases in federal spending. Congress passed the National Sickle Cell Anemia Control Act in 1972, which authorized funds for screening, counseling, information, research, and treatment.

70 Amazingly enough, the first line of the National Sickle Cell Anemia Control Act (Public Law 92-294, S 2676, May 16, 1972) states that approximately two million American blacks have sickle cell anemia, although this figure is accurate only for blacks who have sickle cell trait. About 50,000 Americans have sickle cell disease.

71 Duster (1990), President's Commission (1983a,b), Bowman (1977, 1978), Powledge (1974), Bristow (1974), Lappé (1979), and Keck (1973–1974) discuss public sickle cell screening programs and the spread of test results beyond the individuals tested.

72 In one survey of forty major life insurance companies, 50 percent of the companies reported that they had raised their pre-

miums for individuals with sickle cell trait (Europe, 1973). In-
surers pursued this policy despite the fact that scientific
studies have shown no difference in life expectancy between
people with sickle cell trait and those without the trait. Scientists who claim adverse effects from the trait generally maintain that it affects morbidity rather than mortality (Calabrese,
1984; Kevles, 1985; and Bowman, 1977).

73 For insightful historical and sociological accounts of discrimination by sex, race, and ethnicity, see Reskin (1984), Lieberson
(1980), Gordon et al. (1982), Kessler-Harris (1982), Edwards et
al. (1975), Kanter (1977), and Baxandall et al. (1976).

74 Chapter 7 examines policy alternatives to susceptibility policies further.

5. POWER AND CONTROL IN INDUSTRIAL MEDICINE

Epigraphs: Stokinger and Scheel (1973:572); Samuel, U.S. Congress
hearings (October 14, 1981:35).

1 See Carey et al. (1990), President's Commission (1983a,b),
Holtzman (1989), Blank (1981), and National Academy of Sciences (1975).

2 NIOSH (1982). See also *National Occupational Hazards Survey*,
Volume 3, Table VIII A (Summary of NOHS Estimates)
(1977:30).

3 See Russoniello and Ehrlich (1986), Holtzman (1989), and Harris (1983). An industrial production worker for a chemical company, in a personal interview, points to the limited ability applicants have to discover how medical tests influence hiring:
"Pre-employment tests, I don't know. I think they hire the
workhorses – those that are very fit and don't have problems
from past jobs, but I can't prove it. Neither can people who
don't get hired in the first place."

4 This is despite local, state, and national "right-to-know" measures enacted in the 1980s and early 1990s making hazard
information on toxic chemicals more readily available. For discussion of the limited information employees have about the
health risks of toxic chemicals they work with, see Goldsmith
(1987), Brown (1985), U.S. House Subcommittee on Health and
Safety (1987), Ashford and Caldart (1985), and "Proposed hazards identification standard," OSHA, Department of Labor, 46
Federal Register 4412–4453 (January 16, 1981).

5 This statement appears in the preamble to the initial OSHA Access to Employee Exposure and Medical Records Standard (1980a:35225). See also Brown (1985) and Ashford and Caldart (1985).

6 States with right-to-know laws covering industrial toxic chemical hazards are Alabama, Alaska, California, Connecticut, Delaware, Florida, Illinois, Iowa, Louisiana, Maine, Maryland, Massachusetts, Michigan, Minnesota, Missouri, Montana, New Hampshire, New Jersey, New York, North Carolina, North Dakota, Oklahoma, Oregon, Pennsylvania, Rhode Island, Tennessee, Washington, West Virginia, Wisconsin, and Wyoming. See Office of Technology Assessment (1990), Goldsmith (1987), Bureau of National Affairs (1984a), Chess (1986), Hinds and Moran (1983), and Hadley (1982).

7 OSHA first promulgated the access-to-medical-records standard May 23, 1980. The standard subsequently was overturned by the Reagan administration, then enacted in a more delimited form in 1988 (see 29 *Code of Federal Regulations* Section 1910.20 (1990)). Eighty-three percent of "Fortune 500" companies responding to a survey by Linowes reported denying workers access to their medical records (cited in A. Freedman, *Industry Response to Health Risk*, 1981:17). Unless the law has required it, employers generally have resisted extending workers' access to medical information. See Ashford and Caldart (1985), the initial OSHA Access to Employee Exposure and Medical Records Standard (1980a), Rothstein (1984), and the final 1987 OSHA Hazard Communication Standard, requiring that information on chemical hazards be made available to employees (29 *Code of Federal Regulations* Section 1910.1200 (1990)).

8 Ruttenberg and Hudgins (1981) and Ferber, Hill, and Cobb (1976) provide details concerning Allied Chemical Corporation's chemical plant in which 36 of 76 benzidine dye workers developed bladder tumors, including 17 malignancies. In the same plant, 79 workers exposed to other carcinogens developed bladder tumors. Scientific evidence on the hazards of benzidine dyes had been published since 1940. Subsequent engineering controls reduced exposure to benzidine. For discussion of informing workers of the hazards of benzidine dyes in another company (J. S. Young), see National Academy of Sciences (1980:325–327).

9 The chemical antidote (atropine sulfate) masks employees' symptoms of pesticide poisoning and damage to the nervous system stemming from methomyl exposure. By relieving uncomfortable symptoms, use of the antidote provides a false sense of security. Further medical treatment or engineering controls then seem unnecessary and exposed workers are likely to return to work. For detailed discussion of the use of atropine in a DuPont plant in LaPorte, Texas, see David W. Ortlieb (Director, Health and Safety Department, International Chemical Workers Union), "Testimony of the International Chemical Workers Union," at OSHA's public meeting held on the draft standard, "Occupational Exposure to Pesticides During Manufacture and Formulation," March 24, 1981, particularly pp. 1–7 and 16. Further evidence regarding this case is available in company documents and OSHA records.

10 Brodeur (1985) analyzes evidence of employers not informing workers of asbestos exposure. From 10 to 18 percent of U.S. asbestos insulation and shipyard workers may be expected to die of diseases related to asbestos. For details concerning medical surveillance, informing workers, and withholding information in one firm (DuPont), along with employee, union, company physician, and management views of company practices, see OSHA Case Files M7172/012 and H5527/025.

11 Silvia Krekel (Occupational Health Specialist, Oil, Chemical, and Atomic Workers International Union), Statement at NIOSH National Conference on Occupational Health and Safety Issues Affecting Minority Workers, in Krekel (1981).

12 Evidence and discussion of management access to employee medical records appear in Barken and Markowitz (1988); U.S. House Subcommittee on Health and Safety (1987); Field and Baram (1986); "The Privacy Commission recommendations on employee access," in *Individual Rights in the Corporation*, edited by A. Westin (1980); and the initial OSHA access-to-medical-records standard. See also the analysis of company physicians and occupational medicine in this chapter.

13 This statement is from the initial OSHA Access to Employee Exposure and Medical Records Standard (1980a), enacted in 1988 after having been rescinded.

14 See Wertz and Fletcher (1989b) and Rothstein (1984).

15 OSHA Case File M7172/012, page I 24.5, includes the report on company medical practices in which this statement appears.

See DuPont's "Guidelines for the Management of Chronic Occupational Illnesses," which includes instructions for management review of employee medical records in order to determine a diagnosis and whether a disease should be considered occupational in origin.

16 Rothfeder (1989) and Ringen (1980). "Workers' compensation history," *Business Insurance* (June 9, 1980:27) offers an example of these search services. See also Warren J. Smith (Chairman of the Board, Workers' Institute for Safety and Health, and Secretary-Treasurer, Ohio AFL-CIO), Prepared statement for presentation before the U.S. House Subcommittee on Labor Standards (1981).

17 See Holtzman (1989), Hubbard and Henefin (1985), and National Academy of Sciences (1980, 1975).

18 Duster (1990), Holtzman (1989), Carey et al. (1990), and National Academy of Sciences (1975b) discuss sickle cell testing and other cases of genetic screening, largely in nonindustrial settings. The National Academy of Sciences Committee for the Study of Inborn Errors of Metabolism, in their 1975 book reporting on genetic screening, reported that nine of the twelve insurance companies surveyed "charged higher rates for individuals with sickle trait even though mortality curves for such individuals do not differ significantly from blacks without the trait" (p. 126). See also Nelkin and Tancredi (1989).

19 An exception is a California law that restricts circulation of employee medical information, though its reach does not extend beyond the state. California employers may not disclose employee medical information to parties outside the company without the worker's signed authorization. The California Confidentiality of Medical Information Act appears in *California Civil Code Annotated* Section 56.20 (Deering Supplement, 1990). Connecticut law also protects confidentiality of employee medical records (*Connecticut General Statutes Annotated* Section 31-128f (West 1987)).

20 See U.S. House Subcommittee on Health and Safety (1987), Trost (1986), and Epstein (1980, 1979).

21 Burrough and Lubove (1986); Thomas J. Bray, "Hunt for hazards: Protecting the health of DuPont employees is a costly proposition," *Wall Street Journal* (June 28, 1976); Bronson (1977); and "DuPont data show its cancer deaths trailed rate in U.S.," *Wall Street Journal* (July 29, 1976). DuPont claimed that "The

average DuPont worker is 20 times safer than a person in his own home." Company officials also claimed that "The cancer rate for our workers is about 50% that of the general population." See also Pell et al. (1978).

22 Holtzman (1989), Wofsy (1986), Culliton (1983), and Ashford (1983).

23 Goldsmith (1987), U.S. House Subcommittee on Health and Safety (1987), Cain (1986), McCaffrey (1982), and Ashford (1976). The American Medical Association also opposed the OSHA standard on employee access to medical and exposure records, submitting a letter to the Senate Subcommittee on Investigations and General Oversight, Committee on Labor and Human Resources, which conducted hearings on OSHA (October 26, 1982, letter from James H. Sammons, Executive Vice President, American Medical Association, to Senator Paula Hawkins, Senate Subcommittee Chair).

24 Dow officials expressed their opposition to the OSHA Access to Employee Exposure and Medical Records proposed standard (29 *Code of Federal Regulations* Section 1910.20) in extensive statements submitted to the Agency. See OSHA Docket H-112, particularly the March 30, 1979, statement by D. J. Pagel (senior attorney, Dow Chemical U.S.A.). For DuPont's opposition to the proposed standard, see the September 21, 1978, statement by Eugene L. Grimm and E. Julia Lambeth (attorneys, E. I. duPont de Nemours and Co.,) in OSHA Docket H-112.

25 See U.S. House Subcommittee on Health and Safety (1987, 1981) and OSHA (1980a).

26 Englehardt and Kaplan (1987), U.S. House Subcommittee on Health and Safety (1987), and U.S. Congress (1981, 1982a,b) discuss companies' use of evidence regarding chemical hazards. For examples of conflict between industry and government over industry use of data on health hazards, see Salter (1988), Jackall (1988), and Bronson (1977).

27 See, for example, Nelkin and Brown (1984), Tversky and Kahneman (1981), Schwing and Albers (1980), and Fischhoff et al. (1981).

28 Mazzocchi (1980). See also Raines (1986) and Field and Baram (1986).

29 See Field and Baram (1986), Raines (1986), Rothstein (1984), and Mendeloff (1979).

30 See Kazis and Grossman (1982) and Duerksen (1982) for examples of such dilemmas.

31 Jack Kilian (as corporate scientist and medical director of Dow Chemical's Texas Division), in Wright et al. (1979:147).

32 For examples of this approach, see Hunt (1986) and U.S. Congress (1981).

33 Scientists with Western Electric Company, for example, in describing their company's medical surveillance program, state: "Many highly susceptible employees are initially 'screened away' from high risk jobs by the supervisor, using employee medical work restrictions information" (Barrett and Belk, 1977:736). This article examines the computerized occupational medical surveillance program in Western Electric Company. See also Leach et al. (1981).

34 Boden (1986), NIOSH (1982), and Ashford (1976) discuss health hazard protections in small companies.

35 Paul Kotin (Corporate Medical Director, Johns-Manville Corporation) in Wright et al. (1979:152).

36 Max Rogers (Chief Surgeon, Southern Railway Company), Statement to the Genetic Screening Hearings, U.S. Congress (1981:42 and 49). Rogers stated that: "All of the X-rays could be paid for by just a very few expensive case settlements." In 1980, the company paid $13,539,507 to settle employee personal injury claims. The railroad industry as a whole paid more than $343 million for personal injury claims (U.S. Congress, 1981:43). Trends in medical expenses and jury verdicts further boost company costs for employee injuries.

37 Ford, "Orthopedic Considerations," in Summary Report and Proceedings of the Conference on Low Back X-Rays in Preemployment Physical Examinations, American College of Radiology, Tucson, Arizona, January 11–14, 1973:33, 39–40, cited in Rockey et al. (1979:203).

38 According to Public Health Service figures, 3,000,000 low-back X-rays are performed each year, as many as 1,200,000 of which are conducted on a preemployment basis. Precise figures are not available (U.S. Congress, 1981:101 and 92).

39 The 4 percent figure is from Gilbert Omenn (Professor of Medicine and Environmental Health, University of Washington), who recommends that routine X-ray screening be discontinued (Harris, 1983; and National Academy of Sciences, 1980:370). A medical director of a major railroad company that

conducts back X-ray screening estimates that the X-rays can predict disability in 60 percent of the cases (Max Rogers, Chief Surgeon, Southern Railway Company, in U.S. Congress, 1981:114 and 141). For discussion of the limitations of back X-rays in predicting disability, see U.S. Congress (1981:122) and see Rockey et al. (1979:208–213), who finds that back X-rays have a predictive value of only about 2 percent for identifying workers who may have a risk of disk surgery. In other words, 98 percent of those who are refused employment would never require back surgery. Also, of those individuals denied jobs on the basis of X-ray exams, at least 20 percent never will have low-back pain and at least 60 percent never will lose time from work because of such pain.

40 U.S. House Subcommittee on Health and Safety (1987), Rothstein (1984), U.S. Congress (1981), and Mazzocchi (1980).

41 In addition to preemployment tests, many companies conduct periodic liver function tests to assess chemical exposure risks. DuPont, for example, uses periodic liver function screening tests for workers exposed to DMF (dimethylformamide) and DMAC (dimethylacetamide) (U.S. Congress, 1981:265 and 269). Workers with abnormal test results may be removed from jobs. See Wright et al. (1988).

42 Howard D. Samuel (President, Industrial Union Department, AFL-CIO) in submitted testimony, U.S. Congress (October 14, 1981:35).

43 Judkins (1986), Gersuny (1981), Bacow (1980), Berman (1978), and McCaffrey (1982).

44 Biological monitoring as a general approach in occupational health is more prevalent in large firms within Europe than in those in the United States. This may have to do with the strength of labor relative to management in Europe and the United States. In a country like the U.S. in which employers have been more aggressive and successful in their pursuits compared with labor, the types of new technologies and concepts of workplace risk they favor are more likely to flourish. Jacoby (1985) and Bendix (1956) examine the history of labor–management relations in the United States. Lowry (1986) discusses biological monitoring tests used in or recommended by European countries.

45 A study by the Labor Occupational Health Program (1980) finds that 82 percent of union contracts contain health and

safety clauses. A Bureau of National Affairs (1983) study arrives at the same percentage.

46　Bureau of National Affairs (1987), Bacow (1980), and Labor Occupational Health Program (1980).

47　See Bureau of National Affairs (1987).

48　Thirty percent of all manufacturing contracts require medical examinations, including 86 percent in petroleum and 67 percent in the rubber industries. Of these, 31 percent – or less than one-tenth of the total contracts – require physical exams for new hires; 76 percent require physical exams periodically or at management's request. See Bureau of National Affairs (1983:108–111).

49　See, for example, Nelkin and Tancredi (1989), Holtzman (1989), Stevens (1990), Bompey (1986), Russoniello and Ehrlich (1986), and Lewy (1983).

50　See U.S. House Subcommittee on Health and Safety (1987, 1981), Walsh (1987), OSHA (1980a), and *Journal of Occupational Medicine* (1978).

51　American Occupational Medical Association Code of Ethical Conduct (1976).

52　Office of Technology Assessment (1990), Ashford and Caldart (1985), Barken and Markowitz (1988), Wertz and Fletcher (1989b), and Rothstein (1984) consider laws affecting the distribution of employee medical information.

53　See Raines (1986), Billauer (1985), Field and Baram (1986), Freidson (1986), Rothstein (1984), and McGarity and Schroeder (1981).

54　Howard D. Samuel (President, Industrial Union Department, AFL-CIO) in submitted testimony, U.S. Congress (1981:35).

55　James English (Associate General Counsel, United Steelworkers Union of America), National Academy of Sciences (1980:385).

56　Ahmed Nasr (Assistant Director, Health, Safety, and Human Factors Laboratory, Eastman Kodak), National Academy of Sciences (1980:319).

57　These include Huber (1988), Brown (1980), Smith (1979), McLean et al. (1978), and Thaler and Rosen (1976). Adam Smith argued in 1776 that workers choose hazardous jobs because they receive higher wages.

58　See Passell (1989a,b), U.S. President (1982), McCaffrey (1982), and Zeckhauser and Nichol (1979). Economists and other policy officials in government organizations such as the Office of

Management and Budget (OMB) in the Executive Office of the President, Office of the Assistant Secretary for Policy, Evaluation, and Research (ASPER) in the U.S. Department of Labor, and Council of Economic Advisers (CEA) in the Executive Office of the President have had a growing impact in the late 1970s and 1980s on government policy. They have argued for curtailed standard-setting and expanded market incentives. James Miller III, as head of the Federal Trade Commission and later of the Office of Management and Budget, expressed this perspective: "Imperfect products should be available because consumers have different preferences for defect avoidance" (Green, 1983:14–17). See also Huber (1988).

59 Hazard-pay arguments rely primarily on data concerning injury, not illness. When illnesses are included in the data sets, they are more likely to be acute rather than chronic and long-term. Despite its limited use of disease statistics, the hazard-pay model has influenced government and industry policy toward chronic health risks as well as safety.

60 See U.S. House Subcommittee on Health and Safety (1987) and Nelkin and Brown (1984).

61 On a community scale, the choice between work and health surfaced in a dispute over a Tacoma, Washington, smelter in 1983. The U.S. Environmental Protection Agency called for a citywide vote that would help determine how strictly arsenic emissions would be regulated. Government and industry officials cast the dilemma as a choice between jobs for the community or improved health that would result from tighter chemical controls or plant closure. For discussion of this case, see Shabecoff (1983).

62 Daniels (1985), President's Commission (1983a,b), and Wikler (1978) analyze issues of choice for health hazards outside the workplace, including information constraints.

63 In a related analysis of justice in health care decisions, Daniels (1985) concurs that employee choice is limited. He refers to hazard-pay bargains as "quasi-coercive," largely because workers who accept dangerous jobs have unfairly or unjustly restricted alternatives.

64 For analytic models that discuss worker irrationality in risk perception due to psychological characteristics, cultural biases, and political distortion, see Boxer (1985), Schwing and Albers (1980), and Douglas and Wildavsky (1982).

65 Viscusi does draw on several survey studies, along with his other data sources. In addition to widely used national surveys such as the University of Michigan Survey of Working Conditions, he analyzes surveys with unusual methods, such as a study of chemical workers in which interviews of employees regarding working conditions and risk perceptions were conducted by managers (Viscusi and O'Connor, 1984).

66 Robinson (1987b) discusses evidence that quit rates are lower in jobs workers view to be hazardous than in those they view to be safe.

67 Worrall and Butler (1983) and Leigh (1982) provide evidence for the higher unionization rates of more hazardous jobs. Data that Robinson (1986a) examines at the industrial level of analysis suggest that industries producing more injuries and illnesses pay more than safer industries. However, once the extent of unionization is controlled, the relationship disappears. Riskier industries initially seem to pay more because of risk, but the fact that they also are more extensively unionized explains the higher wages, since unionized industries typically pay more.

68 See Freeman (1980). Robinson (1987b) identifies another reason workers in more hazardous jobs may not quit. He points to an economic externality that undercuts Viscusi's argument that managers will improve working conditions because of the turnover costs produced when workers in more hazardous jobs quit. Individual workers have an incentive to keep their jobs and hope that other workers will quit because it is those who leave who pay the unemployment and job-search costs of quitting. This reduces the number of quits and the pressure these quits exert on management to reduce work hazards.

69 Robinson (1986a:667) concludes that: "figures presented here certainly do not indicate that workers are fully and adequately compensated for the risks they take, nor that firms face the appropriate level and mix of incentives to invest in protective measures." He analyzes five survey data sets, including the 1982 and 1980 National Longitudinal Survey and 1977 Quality of Employment Survey.

70 A study by the U.S. Department of Labor (1980) indicates that employees exposed to occupational hazards underestimate chronic disease effects. Workers assess the cause of other types

of occupational hazards more accurately – that is, their reports are more consistent with scientific data sources.

71 Thus Robinson (1986:4) states: "Employers will be motivated both to hire disadvantaged workers for risky jobs and, where necessary, to reduce the level of skill and on-the-job training necessary in risky jobs to avoid the need for skilled workers."

72 See Davis and Rowland (1980), Robinson (1987a, 1984), and Lucas (1974). Research on the segmented or dual labor market confirming this pattern includes: Berger and Piore (1980), Edwards (1979), Harrison and Sum (1979), and Chapter 4.

73 Robinson (1986b), in analyzing large national data sets, finds that employees in hazardous jobs and industries are more likely to lose their jobs through layoff or plant closure than workers in safer jobs. In addition, they have poorer promotion possibilities, significantly less worker autonomy, and less on-the-job training (1988a). Further, these workers are considerably more likely to describe their jobs as uncreative, meaningless, and monotonous.

74 New Directions News 6 (May 1980) discusses the subcontracting of hazardous work to nonunion shops.

75 Bureau of National Affairs (1987) examines these agreements.

76 The University of Michigan Quality of Employment Surveys reveal that unionized workers know more about occupational health hazards than unorganized workers.

77 See Szasz (1984), McCaffrey (1982), and Ferguson and LaVeen (1981).

78 Viscusi endorses susceptibility policies, including the use of physical exams and personal characteristics requirements: "At the time of hiring, workers should then be screened not only on the basis of their productivity, but also on their probabilities of illness or injury. . . . This monitoring continues after the period of employment has begun . . . [A]n enterprise will acquire information concerning the workers' risk propensity in much the same manner as it does for workers' productivity" (1979:96). "[T]he economy functions much more effectively if the differences in individual productivity on different jobs are reflected in the job matchups. An individual's sensitivity to various hazards or proclivity toward accidents is simply one aspect of his overall productivity. If this heterogeneity is exploited in matching up workers to jobs rather than sup-

pressed, the overall safety and efficiency of the economy will be enhanced" (1983:135).

79 See, for example, Holtzman (1989), Carey et al. (1990), President's Commission (1983a,b), Sorenson (1971), Reilly (1977), Bergsma (1974), Lappé et al. (1972), and Bristow (1974).

80 Some public genetic screening programs have been mandatory. These have included PKU screening for newborns and sickle cell screening for marriage license applicants, school children, and prison inmates. Supporters of these programs have justified them largely on public health grounds. In the case of some compulsory screening, however, effective treatment for the abnormalities has been unavailable and actual preventive health effects of screening have not been demonstrated. For discussion of mandatory public genetic screening, see Duster (1990), President's Commission (1983a), Lappé (1979), U.S. Department of Health and Human Services (1980), Annas (1982), and Powledge (1974).

81 Sources discussing DuPont's screening program include journal articles (*Journal of Occupational Medicine*, 1986; Holden, 1982; Reinhardt, 1978; Lavine, 1982; Severo, 1980b; West, 1982; and Wright et al., 1979), U.S. House Subcommittee hearings (U.S. Congress, 1981, 1982a,b), *New York Times* front-page coverage (Severo, 1980a), newspaper editorials (*New York Times*, 1980b; *Washington Post*, 1980a,b; *Hartford Courant*, 1980; and *Philadelphia Inquirer*, 1982), professional conferences (American Conference of Governmental Industrial Hygienists, 1982; National Academy of Sciences Institute of Medicine, 1980), other news stories (Otten, 1986; Harris, 1983; MacNeil–Lehrer Report, 1982; and Severo, 1982a, 1981), and editorial letters (Shapiro, 1980, and Jefferson, 1980).

82 Duster (1990), Lappé (1979), and National Academy of Sciences (1975) examine the involvement of populations-at-risk in public genetic screening programs.

83 Office of Technology Assessment (1990) and Lappé (1979). For discussion of DuPont's testing initiation, see Severo (1980b), U.S. Congress (1981), and Jefferson (1980).

84 U.S. Congress (1981:281). The DuPont Haskell Laboratory Director did not describe the program as voluntary in his *Journal of Occupational Medicine* article (Reinhardt, 1978).

85 U.S. Congress (1981:281–284), Severo (1980a), and Reinhardt (1978).

86 See Rapp (1988), Neal-Cooper and Scott (1988), Beeson and Golbus (1985), and President's Commission (1983a), particularly Chapter 1 on the Evolution and Status of Genetic Services. The major focus of counseling advocates has been nondirective services. However, critics of this approach maintain that nondirectiveness neither exists nor is desirable. They argue that counselors provide verbal and nonverbal suggestions of actions they believe to be correct and that clients seek firm direction about problem solving from counselors along with technical information and psychological support. Counseling is even more unlikely to be nondirective when employers provide it in industry settings.

87 Bruce Karrh (Corporate Medical Director, DuPont) in Severo (1980a). Karrh describes the purpose of the testing program: "Sickle-cell testing is . . . performed solely as a personal service for our Black employees and play[s] no role in hiring or job placement decisions" (U.S. Congress, 1981:266).

88 Charles Reinhardt (Director, Haskell Laboratory for Toxicology and Industrial Medicine, E. I. du Pont de Nemours and Co.) (1978:320). Low hemoglobin counts refer to less than 14 grams per 100 milliliters of blood.

89 *New York Times* journalist Richard Severo (1980a) claimed in a front-page story that DuPont screens blacks out of jobs. He referred to statements by Charles Reinhardt (Director, DuPont Haskell Laboratory), William Golt (President, DuPont Chemical Workers Association), and others as evidence that blacks with sickle cell trait lose jobs as a result of DuPont screening. Congressional investigation and media coverage put DuPont officials in a defensive posture. The corporate medical director testified before U.S. House Subcommittee hearings that blacks with sickle cell trait were not screened out of jobs and that Severo had misconstrued or deliberately misrepresented evidence that screening affects job placement.

90 For example, see Shapiro (1980) and U.S. Congress (1981, particularly 281–282). Under other circumstances and prior to the extensive controversy, DuPont officials discussed job placement goals of workplace screening (Reinhardt, 1978, and Karrh, 1979).

91 See Holtzman (1989), Carey et al. (1990), Nelkin and Tancredi (1989), Kolata (1986), Rothstein (1984), and section "Employer Use and Abuse of Information," above.

92   Employees' test results showing they carry the sickle cell trait
      is included in their medical file, to which company officials
      have access, even though the corporate medical director
      claims that DuPont conducts sickle cell tests only for em-
      ployees' own use (U.S. Congress, 1981:282–284).

93   U.S. Congress (1981:264–285) examines the company's SAT
      and G-6-PD testing. The DuPont medical director maintains
      that he had been unaware that other corporate officials decid-
      ed to remove workers with G-6-PD deficiency from jobs.

94   Lucid attempts to draw parallels between safeguards for work-
      place screening and those for public programs include
      Holtzman (1989), Lappé (1983), and Murray (1983). In their
      1983 report on Screening and Counseling for Genetic Condi-
      tions, the President's Commission for the Study of Ethical
      Problems in Medicine and Biomedical and Behavioral Research
      focused their attention on genetic screening in public pro-
      grams and private medical practice. They discussed specific
      work settings for screening very little, yet argued that: "[T]he
      various reasons for screening and counseling or the settings in
      which they take place do not in themselves provide any basis
      for the adoption of different policies toward participants"
      (President's Commission, 1983a:3).

95   Bruce Karrh (Corporate Medical Director of DuPont) states:
      "Potential abuses are always there. . . . People who want to
      can figure out ways to discriminate without using genetic
      tests" (Harris, 1983).

96   The final OSHA hazard communication standard appears in
      29 *Code of Federal Regulations* Section 1910.1200 (1990), in effect
      beginning in 1987. The employee access-to-medical-records
      standard appears at 29 *Code of Federal Regulations* Section
      1910.20 (1990).

97   See Verespej (1987) and U.S. House Subcommittee on Health
      and Safety (1987) for discussion of the High-Risk Worker Noti-
      fication Act, still not passed as of 1990. The bill would require
      that past and present employees who have been exposed to
      hazardous substances in the workplace during the past thirty
      years be notified individually.

98   The OSHA lead standard appears in 29 *Code of Federal Regula-
      tions* Section 1910.1025 (1990). See also Goerth (1983b), Jen-
      nings (1982), and Beliles (1982).

99 Eula Bingham (Assistant Secretary of Labor for Safety and Health and Director of OSHA) (1980a:820). OSHA officials in the Carter administration emphasized the benefit of medical removal protection and deplored its absence in other standards. Bingham's comment and the one cited just before it in the text reflect the more favorable approach to medical removal protection of OSHA in the 1970s, compared with the Reagan and Bush administrations of the 1980s and early 1990s.

100 U.S. House Subcommittee on Health and Safety (1987), Szasz (1984), McCaffrey (1982), and Calavita (1983) discuss the transformation of OSHA health rules over the 1970s and 1980s.

101 Knut Ringen (project director, Workers' Institute for Safety and Health) (1980:26).

102 Michael Wright (industrial hygienist, United Steelworkers of America) (1979:145).

6. WHO BEARS THE BURDEN? THE LEGAL AND ECONOMIC CONTEXT OF OCCUPATIONAL DISEASE

Epigraphs: Health Policy Official, U.S. Department of Labor, personal interview; Seminario, in Utidjian et al. (1979:170–171).

1 Leon Eisenberg (Professor, Department of Psychiatry, Harvard Medical School) in National Academy of Sciences (1980:233).

2 Representative Albert Gore, Jr. (Chair, Subcommittee on Investigations and Oversight, House Committee on Science and Technology) in his opening statement at Hearings on Genetic Screening and the Handling of High-Risk Groups in the Workplace, U.S. Congress (1981).

3 Mintz (1984), McCaffrey (1982), Ruttenberg and Hudgins (1981), and Mendeloff (1979).

4 See Jacobs and Chovil (1983). Allen (1981) finds that hazardous working conditions are associated with higher rates of absenteeism than found under safer conditions. Dangerous work also is associated with unauthorized wildcat strikes (Byrne and King, 1986). Viscusi (1983) presents data on turnover and training costs that stem from employee awareness of work hazards. Companies with high training costs have a

special interest in screening workers since for them, turnover expenses make retaining workers particularly desirable.

5 Bureau of Labor Statistics (1990). Robinson (1988b) documents the rise in illness rates in manufacturing, construction, and the trade sector in recent decades. Acute occupational illnesses include circulatory disease, systemic poisoning, mental disorders, dermatitis, eye disease, infective or parasitic disease, inflammation of bones or muscles, radiation effects, and serum and toxic hepatitis. Disabling injury rates also rose sharply for most years since 1958 (Robinson, 1988b; Viscusi, 1983; and Mendeloff, 1979).

6 The U.S. Bureau of Labor Statistics acknowledges that their statistics understate chronic occupational illnesses. The Bureau of Labor Statistics (1990:2) states that while their figures are a valid measure of recognized acute cases, they do not adequately reflect the magnitude of occupational illnesses such as cancers, which are chronic and long-latent in nature, because these illnesses "often are difficult to relate to the workplace and are not adequately recognized and recorded. These long-term latent illnesses are believed to be understated in the survey's illness measures."

7 See Rothstein (1989) and Jacobs and Chovil (1986). Guthier (1986), Kelly (1986), Holtzman (1989), and Baram (1985) discuss insurance company pressure on manufacturing companies to reduce medical costs and undertake health screening programs.

8 See Shor (1987), Robinson (1988b), Raines (1986), the U.S. Department of Labor Interim Report to Congress on Occupational Disease (1980), Shabecoff (1979), Kutchins (1981), and Ashford (1976:416). Despite provisions expanding workers' compensation coverage, the proportion of employees' work-related disease it covers remains small. In the case of asbestos, employees who claim damage from asbestos exposure at work are more likely to seek tort lawsuits than they are to pursue workers' compensation benefits.

9 See Rothstein (1989), Hadler (1986), and Boden (1986).

10 David Brusick (Director, Department of Genetics and Cell Biology, Litton Bionetics) in National Academy of Sciences (1980:393).

11 Office of Technology Assessment (1990), Raines (1986), Field and Baram (1986), Rothstein (1984), McGarity and Schroeder

(1981), and Peters (1984) examine legal trends in statutory and case law that expand employer liability for occupational disease.

12 An attorney for Southern Railway Company, a major railroad, explains that his company could be sued if a worker considered at high risk on the basis of a medical test subsequently develops health problems, "on the premise that we were aware of the potential danger and we knowingly permitted the man to go to work" (Wiley Mitchell, General Solicitor, Southern Railway Company, in U.S. Congress, 1981:115).

13 Some advocates of monitoring studies argue that ultimately the tests may help limit employer costs. Through genetic monitoring, chemical hazards could be located and controlled, thereby curtailing disease rates.

14 Max Rogers (Chief Surgeon, Southern Railway Company) in his statement at the 1973 Conference on Low Back X-Rays, quoted in U.S. Congress (1981:116).

15 Ruttenberg and Powers (1986), Raines (1986), U.S. Department of Labor (1980), U.S. House Subcommittee on Labor Standards (1981), Bureau of National Affairs (1979), Shor (1979), and Shabecoff (1979) examine income sources for victims of occupational disease.

16 Howard D. Samuel (President, Industrial Union Department, AFL-CIO), U.S. Congress (1981:34).

17 For other examples, see Boden (1986) and Ruttenberg and Powers (1986). Boden concludes from an analysis of costs and benefits of screening workers that "Employers who maximize the benefits to them of medical screening may reduce the net social benefits of screening" (p. 751).

18 See Jackall (1988), Szasz (1984), Pertschuk (1982), McCaffrey (1982), Green and Waitzman (1981), Kelman (1980), Hadley (1982), and Wilson (1980).

19 Manville Corporation filed a petition for reorganization under Chapter 11 of the Federal Bankruptcy Code in 1982. Manville cited over 16,500 current asbestos-related lawsuits pending against them. They estimated that over the next 20 years the company would be involved in 32,000 more lawsuits, with over $2 billion in potential liability. Brodeur (1985) examines this case in detail.

20 Business has not considered workers' compensation provisions that shield them from liability to be burdensome govern-

ment regulation. However, many have opposed and referred to as unwarranted interference recent developments broadening coverage to apply to more workers and circumstances. U.S. Department of Labor (1980), Raines (1986), and Field and Baram (1986) provide evidence of workers' compensation payments for occupational disease. Berman (1978) offers insight into the history of business interest in workers' compensation.

21 For example, see Brodeur (1985) and Ruttenberg and Hudgins (1981). Perhaps most remarkably, the tobacco industry has complained about government regulation but has benefited from large government subsidies. See Epstein (1979).

22 By statute, the corporate tax rate was 46 percent in 1983. But the effective rate – the amount actually paid – was only 16.7 percent, down from 21.8 percent in 1980. The difference between the statutory rate and the effective rate reflects corporate tax breaks. The chemical industry generally pays very low taxes – in 1983 an effective tax rate of −1 percent. In other words, the industry received a tax refund. The motor vehicles industry had an effective tax rate of 3.5 percent, with other low tax rates for electronics and appliances (7.4%) and telecommunications (4.8%), utilities (7.1%), railroad (3.3%), and paper and wood (−0.5%). Major causes of low corporate tax rates have included the investment tax credit and the accelerated cost recovery system, which have allowed quick write-offs for investment in plants and equipment. Corporations have complained about the heavy burden of government spending even though corporate taxes have been falling dramatically over the past 25 years. The corporate tax share of the federal tax burden was 6.2 percent in 1983, down from 12.5 percent in 1980 and 26.5 percent in 1950. Individuals paid 48.1 percent in 1983, up from 44.2 percent in 1976. The remaining government tax revenue comes from Social Security taxes, excise taxes, and other receipts (Birnbaum, 1984). See also Bradshaw and Vogel (1981) and Domhoff (1978).

23 Ashford and Caldart (1985) and Baram (1984).

24 Cain (1986), U.S. House Subcommittee on Health and Safety (1987), Verespej (1987), Szasz (1984), Chess (1986), Calavita (1983), Rothstein (1986), Ashford and Caldart (1985), and Hadley (1982:208–215).

25 McCaffrey (1982), Pertschuk (1982), Wilson (1980), Berman (1978), and Ashford (1976) offer accounts of the history of new

regulation in occupational and environmental health and safety and the forces that shape it. Although workplace regulation and occupational health law in general reflect corporations' disproportionate power, labor, consumer, and public interest organizations have managed to have considerable influence, especially in the new regulation of occupational and environmental hazards.

26 Representative Albert Gore, Jr. (Chair, Subcommittee on Investigations and Oversight, House Committee on Science and Technology), in his opening statement at Hearings on Genetic Screening and the Handling of High-Risk Groups in the Workplace, U.S. Congress (1981:2).

27 Bruce W. Karrh (Corporate Medical Director, E. I. duPont de Nemours and Co.), in U.S. Congress (1981:275).

28 National Institute for Occupational Safety and Health (NIOSH) is within the Center for Disease Control, Department of Health and Human Services; Occupational Safety and Health Administration (OSHA) and Equal Employment Opportunity Commission (EEOC) are within the U.S. Department of Labor.

29 29 *United States Code* Sections 654(5)(a)(1) and 655(b)(5)(1988).

30 29 *United States Code* Section 651(b)(1988).

31 Richard Severo, "Federal mandate for gene tests disturbs U.S. job safety official – Part four," in Severo (February 6, 1980a).

32 Richard Severo, "Genetic tests by industry raise questions on rights of workers – Part one," in Severo (February 3, 1980a).

33 This clause is contained in an OSHA rule promulgated for general industry, appearing in 29 *Code of Federal Regulations* Section 1910.1003(g)(1)(i)(1990).

34 Eula Bingham, press release appearing in Department of Labor Office of Information News, USDL 80-107 (February 20, 1980).

35 Eula Bingham, Department of Labor Office of Information News, USDL 80-107 (February 20, 1980). This view also appeared in Bingham (1980b). In a personal interview as OSHA Director, Bingham told me: "There never has been a provision or requirement for genetic screening in OSHA standards." In a letter sent to corporate medical directors in April 1978, with primary emphasis on fetal exclusion policies, Bingham stated: "Employers should exhaust all possible avenues of worker protection (be they engineering controls, work practices, personal protective equipment, etc.) before considering the adoption of exclusionary employment practices."

36 The ACGIH, a private standard-making organization, put forward the threshold limit values (TLVs) as safe exposure levels, as discussed in Chapter 3. Salter (1988) examines this standard-making activity by the ACGIH and the response to proposed standards in the political arena. In addition to the 450 TLV standards OSHA adopted from ACGIH in 1971, OSHA developed 24 standards regulating other substances.

37 29 *Code of Federal Regulations* Section 1910.1025(k)(1990). The medical surveillance section of the lead standard lays out further details of the medical removal protection provision.

38 Medical removal protection and rate retention provisions appear in the benzene standard (29 *Code of Federal Regulations* Section 1910.1028(i)(8) and (i)(9)). Limited medical transfer protections appear in the vinyl chloride standard (29 *Code of Federal Regulations* Section 1910.1017(k)(5)(1990)); and in the asbestos standard (29 *Code of Federal Regulations* Section 1910.1001(g)(3)(iv)(1990)), which provides medical transfer and rate retention for employees for whom respirators are ineffective, but only if another job is available. Respirator-related transfer and rate retention provisions are included in the cotton dust standard (29 *Code of Federal Regulations* Section 1910.1043(f)(2)(iv)(1990)).

39 An exception may be exclusion of women of childbearing potential, as discussed at length in Chapter 4.

40 *Christman* v. *American Cyanamid Company*, No. 80-0024 (N.D. W. Va., filed January 30, 1980). 9 OSHC ¶1596, 1981 OSHD 25,338 (1981), affirmed, *Oil, Chemical, and Atomic Workers International Union* v. *American Cyanamid Company*, 741 F.2d 444 (D.C. Cir. 1984).

41 This scientist added: "There may be extreme cases that present such an extreme risk that you just can't sanction it. But in the main, we're against singling out susceptible workers."

42 The linkage of testicular atrophy and Ordram is an example of the first method. The discovery of reproductive problems with DBCP is an example of the second method, since further NIOSH research work and regulatory action was initiated after workers discovered they had conceived few children.

43 The NIOSH ethylene oxide study employed two types of cytogenetic assays: sister chromatid exchange test and an evaluation of chromosomal aberrations. Lowry (1986) examines NIOSH's active interest in monitoring. NIOSH and OSHA offi-

cials generally have been more favorable toward genetic monitoring than toward genetic screening. Their perspective on monitoring usually falls under the "second view" of genetic monitoring – "Support for Monitoring," as discussed in Chapter 3.

44 Meinhardt (1981), the NIOSH protocol for the Texas study, discusses this perspective and gives details of their methodology.

45 42 *United States Code* Section 2000e-2(a)(1)(1988). Title VII forbids employment discrimination on grounds of race, sex, color, religion, pregnancy, or national origin.

46 42 *United States Code* Section 2000e-2(a)(2)(1988).

47 42 *United States Code* Section 2000e-2e (1988).

48 Greenhouse (1991), Kilborn (1991), Lewin (1990), Office of Technology Assessment (1990), Andrews (1987), Rothstein (1986), Bertin (1983), and Williams (1981) discuss the restricted use of specific employer defenses of BFOQ and business necessity in employment discrimination cases under Title VII.

49 Wermiel (1991), Hagar (1990), Savage (1990), Postol (1988), McElveen (1986), Rothstein (1984), and Williams (1981) examine these cases in the context of Title VII. See also the discussion of the Johnson Controls fetal exclusion policy in Bureau of National Affairs, *United States Law Week* 59, No. 36 (March 20, 1991): 4209–4219; in 886 *Federal Reporter* F2d (November 13, 1989):871–921; and in Kilborn (1991, 1990).

50 Two EEOC cases of blacks excluded because they had pseudofolliculitis barbae (PSB), a skin disorder, are *EEOC* v. *Greyhound*; and *EEOC* v. *Trailways Lines, Inc.*

51 EEOC Decision #81-8, 1981 CCH EEOC Dec. 6764 (1981).

52 Office of Technology Assessment (1990), Rothstein (1984), Holtzman (1989), and General Accounting Office (1982). Other cases of sickle cell anemia may have been filed with the EEOC. Since the EEOC decision on sickle cell anemia has been transmitted to the EEOC field offices, the national office is not necessarily aware of those cases.

53 This discussion of cases and decisions is not exhaustive. Other Title VII cases may relate to health-related exclusion.

54 The Rehabilitation Act of 1973, as amended, appears in 29 *United States Code* Sections 701 to 796 (1988). Title V of the Act includes the major provisions related to employment of the handicapped.

55 Section 503 of the Rehabilitation Act generally does not allow for private lawsuits, according to courts that have addressed the question. Section 504 may allow private action in specific circumstances.

56 Andrews (1987), Office of Technology Assessment (1990), Postol (1988), Rothstein (1984), U.S. Congress (1982a:110), and General Accounting Office (1982) discuss potential applications of the Rehabilitation Act to people who may be susceptible. The Americans with Disabilities Act of 1990 may also apply to workers seen as at increased risk based on genetic factors.

57 Mark Rothstein (Professor of Law, West Virginia University), "Some legal aspects of biochemical genetic and cytogenetic screening in the workplace," in Prepared Statement, U.S. Congress (1982a:103). See also Office of Technology Assessment (1990) and Rothstein (1986).

58 See Viscusi and O'Connor (1984), Calavita (1983), Trost (1985), and Provost (1982). A 1985 Office of Technology Assessment report on occupational health and safety government regulation found that health and safety protections were minimally enforced under the Reagan administration. Examples of eased regulation include more lenient inspection schedules, reduced penalties, and slower rule-making (Trost, 1985).

59 The New Jersey law (*New Jersey Statutes Annotated* Section 10:5-5(y)(1989 Supplement)) was enacted in 1981 as an amendment to the state "Law against Discrimination" (L. 1945, c. 169 p. 589, section 1). The law states that it is unlawful employment practice or discrimination for an employer "to refuse to hire or employ or to bar or to discharge from employment such individual or to discriminate against such individual in compensation or in terms, conditions or privileges of employment" anyone because of their "atypical hereditary cellular or blood trait," including "sickle cell trait, hemoglobin C trait, thalassemia trait, Tay-Sachs trait, or cystic fibrosis trait." This law applies to employers using genetic information from a medical history as well as test results from screening programs they have conducted.

60 *North Carolina General Statutes* Section 95-28.1 (Michie 1989); *Louisiana Statutes Annotated* Sections 23:1001–1004 (West 1985); and *Florida Statutes Annotated* Section 448.075 (West 1981).

61 The Connecticut Reproductive Hazards Act (*Connecticut General Statutes Annotated* Sections 46a-60(a)(7-10)(West 1986)). Office of Technology Assessment (1990), Andrews (1987), and Rothstein (1984) discuss other state laws.

62 "The Genetic Testing and Employment Act," proposed by Frank Barbaro, Albany Assemblyman of New York State, February 5, 1980. Barbaro referred to genetic testing as "a repugnant invasion of privacy of the individual" (*New York Times*, 1980c).

63 Other corporate officials emphasize the reservations that employers have about genetic screening, stemming partly from adverse publicity. A trade association representative, for example, states: "Genetic screening is a topic that all the companies want to stay as far away from as possible. They've been accused by the media of all sorts of things. And then there's the congressional investigation."

7. THE SOCIAL CONSTRUCTION OF WORKPLACE HAZARDS: CONCLUSIONS AND POLICY IMPLICATIONS

1 See, for example, Perrow (1984), Starr (1982), Bosk (1979), Freidson (1973), and Nelkin (1984).

2 Under federal OSHA guidelines, "feasibility" encompasses technological feasibility. That is, government standards must offer protection as strict as it is technologically feasible. To what extent OSHA rules must be economically feasible as well for particular companies and industries has been controversial, contributing to extensive litigation. Case law indicates that OSHA regulation can be stringent enough to drive companies, but not entire industries, out of business. See Rothstein (1984) and Daniels (1985).

3 Brown (1984), Ruttenberg (1982), and Epstein (1979) discuss cost-saving emissions-control technology used to reduce vinyl chloride exposure. See Jackall (1988) for discussion of the OSHA cotton dust case, in which industry benefited financially from the technological innovation that government regulation encouraged, even though executives fought OSHA on regulating cotton dust.

4 The High-Risk Worker Notification Act, still not passed as of 1990, would extend worker notification of health hazards in

the workplace substantially. See U.S House Subcommittee on Health and Safety (1987) and Verespej (1987). In addition, information that employees are given should not also be provided to insurance and credit companies.

5 The major federal OSHA rule expanding the chemical hazard information available to workers is the "hazard communication" standard: 29 *Code of Federal Regulations* Section 1910.1200 (1990). The hazard communication standard was promulgated by OSHA in 1980 but rescinded by the Reagan administration and not put into effect until 1987. Without federal protection, many states and localities enacted "right-to-know" laws (Goldsmith, 1987, and Bureau of National Affairs, 1984a). Faced with a wide array of local and state laws that disturbed industry, the Reagan administration proposed a federal right-to-know standard that was narrower than the measure put forth in the Carter administration.

6 The OSHA lead standard appears at 29 *Code of Federal Regulations* 1910.1025 (1990). The Medical Surveillance section of the lead standard gives details on the medical removal protection provision.

7 This approach to reproductive hazards appears in the OSHA lead standard. Its requirements apply equally to men and women workers who plan to parent children. After lengthy hearings and investigation, OSHA concluded that lead has profound adverse effects on the reproductive health of both male and female workers, including effects prior to conception. Under the lead standard, employees of both sexes who are planning to become parents (and who have blood lead levels over 30 $\mu g/100g$) have the right to a temporary transfer to other jobs and to retain their wage rates and seniority during the transfer period (29 *Code of Federal Regulations* 1910.1025 (1990)). The Connecticut Reproductive Hazards Act (*Connecticut General Statutes Annotated* Sections 46a-60(a)(7-10)(West 1986) requires employers to make reasonable efforts to transfer pregnant employees to temporary jobs or otherwise protect the reproductive health of employees.

8 Medical removal protection generally applies to current employees, not job applicants. In the case of medical tests for job applicants, too, the scientific basis for locating high-risk individuals and linking their personal characteristics to workplace exposures should be strong, and the focus should be on reduc-

ing exposure hazards. In addition, in order for the exclusion of job applicants to be considered, the risk of disease for high-risk workers should be large; the number of people affected should be small; reliable and confidential medical information should be given to the job applicants; and racial, ethnic, or sexual groups should not be singled out.

9 Dietz and Rycroft (1987), Shrader-Frechette (1985), Fischhoff et al. (1981), and Heimer (1985) offer insight into social factors that underlie risk and its assessment. Short (1984) concurs that risk analysis is a crucial area of investigation that warrants major sociological attention.

APPENDIX: RESEARCH DESIGN

1 Trade associations are similar to unions, in that they represent their member company officials and corporations in many of the same ways that unions represent their employee members.

2 The interviews for this research were approved by the University of California, Berkeley, Committee for the Protection of Human Subjects (Human Subjects 82-10-2 NICHD and 85-3-55 NSF). Approval was obtained when the research was begun as part of a National Institute of Child Health and Human Development project, entitled "Social and Political Issues in the New Genetics" (NICHD 5 RO1 HD13897-03), and was continued under a grant from the National Science Foundation (NSF SES 84-12298). In addition to this study, findings from this research appear in research reports and articles, including Draper (1984a,b, 1986, 1987, 1991). This research was based in the University of California, Berkeley, Department of Sociology and Institute for the Study of Social Change, and continued in the Stanford University and University of Southern California Departments of Sociology.

3 See, for example, Daniels (1988), Lynn (1986), Office of Technology Assessment (1983), and Harris and Associates (1980).

4 For discussion of intensive interview data and analysis, and the constructed social world they can illuminate, see Lofland and Lofland (1984), Emerson (1983), and Glaser and Strauss (1967).

Glossary

carcinogenic   causing cancer.

chromosome   the structure in the cell nucleus that stores and transmits genetic information.

cytogenetics   the branch of genetics concerned with the structure and function of the cell, especially the chromosomes.

DNA   deoxyribonucleic acid: the genetic material of all cells.

EEOC   Equal Employment Opportunity Commission: the federal agency charged with administering Title VII of the Civil Rights Act of 1964 and the Age Discrimination in Employment Act.

EPA   Environmental Protection Agency: the federal agency charged with regulating hazards present in the environment.

epidemiology   the study of the prevalence and spread of disease in a human population.

externalities   social costs not borne by business, particular companies, or industries.

false positive   test result that inaccurately appears to be positive.

fetal exclusion   policies in which women are excluded from jobs in the attempt to prevent damage to fetuses from chemical exposure.

genetic monitoring   the periodic testing of workers to assess damage to their DNA or chromosomes from exposure to hazardous substances or agents.

genetic paradigm   a general perspective that traces human behavior or disease to inborn biological factors.

genetic screening   a one-time test to determine the presence of particular genetic traits in individuals, such as those that might cause workers to be at increased risk for disease.

genetics   the branch of science that deals with heredity.

G-6-PD glucose-6-phosphate-dchydrogenase deficiency: a genetic red blood cell condition characterized by an enzyme deficiency that can result in anemia.

hemoglobin the oxygen-carrying part of the blood.

heterozygote an individual possessing alternative forms of a gene (a variant gene and a normal gene, for example) instead of a pair of matching genes at a specific physical position on a chromosome. Heterozygotes sometimes are called carriers. These individuals may be more likely to develop disease under certain conditions.

homozygote an individual possessing an identical pair of genes, either both normal or both variant, at a specific physical position on a chromosome.

medical removal protection (MRP) procedure or legal requirement in which employees affected adversely by exposure to a toxic substance are removed from further exposure until they are medically advised or legally allowed to return.

mutagenic causing chromosomal changes.

negligence an act that a reasonably prudent person would not perform or an omission of what a reasonably prudent person would do.

NIOSH National Institute for Occupational Safety and Health, within the U.S. Department of Health and Human Services: the agency responsible for conducting research and advising OSHA on job safety and health matters.

OSHA the Occupational Safety and Health Administration, within the U.S. Department of Labor: the agency charged with carrying out the federal Occupational Safety and Health Act (29 *United States Code* Sections 651 to 678 (1988)), which requires employers to provide employees with a safe and healthful workplace.

rate retention maintenance of wage and benefit levels during a period of medical removal from a job.

Rehabilitation Act the 1973 federal law (29 *United States Code* Sections 701 to 796 (1988)) prohibiting employment discrimination against handicapped individuals.

SAT serum alpha$_1$-antitripsin deficiency: the lack of the serum protein that protects lungs from protein-decomposing enzymes. This genetic trait is correlated with susceptibility to emphysema.

sickle cell disease a blood disease that causes distorted, sickle-shaped red blood cells and can produce symptoms ranging from minor to life-threatening.

sickle cell trait   a genetic condition characterized by the presence of an abnormal molecule in the red blood cells. Health hazards from this heterozygous trait generally are considered minimal or nonexistent.

susceptibility   biological predisposition to harmful effects of a chemical or other agent.

teratogenic   causing abnormal development of the embryo.

Title VII   part of the Civil Rights Act of 1964 (42 *United States Code* Section 2000e (1988)): the federal law prohibiting employment discrimination based on race, color, religion, sex, or national origin.

TLV   threshold limit value: the maximum time-weighted average concentration to which a healthy worker may be exposed up to 8 hours a day for a normal 40-hour week, over a 40- to 50-year working lifetime without becoming ill.

tort   a private or civil wrong, independent of a contract, arising from a violation of a duty.

toxin   a substance that is poisonous, carcinogenic, mutagenic, or teratogenic.

References

Alexander, Victor, Sanford S. Leffingwell, J. William Lloyd, Richard D. Waxweiler, and Richard L. Miller
1980 "Brain cancer in petrochemical workers: A case series report." *American Journal of Industrial Medicine* 1, No. 1:115–123.

Allen, Steven G.
1981 "An empirical model of work attendance." *Review of Economics and Statistics* 63, No. 1 (February):77–87.

American Conference of Governmental Industrial Hygienists
1982 "ACGIH Symposium on Protection of the Sensitive Individual, Tucson, Arizona (November 9–11, 1981)." *Annals of the American Conference of Governmental Industrial Hygienists* 3 (September):1–187.

American Public Health Association
1982 *Health of Minorities and Women.* Publication No. 072. Washington, D.C.

American Society of Law and Medicine; and Boston University Schools of Law, Medicine, and Public Health (sponsors)
1983 Biological Monitoring and Genetic Screening in the Industrial Workplace: Conference Materials. Washington, D.C. (May 12–13).

Ames, Bruce N., Renae Magaw, and Lois Swirsky Gold
1987 "Ranking possible carcinogenic hazards." *Science* 236 (April 17):271–279.

Andrews, Lori B.
1987 *Medical Genetics: A Legal Frontier.* Chicago: American Bar Foundation.

References

Annas, George J.
1982 "Mandatory PKU screening: The other side of the looking glass." *American Journal of Public Health* 72, No. 12 (December):1401–1403.

Antonarakis, S. E.
1989 "Diagnosis of genetic disorders at the DNA level." *New England Journal of Medicine* 320:153–163.

Ashford, Nicholas A.
1976 *Crisis in the Workplace: Occupational Disease and Injury.* Cambridge, Mass.: The MIT Press.
1983 "A framework for examining the effects of industrial funding on academic freedom and the integrity of the university." *Science, Technology, and Human Values* (April).
1987 "New scientific evidence and public health imperatives." *New England Journal of Medicine* 316, No. 17 (April 23):1084–1085.

Ashford, Nicholas A., and Charles Caldart
1985 "The 'right-to-know': Toxic information transfer in the workplace." *Annual Review of Public Health* 6:383–401.

Ashford, Nicholas A., Christine J. Spadafor, and Charles C. Caldart
1984 "Human monitoring: Scientific, legal, and ethical considerations." *Harvard Environmental Law Review* 8, No. 2:263–363.

Ashford, Nicholas A., Christine J. Spadafor, Dale B. Hattis, and Charles C. Caldart
1990 *Monitoring the Worker for Exposure and Disease: Scientific, Legal, and Ethical Considerations in the Use of Biomarkers.* Baltimore: Johns Hopkins University Press.

Atherley, Gordon, Neil Johnston, and Maritza Tennassee
1986 "Biomedical surveillance: Rights conflict with rights." *Journal of Occupational Medicine* 28, No. 10 (October):958–965.

Austin, Susan G., and A. Robert Schnatter
1983 "A case-control study of chemical exposures and brain tumors in petrochemical workers." *Journal of Occupational Medicine* 25, No. 4 (April):313–320.

Bacow, Lawrence S.
1980 *Bargaining for Job Safety and Health.* Cambridge, Mass.: MIT Press.

References

Baram, Michael S.
1984 "The right to know and the duty to disclose hazard information." *American Journal of Public Health* 74, No. 4 (April):385–390.
1985 "Charting the future course for corporate management of genetic and health risks." In Aubrey Milunsky and George J. Annas (editors), *Genetics and the Law III.* New York: Plenum.

Barash, David P.
1977 *Sociobiology and Behavior.* New York: Elsevier.

Barken, Marlene, and James R. Markowitz
1988 "Preparing the company physician to testify at legal proceedings." *Journal of Occupational Medicine* 30, No. 5 (May):405–411.

Barnard, Robert C.
1982 "Legal issues: Reproductive health hazards." *Annals of the American Conference of Governmental Industrial Hygienists* 3 (September):157–163.

Barrett, C. D., and H. D. Belk
1977 "A computerized occupational medical surveillance program." *Journal of Occupational Medicine* 19, No. 11 (November):732–736.

Bassett-Stanford, Mary
1981 "Genetic testing in employment: Employee protection or threat?" *Suffolk University Law Review* 15, No. 5 (December):1187–1217.

Baxandall, Rosalyn, Linda Gordon, and Susan Reverby (editors)
1976 *America's Working Women: A Documentary History – 1600 to the Present.* New York: Vintage Books.

Bayer, Ronald
1982 "Women, work, and reproductive hazards." *Hastings Center Report* 12, No. 5 (October):14–19.
1986 "Biological monitoring in the workplace: Ethical issues." *Journal of Occupational Medicine* 28, No. 10 (October):935–939.

Bazelon, David L.
1979 "Risk and responsibility." *Science* 205, No. 4403 (July 20):277–280.

Beeson, Diane, and Mitchell S. Golbus
1985 "Patient decision-making: Whether or not to have pre-

natal diagnosis and abortion for X-linked conditions." *American Journal of Medical Genetics* 20, No. 1 (January):107–114.

Beliles, Robert P.
1982   "OSHA occupational health standards and the sensitive worker." *Annals of the American Conference of Governmental Industrial Hygienists* 3 (September):71–75.

Bellinger, David, Alan Leviton, Christine Waternaux, Herbert Needleman, and Michael Rabinowitz
1987   "Longitudinal analyses of prenatal and postnatal lead exposure and early cognitive development." *New England Journal of Medicine* 316, No. 17 (April 13):1037–1043.

Bendix, Reinhard
1956   *Work and Authority in Industry: Ideologies of Management in the Course of Industrialization.* New York: Harper and Brothers.

Berger, Peter L., and Thomas Luckmann
1966   *The Social Construction of Reality: A Treatise in the Sociology of Knowledge.* Garden City, N.Y.: Doubleday.

Berger, Suzanne, and Michael J. Piore
1980   *Dualism and Discontinuity in Industrial Societies.* Cambridge: Cambridge University Press.

Bergsma, Daniel (editor)
1974   *Ethical, Social, and Legal Dimensions of Screening for Human Genetic Disease.* New York: Stratton Intercontinental Medical Book Corporation.

Berlin, A., Ralph E. Yodaiken, and B. A. Herman
1984   *Assessment of Toxic Agents at the Workplace: Roles of Ambient and Biological Monitoring* (Conference held in Luxembourg in 1982). Boston: Martinus Nijhoff.

Berman, Daniel M.
1978   *Death on the Job: Occupational Health and Safety Struggles in the United States.* New York: Monthly Review Press.

Bertin, Joan E.
1983   "Workplace bias takes the form of 'fetal protectionism.' " *Legal Times* (August 1):18–20.
1986   "Reproduction, women, and the workplace: Legal issues." In Zena A. Stein and Maureen C. Hatch (editors), *Reproductive Problems in the Workplace, Occupational Medicine: State of the Art Reviews.* Philadelphia: Hanley and Belfus.

References

Beutler, Ernest
  1984   "Sensitivity to drug-induced hemolytic anemia in glucose-6-phosphate dehydrogenase deficiency." In Gilbert S. Omenn and Harry V. Gelboin (editors), *Genetic Variability in Responses to Chemical Exposure, Banbury Report 16*. Cold Spring Harbor, N.Y.: Cold Spring Harbor Laboratory.

Billauer, Barbara Pfeffer
  1985   "The legal liability of the occupational health professional." *Journal of Occupational Medicine* 27, No. 3 (March): 185–188.

Bingham, Eula
  1980a "Occupational safety and health standards." In John M. Last (editor), *Public Health and Preventive Medicine*, 11th ed. New York: Appleton-Century-Crofts.
  1980b "OSHA wants no genetic screening." Letter to the Editor, *New York Times* (March 22).

Birnbaum, Jeffrey H.
  1984   "Congressional study finds corporations paid only 6.2% of U.S. taxes in 1983." *Wall Street Journal* (December 3).

Bishop, Jerry E.
  1984   "Predictive probes: Scientists are focusing on genes predisposing people to illnesses." *Wall Street Journal* (September 12).

Blakeslee, Sandra
  1991   "Research on birth defects turns to flaws in sperm." *New York Times* (January 1).

Blank, Robert H.
  1981   *The Political Implications of Human Genetic Technology*. Boulder, Colo.: Westview Press.

Bloom, Arthur D. (editor)
  1981   *Guidelines for Studies of Human Populations Exposed to Mutagenic and Reproductive Hazards*. White Plains, N.Y.: March of Dimes Birth Defects Foundation.

Bock, Kenneth
  1980   *Human Nature and History: A Response to Sociobiology*. New York: Columbia University Press.

Boden, Leslie I.
  1986   "Impact of workplace characteristics on costs and benefits of medical screening." *Journal of Occupational Medicine* 28, No. 8 (August):751–756.

References

Bompey, Stuart H.
    1986   "Drugs in the workplace: From the batter's box to the boardroom." *Journal of Occupational Medicine* 28, No. 9 (September):825–832.
Bond, Gregory G., Ralph R. Cook, Peter C. Wight, and George H. Flores
    1983   "A case-control study of brain tumor mortality at a Texas chemical plant." *Journal of Occupational Medicine* 25, No. 5 (May):377–386.
Bosk, Charles L.
    1979   *Forgive and Remember: Managing Medical Failure.* Chicago: University of Chicago Press.
Bouchard, Thomas J., David T. Lykken, Matthew McGue, Nancy L. Segal, and Auke Tellegen
    1990   "Sources of human psychological differences: The Minnesota study of twins reared apart." *Science* 250, No. 4978 (October 12):223–228.
Bowman, James E.
    1977   "Genetic screening programs and public policy." *Phylon* 38:117–142.
    1978   "Social, legal, and economic issues in sickle cell programs." In John J. Buckley, Jr. (editor), *Genetics Now: Ethical Issues in Genetic Research.* Washington, D.C.: University Press of America.
Boxer, Peter A.
    1985   "Occupational mass psychogenic illness." *Journal of Occupational Medicine* 27, No. 12 (December):867–872.
Bradshaw, Thorton, and David Vogel (editors)
    1981   *Corporations and Their Critics: Issues and Answers on the Problems of Corporate Social Responsibilities.* New York: McGraw-Hill.
Brandt-Rauf, Paul W.
    1988   "New markers for monitoring occupational cancer: The example of oncogene proteins." *Journal of Occupational Medicine* 30, No. 5 (May):399–404.
Breiger, Heinrich
    1963   "Genetic bases of susceptibility and resistance to toxic agents." *Journal of Occupational Medicine* 5, No. 11 (November):511–515.
Bridbord, K., P. Decoufle, J. F. Fraumeni, Jr., D. G. Hoel, R. N.

References

Hoover, D. P. Rall, U. Saffioti, M. A. Schneiderman, and A. C. Upton

1978   Estimates of the Fraction of Cancer in the United States Related to Occupational Factors. National Cancer Institute, National Institute of Environmental Health Sciences, and National Institute for Occupational Safety and Health (September 15). [Appears in Peto and Schneiderman, 1981.]

Bridges, Bryn A., Byron E. Butterworth, and I. Bernard Weinstein (editors)

1982   *Indicators of Genotoxic Exposure, Banbury Report 13.* Cold Spring Harbor, N.Y.: Cold Spring Harbor Laboratory.

Bristow, Lonnie

1974   "The myth of sickle cell trait." *Western Journal of Medicine* 121 (July):77–82.

Brodeur, Paul

1985   *Outrageous Misconduct: The Asbestos Industry on Trial.* New York: Pantheon Books.

1989   "Annals of radiation: The hazards of electromagnetic fields III – Video-display terminals." *The New Yorker* (June 26):39–68.

Brodine, C. E., and D. E. Uddin

1977   "Medical aspects of sickle hemoglobin in military personnel." *Journal of the National Medical Association* 69, No. 1:29–32.

Bronson, Gail

1977   "Confrontation of DuPont, health agency is sparked by employees' cancer worries." *Wall Street Journal* (February 11).

1978   "Industry focuses on hypersusceptible workers prone to allergies, other maladies caused on the job." *Wall Street Journal* (March 23).

1979a   "Allied Chemical compensates five women laid off to protect childbearing ability." *Wall Street Journal* (January 5).

1979b   "Bitter reaction: Issue of fetal damage stirs women workers at chemical plants." *Wall Street Journal* (February 9).

Brown, Charles

1980   "Equalizing differences in the labor market." *Quarterly Journal of Economics* 94 (February):113–134.

References

Brown, Michael S.
  1984   "Setting occupational health standards: The vinyl chloride
          case." In Dorothy Nelkin (editor), *Controversy: Politics of
          Technical Decisions*, 2nd ed. Beverly Hills, Calif.: Sage.
  1985   "Disputed knowledge: Worker access to hazard informa-
          tion." In Dorothy Nelkin (editor), *The Language of Risk:
          Conflicting Perspectives on Occupational Health*. Beverly
          Hills, Calif.: Sage.
Bureau of the Census, U.S. Department of Commerce
  1954   *United States Census of Population: 1950: Occupation by Indus-
          try*, Subject Reports, Volume IV Part 1, Chapter C. Wash-
          ington, D.C.: U.S. Government Printing Office.
  1963   *United States Census of Population: 1960: Occupation by Indus-
          try*, Subjects Reports, Volume II 7C. Washington, D.C.:
          U.S. Government Printing Office.
  1967   *United States Census of Population: 1960: Industrial Charac-
          teristics*, Subject Reports, Volume II 7F. Washington, D.C.:
          U.S. Government Printing Office.
  1972   *1970 Census of Population: Occupation by Industry*, Subject
          Reports, Volume II 7C. Washington, D.C.: U.S. Govern-
          ment Printing Office.
  1983   *Statistical Abstract of the United States: 1984*, 104th ed. Wash-
          ington, D.C.: U.S. Government Printing Office.
  1984   *1980 Census of Population: Occupation by Industry*, Subject
          Reports, Volume II 7C. Washington, D.C.: U.S. Govern-
          ment Printing Office.
  1988   *Fertility of American Women: June 1987.* Current Population
          Reports, Population Characteristics Series P-20, No. 427.
          Washington, D.C.: U.S. Government Printing Office.
  1990   *Statistical Abstract of the United States: 1990*, 110th ed. Wash-
          ington, D.C.: U.S. Government Printing Office.
Bureau of Labor Statistics, U.S. Department of Labor
  1972   *Directory of National Unions and Employee Associations: 1971*,
          Bulletin 1750. Washington, D.C.: U.S. Government Print-
          ing Office.
  1985   *Handbook of Labor Statistics*, Bulletin 2217 (June).
  1990   "BLS reports on survey of occupational injuries and ill-
          nesses in 1988." *News*. USDL 90-582. Washington, D.C.:
          U.S. Government Printing Office (November 14).
  1991   *Employment and Earnings*, Volume 38, Number 1 (January).

References

Bureau of National Affairs, Inc.
  1979   Statements of Secretary Marshall, AFL-CIO Industrial
          Union Department, and Steelworkers on National Work-
          ers' Compensation Standards Act. Washington, D.C.
          (April 3).
  1981   "Conference urges more research on job risks faced by
          minorities." *Daily Labor Report*, Current Developments
          Section, Number 136 (July 16):A1–A3.
  1982   *Directory of U.S. Labor Organizations: 1982–1983 Edition*,
          Bulletin 2175 (December), edited by Courtney D. Gifford.
          Washington, D.C.
  1983   *Basic Patterns in Union Contracts*, 10th ed. Washington,
          D.C.
  1984a   *Chemical Right to Know Requirements: Federal and State Laws
          and Regulations, A Status Report*. Washington, D.C.
  1984b   *Directory of U.S. Labor Organizations: 1984–1985 Edition*,
          edited by Courtney D. Gifford. Washington, D.C.
  1987   *Basic Patterns in Union Contracts*, 11th ed. Washington,
          D.C.
Burrough, Bryan, and Seth H. Lubove
  1986   "Credibility gap: Some concerns fudge their safety re-
          cords to cut insurance costs." *Wall Street Journal* (De-
          cember 2):1 and 33.
Byrne, Dennis M., and Randall H. King
  1986   "Wildcat strikes in U.S. manufacturing, 1960–1977."
          Journal of Labor Research 7, No. 2 (Fall):387–402.
Cain, Carol
  1986   "Employer groups oppose hazardous substance bills."
          Business Insurance 20 (May 26):2 and 86.
Calabrese, Edward J.
  1978   *Pollutants and High Risk Groups: The Biological Basis of En-
          hanced Susceptibility to Environmental and Occupational Pol-
          lutants*. New York: John Wiley and Sons.
  1979   "Pollutants and high risk groups." *Environmental Health
          Perspectives* 29 (April):1–176.
  1984   *Ecogenetics: Genetic Variation in Susceptibility to Environ-
          mental Agents*. New York: John Wiley and Sons.
  1986   "Ecogenetics: Historical foundation and current status."
          Journal of Occupational Medicine 28, No. 10 (October):
          1096–1102.

References

Calavita, Kitty
  1983 "The demise of the Occupational Safety and Health Administration: A case study in symbolic action." *Social Problems* 30, No. 4 (April):437–448.
Caplan, Arthur L.
  1978 *The Sociobiology Debate: Readings on the Ethical and Scientific Issues Concerning Sociobiology.* New York: Harper & Row.
Carey, John, with Joan O'C. Hamilton, Laura Jereski, and Emily T. Smith
  1990 "The genetic age." *Business Week* No. 3161 (May 28):68–83.
Carrano, Anthony V.
  1982 "Sister chromatid exchange as an indicator of human exposure." In Bryn A. Bridges, Byron E. Butterworth, and I. Bernard Weinstein (editors), *Indicators of Genotoxic Exposure, Banbury Report 13.* Cold Spring Harbor, N.Y.: Cold Spring Harbor Laboratory.
  1986 "Chromosomal alterations as markers of exposure and effect." *Journal of Occupational Medicine* 28, No. 10 (October):1112–1116.
Carrano, Anthony V., and A. T. Natarajan
  1988 "Considerations for population monitoring using cytogenetic techniques." *Mutation Research* 204, No. 3 (March): 379–406.
Chase, Allan
  1977 *The Legacy of Malthus.* New York: Alfred A. Knopf.
Chavkin, Wendy (editor)
  1984 *Double Exposure: Women's Health Hazards on the Job and at Home.* New York: Monthly Review Press.
Chemical Week
  1982 "A test for cancer prone people." (August 18):23.
Chess, Caron
  1986 "Looking behind the factory gates." *Technology Review* (August/September):42–53.
Coalition for Reproductive Rights of Workers (CRROW)
  1980 *Reproductive Hazards in the Workplace: A Resource Guide.* Washington, D.C.: CRROW.
Collins, H. M.
  1981 "Knowledge and controversy: Studies of modern natural science – (Special issue)." *Social Studies of Science* 11, No. 1 (February):1–158.

References

Cooper, W. Clark
  1973   "Indicators of susceptibility to industrial chemicals." *Journal of Occupational Medicine* 15, No. 4 (April):355–359.
Corey, Paul N., Mary Jane Ashley, and Moira Chan-Yeung
  1979   "Racial differences in lung function: Search for proportional relationships." *Journal of Occupational Medicine* 21, No. 6 (June):395–398.
Council on Environmental Quality
  1981   *Chemical Hazards to Human Reproduction.* Prepared by Clement Associates, Inc. Washington, D.C.: U.S. Government Printing Office.
Culliton, Barbara J.
  1983   "Academe and industry debate partnership." *Science* 219 (January 14):150–151.
Currie, Elliott
  1985   *Confronting Crime: An American Challenge.* New York: Pantheon.
Dabney, Betty
  1981   "The role of human genetic monitoring in the workplace." *Journal of Occupational Medicine* 23, No. 9 (September):626–631.
Daniels, Cynthia, Maureen Paul, and Robert Rosofsky
  1988   *Family, Work, and Health.* Boston: Commonwealth of Massachusetts.
Daniels, Norman
  1985   *Just Health Care.* New York: Cambridge University Press.
Davidson, Joe
  1985   "U.S. study cites 'distressing disparity' in health conditions for blacks, whites." *Wall Street Journal* (October 15).
Davis, Devra Lee, Kenneth Bridbord, and Marvin Schneiderman
  1981   "Estimating cancer causes: Problems in methodology, production, and trends." In Richard Peto and Marvin Schneiderman (editors), *Quantification of Occupational Cancer, Banbury Report 9.* Cold Spring Harbor, N.Y.: Cold Spring Harbor Laboratory.
  1983   "Cancer prevention: Assessing causes, exposures, and recent trends in mortality for U.S. males, 1968–1978." *International Journal of Health Services* 13, No. 3:337–367.

References

Davis, Morris E.
    1977   "Occupational hazards and black workers." *Urban Health*
            6, No. 5 (August):16–18.
    1980   "The impact of workplace health and safety on black
            workers: Assessment and prognosis." *Labor Law Journal*
            31, No. 12 (December):723–732.
Davis, Morris E., and Andrew S. Rowland
    1980   *Occupational Disease among Black Workers: An Annotated
            Bibliography.* Berkeley: University of California, Labor Oc-
            cupational Health Program.
    1983   "Problems faced by minority workers." In Barry S. Levy
            and David H. Wegman (editors), *Occupational Health: Rec-
            ognizing and Preventing Work-Related Disease.* Boston: Lit-
            tle, Brown.
Dawkins, Richard
    1976   *The Selfish Gene.* New York: Oxford University Press.
Dietz, Thomas, and Robert W. Rycroft
    1987   *The Risk Professionals.* New York: Russell Sage Foundation.
Doll, Richard
    1981   "Relevance of epidemiology to policies for the preven-
            tion of cancer." *Journal of Occupational Medicine* 23, No. 9
            (September):601–609.
Doll, Richard, and Richard Peto
    1981   "The causes of cancer: Quantitative estimates of avoida-
            ble risks of cancer in the United States today." *Journal of
            the National Cancer Institute* 66:1191–1308.
Domhoff, G. William
    1978   *The Powers That Be.* New York: Random House.
Donovan, Jenny L.
    1984   "Ethnicity and health: A research review." *Social Science
            and Medicine* 19, No. 7:663–670.
Douglas, Mary, and Aaron Wildavsky
    1982   *Risk and Culture: An Essay on the Selection of Technological
            and Environmental Dangers.* Berkeley: University of Cal-
            ifornia Press.
Draper, Elaine
    1984a   "Risk by choice? Knowledge and power in the hazardous
            workplace." *Contemporary Sociology* 13, No. 6 (Novem-
            ber):688–691.
    1984b   "Toxic chemicals and women workers: Exclusionary
            policies in industry." Paper presented at the Annual

Meeting of the American Sociological Association, San Antonio, Texas (August 27).

1986   "High-risk workers or high-risk work? Genetic susceptibility policies in the hazardous workplace." *International Journal of Sociology and Social Policy* 6, No. 4 (Fall):12–28.

1987   "Labor–management conflict over workers at risk." Paper presented at the Annual Meeting of the American Sociological Association, Chicago (August 19).

1991   "Fetal exclusion policies and gendered constructions of suitable work." Paper presented at the Annual Meeting of the American Sociological Association, Cincinnati, (August 25).

Duerksen, Christopher J.

1982   *Dow vs. California: A Turning Point in the Envirobusiness Struggle.* Washington, D.C.: The Conservation Foundation.

Duster, Troy

1990   *Back Door to Eugenics.* New York: Routledge, Chapman, and Hall.

Duster, Troy, and Karen Garrett (editors)

1984   *Cultural Perspectives on Biological Knowledge.* Norwood, N.J.: Ablex.

Edelstein, Stuart J.

1986   *The Sickled Cell: From Myths to Molecules.* Cambridge, Mass.: Harvard University Press.

Edwards, Richard

1979   *Contested Terrain: The Transformation of the Workplace in the Twentieth Century.* New York: Basic Books.

Edwards, Richard C., David M. Gordon, and Michael Reich (editors)

1975   *Labor Market Segmentation.* Lexington, Mass.: D. C. Heath.

Emerson, Robert M. (editor)

1983   *Contemporary Field Research: A Collection of Readings.* Boston: Little, Brown.

Englehardt, Tristan H., and Arthur L. Kaplan (editors)

1987   *Scientific Controversies: Case Studies in the Resolution and Closure of Disputes in Science and Technology.* New York: Cambridge University Press.

Environmental Health Perspectives

1987a   The Role of Biomarkers in Reproductive and Developmental Toxicology – Special Issue (Conference held in Washington, D.C., January 12–13, 1987). Vol. 74 (October):1–199.

1987b The Environment and Human Health: Achievement and New Directions – Special Issue (Conference held in Research Triangle Park, North Carolina, December 3–6, 1986). Vol. 75 (November):1–150.

Epstein, Samuel S.
1979 *The Politics of Cancer.* New York: Anchor Books.
1980 "2,4,5-T and the Dow track record." Statement on Behalf of the Interfaith Center on Corporate Responsibility, Press Release (May 9).

Epstein, Samuel S., and Joel B. Swartz
1981 "Fallacies of lifestyle cancer theories." *Nature* 289, No. 5794 (January 15):127–130.

Equal Employment Opportunity Commission, Department of Labor
1980 "Interpretive guidelines on employment discrimination and reproductive hazards" [later withdrawn], 45 *Federal Register* (February 1):7514–7517.

Etzioni, Amitai
1973 *Genetic Fix: The Next Technological Revolution.* New York: Harper & Row.

Europe, J.
1973 "Sickle cell trait: An important barrier to employment." In Legislative and Socio-Economic Aspects of Sickle Cell Disease. Proceedings of Symposia sponsored by the Comprehensive Sickle Cell Center, Harlem Hospital–Columbia University (January 12–February 23).

Evans, H. John
1988 "Mutation cytogenetics: Past, present, and future." *Mutation Research* 204, No. 3 (March):355–365.

Eysenck, Hans
1971 *Race, Intelligence, and Education.* London: Temple Smith.
1973 *The Inequality of Man.* London: Temple Smith.

Fabricant, Jill D., and Marvin S. Legator
1981 "Etiology, role, and detection of chromosomal aberrations in man." *Journal of Occupational Medicine* 23, No. 9 (September):617–625.

Farley, Reynolds, and Walter R. Allen
1987 *The Color Line and the Quality of Life in America.* New York: Russell Sage Foundation.

References

Ferber, Kelvin H., William J. Hill, and Donald A. Cobb
1976 "An assessment of the effect of improved working conditions on bladder tumor incidence in a benzidine manufacturing facility." *American Industrial Hygiene Association Journal* 37, No. 1 (January):61–68.

Ferguson, Allen R., and E. Phillip LaVeen (editors)
1981 *The Benefits of Health and Safety Regulation*. Boston: Ballinger.

Field, Robert I., and Michael S. Baram
1986 "Screening and monitoring data as evidence in legal proceedings." *Journal of Occupational Medicine* 28, No. 10 (October):946–950.

Fischhoff, Baruch, Sarah Lichtenstein, Paul Slovic, Stephen L. Derby, and Ralph L. Keeney
1981 *Acceptable Risk*. Cambridge: Cambridge University Press.

Fleck, Ludwik
1979 *Genesis and Development of a Scientific Fact*. Chicago: University of Chicago Press.

Fletcher, Joseph F.
1980 "Knowledge, risk, and the right to reproduce: A limiting principle." In Aubrey Milunsky and George J. Annas (editors), *Genetics and the Law II*. New York: Plenum Press.

Fraumeni, Joseph F., Jr.
1975 *Persons at High Risk of Cancer: An Approach to Cancer Etiology and Control*. New York: Academic Press.

Freeman, Richard B.
1980 "The exit-voice tradeoff in the labor market: Unionism, job tenure, quits, and separations." *Quarterly Journal of Economics* 94, No. 4 (June):643–673.

Freidson, Eliot
1973 *The Profession of Medicine: A Study of the Sociology of Applied Knowledge*. New York: Dodd, Mead.
1986 *Professional Powers: A Study of the Institutionalization of Formal Knowledge*. Chicago: University of Chicago Press.

Fujimura, Joan
1988 "The molecular biological bandwagon in cancer research: Where social worlds meet." *Social Problems* 35, No. 3 (June):261–283.

General Accounting Office
1982 "Statement of facts regarding protection of the handicapped from employment discrimination." Report pre-

pared for the Subcommittee on Investigations and Oversight, Committee on Science and Technology, U.S. House of Representatives.

Gershon, Elliot, et al. (editors)
  1980 *Genetic Strategies in Psychobiology and Psychiatry.* Pacific Grove, Calif.: Boxwood Press.

Gersuny, Carl
  1981 *Work Hazards and Industrial Conflict.* Hanover, N.H.: University Press of New England.

Gilbert, G. Nigel, and Michael Mulkay
  1984 *Opening Pandora's Box: A Sociological Analysis of Scientists' Discourse.* New York: Cambridge University Press.

Glaser, Barney, and Anselm Strauss
  1967 *The Discovery of Grounded Theory: Strategies for Qualitative Research.* Chicago: Aldine.

Goerth, Charles R.
  1983a "Genetic screening and the law: Question waiting for an answer." *Occupational Health and Safety* (April):49–51.
  1983b "Medical removal protection." *Occupational Health and Safety* (February):29–31.

Goffman, Erving
  1963 *Stigma: Notes on the Management of Spoiled Identity.* Englewood Cliffs, N.J.: Prentice-Hall.

Goldsmith, Willis J.
  1987 "The expanding scope of employers' duties under the hazard communication standard and state and local right-to-know laws." *Employee Relations Law Journal* (Spring):705–711.

Gordon, David M., Richard Edwards, and Michael Reich
  1982 *Segmented Work, Divided Workers: The Historical Transformation of Labor in the United States.* New York: Cambridge University Press.

Gordon, Robert A.
  1987 "SES versus IQ in the race–IQ–delinquency model." *International Journal of Sociology and Social Policy* 7, No. 3:30–96.

Gould, Stephen Jay
  1981 *The Mismeasure of Man.* New York: W. W. Norton.

Green, Mark
  1983 "The gang that can't deregulate." *The New Republic* 188, No. 11 (March 21): 14–17.

References

Green, Mark, and Norman Waitzman
    1981 *Business War on the Law: An Analysis of the Benefits of Federal Health/Safety Enforcement.* Washington, D.C.: Corporate Accountability Research Group.

Greenhouse, Linda
    1991 "Court backs right of women to jobs with health risks." *New York Times* (March 21).

Greenwood, Ted
    1984 *Knowledge and Discretion in Government Regulation.* New York: Praeger.

Greer, William R.
    1985 "Value of one life? From $8.37 to $10 million." *New York Times* (June 26).

Guthier, William E.
    1986 "Medical screening and monitoring as noted by the insurance industry." *Journal of Occupational Medicine* 28, No. 8 (August):765–767.

Gutting, Gary (editor)
    1980 *Paradigms and Revolutions: Applications and Appraisals of Thomas Kuhn's Philosophy of Science.* Notre Dame, Ind.: University of Notre Dame Press.

Hadler, Nortin M.
    1986 "Criteria for screening workers for the establishment of disability." *Journal of Occupational Medicine* 28, No. 10 (October):940–945.

Hadley, Joseph E.
    1982 "The 'right-to-know' and the sensitive worker: Access to medical and exposure records and hazard identification." *Annals of the American Conference of Governmental Industrial Hygienists* 3 (September):165–172.

Hagar, Philip
    1990 "State high court rejects job bias to protect women." *Los Angeles Times* (May 18):1 and 34.

Haldane, J. B. S.
    1938 *Heredity and Politics.* London: George Allen and Unwin.

Halperin, William E., Jennifer Ratcliffe, Todd M. Frazier, Lawrence Wilson, Scott P. Becker, and Paul A. Schulte
    1986 "Medical screening in the workplace: Proposed principles." *Journal of Occupational Medicine* 28, No. 8 (August):547–552.

Handler, Philip
   1979   "Some comments on risk assessment." In National Research Council Current Issues and Studies, Annual Report. Washington, D.C.: National Academy of Sciences.
Harris, Curtis C., John J. Mulvihill, Snorri J. Thorgeirsson, and John D. Minna
   1980   "Individual differences in cancer susceptibility." *Annals of Internal Medicine* 92, No. 6 (June):809–825.
Harris, Louis and Associates
   1980   *Risk in a Complex Society.* New York: Marsh and McLennan Companies.
Harris, Richard F.
   1983   "A hard look: Your genes someday may decide where you work." *San Francisco Examiner* (December 7):1 and 12.
Harrison, Bennett, and Andrew Sum
   1979   "The theory of 'dual' or segmented labor markets." *Journal of Economic Issues* 13, No. 3 (September):687–706.
Harsanyi, Zsolt, and Richard Hutton
   1981   *Genetic Prophecy: Beyond the Double Helix.* New York: Bantam Books.
Hartford Courant
   1980   "Factory genes that fit." Editorial (February 16).
Hathaway, James A.
   1978   "Women in the workplace." Testimony before the National Advisory Committee on Occupational Safety and Health, Washington, D.C. (May 2).
Heimer, Carol A.
   1985   *Reactive Risk and Rational Action: Managing Moral Hazard in Insurance Contracts.* Berkeley: University of California Press.
Herrnstein, Richard J.
   1971   "IQ." *The Atlantic* (September):63–64.
Hillman, Carol B.
   1981   "An industrial view." *New York Times* (June 26).
Hinds, Richard deC., and Robert D. Moran
   1983   *OSHA: Toxic Substances in the Workplace.* Washington, D.C.: Practising Law Institute.
Hocking, B.
   1987   "Anthropologic aspects of occupational illness epi-

demics." *Journal of Occupational Medicine* 29, No. 6 (June):526–530.

Holden, Constance
1981 "Air force challenged on sickle trait policy." *Science* 211, No. 4479 (January 16):257.
1982 "Looking at genes in the workplace." *Science* 217, No. 4557 (July 23):336–337.

Holtzman, Neil A.
1989 *Proceed with Caution: Predicting Genetic Risks in the Recombinant DNA Era.* Baltimore: Johns Hopkins University Press.

Howard, Linda G.
1981 "Hazardous substances in the workplace: Implications for the employment rights of women." *University of Pennsylvania Law Review* 129, No. 4 (April):798–855.

Hricko, Andrea (with Melanie Brunt)
1976 *Working for Your Life: A Woman's Guide to Job Health Hazards.* Berkeley: University of California Labor Occupational Health Program; and Washington, D.C.: Public Citizen's Health Research Group.

Huber, Peter W.
1988 *Liability: The Legal Revolution and Its Consequences.* New York: Basic Books.

Hubbard, Ruth
1982a "The fetus as patient." *Ms.* (October):28–32.
1982b "Some legal and policy implications of recent advances in prenatal diagnosis and fetal therapy." *Women's Rights Law Reporter* 7, No. 3 (Spring):201–227.
1986 "Eugenics and prenatal testing." *International Journal of Health Services* 16, No. 2:227–242.

Hubbard, Ruth, and Mary Sue Henefin
1985 "Genetic screening of prospective parents and of workers: Some scientific and social issues." *International Journal of Health Services* 15, No. 2:231–251.

Hunt, Morton
1986 "The total gene screen." *New York Times Magazine* (January 19):33–38+.

Hunt, Vilma R.
1982 "The reproductive system: Sensitivity through the life cycle." *Annals of the American Conference of Governmental Industrial Hygienists* 3 (September):53–59.

References

International Symposium of Biochemical and Cellular Indices of Human Toxicity in Occupational and Environmental Medicine.
    1986   Proceedings. Conference held in Milan, Italy (May 19–22).

Itaya, Sharon S.
    1982   "A unionist's view of the sensitive worker." *Annals of the American Conference of Governmental Industrial Hygienists* 3 (September):111–112.

Jackall, Robert
    1988   *Moral Mazes: The World of Corporate Managers*. New York: Oxford University Press.

Jacobs, Philip, and Alan Chovil
    1983   "Economic evaluation of corporate medical programs." *Journal of Occupational Medicine* 25, No. 4 (April):273–278.

Jacoby, Sanford M.
    1985   *Employing Bureaucracy: Managers, Unions, and the Transformation of Work in American Industry, 1900–1945*. New York: Columbia University Press.

Jefferson, E. G.
    1980   "DuPont and sickle-cell tests." *Washington Post*, Letter to the Editor (March 16).

Jencks, Christopher
    1987   "Genes and crime." *New York Review of Books* (February 12):33–41.

Jennings, Robert L., Jr.
    1982   "Medical removal protection and the sensitive worker." *Annals of the American Conference of Governmental Industrial Hygienists* 3 (September):147–150.

Jensen, Arthur R.
    1969   "How much can we boost IQ and scholastic achievement?" *Harvard Educational Review* 39:1–123.
    1977   "Race and the genetics of intelligence: A reply to Lewontin." In Adela S. Baer (editor), *Heredity and Society: Readings in Social Genetics*, 2nd ed. New York: Macmillan.

Jensen, Wallace N.
    1962   "Hereditary and chemically induced anemia." *Archives of Environmental Health* 5, No. 2 (August):212–216.

Jones, James H.
    1981   *Bad Blood: The Tuskegee Syphilis Experiment*. New York: Free Press.

References

Jones, Stephen R., Richard A. Binder, and Everett M. Donowho, Jr.
1970 "Sudden death in sickle cell trait." *New England Journal of Medicine* 282, No. 6 (February 5):323–325.

Journal of Occupational Medicine
1978 "Medical groups protest OSHA proposal regarding access to medical records: Statements of AOMA, AAOM, and AMA." Vol. 20, No. 11 (November):769–772.
1986 Medical Screening and Biological Monitoring for the Effects of Exposure in the Workplace (Conference held in Cincinnati July 10–13, 1984). Vol. 28, Nos. 8 and 10 (August and October).

Judkins, Bennett M.
1986 *We Offer Ourselves as Evidence: Toward Workers' Control of Occupational Health.* New York: Greenwood Press.

Kanter, Rosabeth Moss
1977 *Men and Women of the Corporation.* New York: Basic Books.

Kark, John A., David M. Posey, Harold R. Schumacher, and Charles J. Ruehle
1987 "Sickle cell trait as a risk factor for sudden death in physical training." *New England Journal of Medicine* 317, No. 13 (September 24):781–787.

Karrh, Bruce W.
1979 The confidentiality of occupational medical data." *Journal of Occupational Medicine* 21, No. 3 (March):157–160.

Kaye, Harold L.
1986 *The Social Meaning of Modern Biology.* New Haven, Conn.: Yale University Press.

Kazis, Richard, and Richard L. Grossman
1982 *Fear at Work: Job Blackmail, Labor, and the Environment.* New York: Pilgrim Press.

Keck, John S.
1973–1974 "Sickle cell legislation: Beneficence or 'The new ghetto hustle'?" *Journal of Family Law* 13, No. 2:278–311.

Keller, Evelyn Fox
1984 *Reflections on Gender and Science.* New Haven, Conn.: Yale University Press.

Kelly, Ambrose B.
1986 "Loss control and its place in the insurance industry." *Journal of Occupational Medicine* 28, No. 8 (August):768–771.

Kelman, Steven
1980 *Regulating America, Regulating Sweden: A Comparative Study*

of Occupational Safety and Health Policy. Cambridge, Mass.: MIT Press.

Kessler-Harris, Alice
1982 *Out to Work: A History of Wage-Earning Women in the United States.* New York: Oxford University Press.

Kety, Seymour S.
1976 "Genetic aspects of schizophrenia." *Psychiatric Annals* 6:6–15.

Kevles, Daniel J.
1985 *In the Name of Eugenics: Genetics and the Uses of Human Heredity.* New York: Alfred A. Knopf.

Khoury, Muin J., Carol A. Newill, and Gary A. Chase
1985 "Epidemiological evaluation of screening for risk factors: Application to genetic screening." *American Journal of Public Health* 75, No. 10 (October):1204–1208.

Kilborn, Peter T.
1991 "Employers left with many decisions." *New York Times* (March 21).
1990 "Who decides who works at jobs imperiling fetuses?" *New York Times* (September 2).

Kilian, D. J., D. J. Picciano, and C. B. Jacobson
1975 "Industrial monitoring: A cytogenetic approach." *Annals of the New York Academy of Sciences* 269 (December 31):4–11.

King, Mary-Claire
1984 "Genetic and epidemiologic approaches to detecting genetic susceptibility to chemical exposures." In Gilbert S. Omenn and Harry V. Gelboin (editors), *Genetic Variability in Responses to Chemical Exposure, Banbury Report 16.* Cold Spring Harbor, N.Y.: Cold Spring Harbor Laboratory.

King, Mary-Claire, Geraldine M. Lee, Nancy B. Spinner, Glenys Thomson, and Margaret R. Wrensch
1984 "Genetic epidemiology." *Annual Review of Public Health* 5:1–52.

Knorr-Cetina, Karin D., and Michael Mulkay (editors)
1983 *Science Observed: Perspectives on the Social Study of Science.* Beverly Hills, Calif.: Sage.

Knudson, A. G., Jr.
1977 "Genetic predisposition to cancer." In H. Hiatt et al. (edi-

tors), *Origins of Cancer.* Cold Spring Harbor, N.Y.: Cold
Spring Harbor Laboratory.

Kolata, Gina

1986 "Genetic screening raises questions for employers and in-
surers." *Science* 232, No. 4748 (April 18):317–319.

1989 "Scientists pinpoint genetic changes that predict cancer."
New York Times (May 16).

Kotelchuck, David, Robert Forer, Joan Drake, and Jacqueline Pope

1978 "Occupational injuries and illness among black workers."
Health PAC Bulletin Nos. 81–82 (April):33–34.

Kotin, Paul

1977 "Hypersusceptibility: Role in worker selection." Paper
Presented to the Joint Conference on Occupational
Health, Sponsored by American Academy of Occupa-
tional Medicine (October 7).

Kouri, Richard E., Arthur S. Levine, Brenda K. Edwards, Theodore
L. McLemore, Elliot S. Vesell, and Daniel W. Nebert

1984 "Sources of interindividual variations in aryl hydrocarbon
hydroxylase in mitogen-activated human lymphocytes."
In Gilbert S. Omenn and Harry V. Gelboin (editors), *Ge-
netic Variability in Responses to Chemical Exposure, Banbury
Report 16.* Cold Spring Harbor, N.Y.: Cold Spring Harbor
Laboratory.

Krekel, Silvia

1981 Statement Delivered at the NIOSH National Conference
on Occupational Health and Safety Issues Affecting Minority Workers (July).

Krieger, Linda J., and Patricia N. Cooney

1983 "The Miller-Wohl controversy: Equal treatment, positive action, and the meaning of women's equality." *Gold-
en Gate University Law Review* 13, No. 3 (Summer):513–
572.

Kuhn, Thomas S.

1970 *The Structure of Scientific Revolutions.* 2nd ed. Chicago: University of Chicago Press.

Kurzman, Dan

1987 *A Killing Wind: Inside Union Carbide and the Bhopal Catastrophe.* New York: McGraw-Hill.

Kutchins, A.

1981 "The most exclusive remedy is no remedy at all: Workers' compensation coverage for occupational diseases." *Labor Law Journal* 32, No. 4 (April):212–228.

Labor Occupational Health Program
  1980   *Workplace Health and Safety: A Guide to Collective Bargaining.* Berkeley: Institute of Industrial Relations, University of California, Berkeley.

Landrigan, Philip J.
  1982   "Letter to Mr. Justin F. Cooper, Vice President, Texaco Chemical Company." Cincinnati, Ohio: National Institute for Occupational Safety and Health, Division of Surveillance, Hazard Evaluations, and Field Studies (January 5).

Lappé, Marc
  1979   *Genetic Politics: The Limits of Biological Control.* New York: Simon and Schuster.
  1983   "Ethical issues in testing for differential sensitivity to occupational hazards." *Journal of Occupational Medicine* 25, No. 11 (November):797–808.
  1988   "Ethical issues in genetic screening for susceptibility to chronic lung disease." *Journal of Occupational Medicine* 30, No. 6 (June):493–501.

Lappé, Marc, James M. Gustafson, and Richard Robin (Genetics Research Group)
  1972   "Ethical and social issues in screening for genetic disease." *New England Journal of Medicine* 286, No. 21 (May 25):1129–1132.

Last, John (editor)
  1980   *Public Health and Preventive Medicine,* 11th ed. New York: Appleton-Century-Crofts.

Latour, Bruno, and Steve Woolgar
  1979   *Laboratory Life: The Social Construction of Scientific Facts.* Beverly Hills, Calif.: Sage.

Lavine, Mary P.
  1982   "Industrial screening programs for workers: Ethical and policy problems." *Environment* 24, No. 5 (June):26–38.

Leach, L., S. E. Reiss, E. J. Kerfoot, and P. L. Lubs
  1981   "Occupational health survey: An evaluation of potential health hazards in the workplace." *American Industrial Hygiene Association Journal* 42, No. 2 (February):160–164.

Leary, Warren E.
  1991   "Hypertension among blacks tied to bias, poverty, and diet." *New York Times* (February 6).

References

LeClercq, Gary R.
  1983   "Workplace reproductive risk: Corporate responsibil-
          ities." *Annals of the American Conference of Governmental
          Industrial Hygienists* 4 (March): 49–53.
Legator, Marvin S.
  1981   "Statement by Dr. Marvin Legator, Director of the Divi-
          sion of Genetic Toxicology of the University of Texas
          Medical Branch (Galveston)." Delivered at the Dow
          Chemical Annual Meeting. Midland, Michigan (May 8).
  1982   "Approaches to worker safety: Recognizing the sensitive
          individual and genetic monitoring." *Annals of the Ameri-
          can Conference of Governmental Industrial Hygienists* 3 (Sep-
          tember):29–34.
  1987   "The successful experiment that failed." In Tristan H.
          Englehardt and Arthur L. Kaplan (editors), *Scientific Con-
          troversies: Case Studies in the Resolution and Closure of Dis-
          putes in Science and Technology.* New York: Cambridge Uni-
          versity Press.
Leigh, J. Paul
  1982   "Are unionized blue collar jobs more hazardous than
          nonunionized blue collar jobs?" *Journal of Labor Research*
          3, No. 3 (Summer):349–357.
Levine, Adeline Gordon
  1982   *Love Canal: Science, Politics, and People.* Lexington, Mass.:
          Lexington Books.
Levine, Richard J., Patricia B. Blunden, R. Daniel Dalcorso, Thomas B. Starr, and Charles E. Ross
  1983   "Superiority of reproductive histories to sperm counts in
          detecting infertility at a dibromochloropropane manufac-
          turing plant." *Journal of Occupational Medicine* 25, No. 8
          (August):591–597.
Levy, Barry S., and David H. Wegman
  1983   *Occupational Health: Recognizing and Preventing Work-
          Related Disease.* Boston: Little, Brown.
Lewin, Tamar
  1988a   "Companies ignore men's health risk." *New York Times*
          (December 16).
  1988b   "Protecting the baby: Work in pregnancy poses legal
          frontier." *New York Times* (August 2).
  1990   "Battery producer loses a bias case." *New York Times*
          (March 3):8.

References

Lewontin, Richard C., Steven Rose, and Leon J. Kamin
1984 *Not In Our Genes: Biology, Ideology, and Human Nature.* New York: Pantheon Books.

Lewy, Robert
1983 "Preemployment qualitative urine toxicology screening." *Journal of Occupational Medicine* 25, No. 8 (August):579–580.

Lieberson, Stanley
1980 *A Piece of the Pie: Black and White Immigrants since 1880.* Berkeley: University of California Press.

Litwin, S. D. (editor)
1978 *Genetic Determinants of a Pulmonary Disease.* New York: Marcel Dekker.

Lloyd, J. William
1970 "Long-term mortality study of steelworkers, IV, Mortality by work area." *Journal of Occupational Medicine* 12, No. 5 (May):151–157.
1971 "Long-term mortality study of steelworkers, V, Respiratory cancer in coke plant workers." *Journal of Occupational Medicine* 13, No. 2 (February):53–68.

Lofland, John, and Lynn Lofland
1984 *Analyzing Social Settings.* Belmont, Calif.: Wadsworth.

Lowry, Larry K.
1986 "Biological exposure index as a complement to the TLV." *Journal of Occupational Medicine* 28, No. 8 (August):578–582.

Lucas, Robert
1974 "The distribution of job characteristics." *Review of Economic Statistics* 56 (November):530–540.

Luker, Kristin
1984 *Abortion and the Politics of Motherhood.* Berkeley: University of California Press.

Lumsden, Charles J., and E. O. Wilson
1981 *Genes, Mind, and Culture: The Coevolutionary Process.* Cambridge, Mass.: Harvard University Press.

Lynn, Frances M.
1986 "The interplay of science and values in assessing and regulating environmental risks." *Science, Technology, and Human Values* 11, No. 2 (Spring):40–50.

MacCormack, Carol, and Marilyn Strathern (editors)
1980 *Nature, Culture, and Gender.* New York: Cambridge University Press.

References

The MacNeil–Lehrer Report
 1982 "Genetic screening." (July 20).
Mannheim, Karl
 1936 *Ideology and Utopia: An Introduction to the Sociology of Knowledge*. New York: Harcourt, Brace, and World.
 1952 *Essays on the Sociology of Knowledge*. London: Routledge and Kegan Paul.
Marsh, Frank H., and Janet Katz (editors)
 1985 *Biology, Crime, and Ethics: A Study of Biological Explanations for Criminal Behavior*. Cincinnati: Anderson.
Martin, Charles F., and James E. Higgins
 1976 "Byssinosis and other respiratory ailments: A survey of 6,631 cotton textile employees." *Journal of Occupational Medicine* 18, No. 7 (July):455–462.
Maugh, Thomas H. II
 1981 "A new understanding of sickle cell emerges." *Science* 211, No. 4479 (January 16):265–267.
Mazur, Allan, and Leon S. Robertson
 1972 *Biology and Social Behavior*. New York: Free Press.
Mazzocchi, Anthony
 1980 "Genetic confrontation in the workplace." Presented at the University of California, Berkeley (October 17).
McAuliffe, K.
 1987 "Predicting disease." *U.S. News and World Report* 120, No. 20 (May 25):64–69.
McCaffrey, David P.
 1982 *OSHA and the Politics of Health Regulation*. New York: Plenum Press.
McElveen, Junius C., Jr.
 1986 "Reproductive hazards in the workplace: Some legal considerations." *Journal of Occupational Medicine* 28, No. 2 (February):103–109.
McGarity, Thomas O., and Elinor P. Schroeder
 1981 "Risk-oriented employment screening." *Texas Law Review* 59, No. 6 (August):999–1076.
McGuffin, Petar, and Elizabeth Sturt
 1986 "Genetic markers in schizophrenia." *Human Heredity* 36, No. 1 (January-February):65–88.
McKusick, Victor A.
 1988 "The new genetics and clinical medicine: A summing up." *Hospital Practice* 23, No. 7 (July 15):177–191.

References

McLean, R. A., et al.
1978 "Compensating wage differentials for hazardous work: An empirical analysis." *Quarterly Review of Economics and Business* 18, No. 3:97–107.

McMichael, A. J., R. Spirtas, J. F. Gamble, and P. M. Tousey
1976 "Mortality among rubber workers: Relation to specific jobs." *Journal of Occupational Medicine* 18, No. 3 (March): 178–185.

Mednick, Sarnoff A., Patricia Brennan, and Elizabeth Kandel
1988 "Predisposition to violence." *Aggressive Behavior* 14, No. 1:25–33.

Mednick, Sarnoff A., W. F., Gabrelli, Jr., and B. Hutchins
1984 "Genetic influences in criminal convictions: Evidence from an adoption cohort." *Science* 224, No. 4651 (May 25):891–893.

Meier, Barry, and Ron Winslow
1984 "Struggling giant: Union Carbide faces a difficult challenge even without Bhopal." *Wall Street Journal* (December 27).

Meinhardt, Theodore
1981 "Cytogenetic studies of workers exposed to ethylene oxide." Cincinnati, Ohio: National Institute of Occupational Safety and Health, Division of Surveillance, Hazard Evaluations, and Field Studies, Industrywide Studies Branch.

Mendeloff, John
1979 *Regulating Safety: An Economic and Political Analysis of Occupational Safety and Health Policy.* Cambridge, Mass.: MIT Press.

Merton, Robert K.
1973 *The Sociology of Science: Theoretical and Empirical Investigations.* Chicago: University of Chicago Press.
1979 *The Sociology of Science: An Episodic Memoir.* Carbondale, Ill.: Southern Illinois University Press.

Messite, Jacqueline, and Marcus B. Bond
1980 "Reproductive toxicology and occupational exposure." In Carl Zenz (editor), *Developments in Occupational Medicine.* Chicago: Year Book Medical Publishers.

Milkman, Ruth
1987 *Gender at Work: The Dynamics of Job Segregation by Sex during World War II.* Urbana: University of Illinois Press.

References

Mill, John Stuart
  1965 *Principles of Political Economy*. In his *Collected Works*, Vol. 2. Toronto: University of Toronto Press [originally published in 1848].
Mills, C. Wright
  1959 *The Sociological Imagination*. London: Oxford University Press.
Milunsky, Aubrey, and George J. Annas (editors)
  1980 *Genetics and the Law II*. New York: Plenum Press.
Mintz, Benjamin W.
  1984 *OSHA: History, Law, and Policy*. Washington, D.C.: Bureau of National Affairs.
Montagu, Ashley (editor)
  1980 *Sociobiology Examined*. New York: Oxford University Press.
Muir, Calum S.
  1978 "International variation in high-risk populations." In Joseph F. Fraumeni, Jr. (editor), *Persons at High Risk of Cancer: An Approach to Cancer Etiology and Control*. New York: Academic Press.
Mulinare, Joseph, José F. Cordero, J. David Erickson, and Robert J. Berry
  1988 "Periconceptional use of multivitamins and the occurrence of neural tube defects." *Journal of the American Medical Association* 260, No. 21 (December 2):3141–3145.
Murray, Thomas H.
  1983 "Genetic screening in the workplace: Ethical issues." *Journal of Occupational Medicine* 25, No. 6 (June):451–454.
  1985 "Genetic testing at work: How should it be used?" *Technology Review* (May-June):51–59.
National Academy of Sciences
  1975 *Genetic Screening: Programs, Principles, and Research*. Washington, D.C.: National Academy of Sciences, National Research Council, Committee for the Study of Inborn Errors of Metabolism.
National Academy of Sciences, Institute of Medicine
  1980 Genetic Influences on Responses to the Environment: Conference Proceedings. Washington, D.C., July 10–11.
National Center for Health Statistics
  1984 *Health, United States, 1984*.

281

References

National Institute for Occupational Safety and Health (NIOSH)
  1982   *National Occupational Exposure Survey.* U.S. Department of Health, Education, and Welfare, Division of Surveillance, Hazard Evaluations, and Field Studies.
National Research Council (NRC), Committee on Environmental Mutagens
  1983   *Identifying and Estimating the Genetic Impact of Chemical Mutagens.* Washington, D.C.: National Academy Press.
Neal-Cooper, Florence, and Robert B. Scott
  1988   "Genetic counseling in sickle-cell anemia: Experiences with couples at risk." *Public Health Reports* 103, No. 2 (March-April):174–178.
Nelkin, Dorothy
  1987   *How the Press Covers Science and Technology.* New York: W. H. Freeman.
Nelkin, Dorothy (editor)
  1984   *Controversy: Politics of Technical Decisions.* 2nd ed. Beverly Hills, Calif.: Sage.
Nelkin, Dorothy, and Michael S. Brown
  1984   *Workers at Risk: Voices from the Workplace.* Chicago: The University of Chicago Press.
Nelkin, Dorothy, and Laurence Tancredi
  1989   *Dangerous Diagnostics: The Social Power of Biological Information.* New York: Basic Books.
New York Times
  1980a   "Air Force rejects cadets with sickle trait." (February 4).
  1980b   "Banning workers to protect them." Editorial (March 22).
  1980c   "Bill offered in Albany to outlaw gene tests" (February 5).
Nichols, Eve K.
  1988   *Human Gene Therapy.* Cambridge, Mass.: Harvard University Press.
Nugent, Angela
  1983   "Fit for work: The introduction of physical examinations in industry." *Bulletin of the History of Medicine* 57, No. 4 (Winter):578–595.
Occupational Safety and Health Administration, U.S. Department of Labor
  1978   Presentations and Discussion of the Views and Perceptions of Corporate and Union Representatives Regarding the Effects on the Employment of Women That Arise from Safety and Health Considerations.

National Advisory Committee on Occupational Safety and Health (Meeting Transcripts). Washington, D.C. (May 2).

1980a "Access to employee exposure and medical records standard" (initial standard). 45 *Federal Register* 35212–35303 (May 23).

1980b "Identification, classification, and regulation of potential occupational carcinogens." 45 *Federal Register* 5001 (January 22).

Office of Science and Technology Policy, Executive Office of the President

1985 "Chemical Carcinogens: A Review of the Science and Its Associated Principles." 50 *Federal Register*, No. 50.

Office of Technology Assessment, U.S. Congress

1983 *The Role of Genetic Testing in the Prevention of Occupational Disease.* Washington, D.C.: U.S. Government Printing Office.

1985 *Reproductive Health Hazards in the Workplace.* Washington, D.C.: U.S. Government Printing Office.

1990 *Genetics in the Workplace.* Washington, D.C.: U.S. Government Printing Office.

Omenn, Gilbert S.

1982 "Predictive identification of hypersusceptible individuals." *Journal of Occupational Medicine* 24, No. 5 (May): 369–374.

Omenn, Gilbert S., and Harry V. Gelboin (editors)

1984 *Genetic Variability in Responses to Chemical Exposure, Banbury Report 16.* Cold Spring Harbor, N.Y.: Cold Spring Harbor Laboratory.

Otten, Alan L.

1985 "Women's rights vs. fetal rights looms as thorny and divisive issue." *Wall Street Journal* (April 12).

1986 "Probing the cell: Genetic examination of workers is an issue of growing urgency." *Wall Street Journal* (February 24).

Palca, Joseph

1988 "National Research Council endorses genome project." *Nature* 331, No. 6156 (February 11):467.

Passell, Peter

1989a "Life's risks: Balancing fear against reality of statistics." *New York Times* (May 8).

1989b "Making a risky life bearable: Better data, clearer choices." *New York Times* (May 9).

Pell, Sidney, Maureen T. O'Berg, and Bruce W. Karrh
1978 "Cancer epidemiologic surveillance in the DuPont Company." *Journal of Occupational Medicine* 20, No. 11 (November):725–740.

Percy, Constance, Edward Stanek, and Lynn Gloeckler
1981 "Accuracy of cancer death statistics and its effect on cancer mortality statistics." *American Journal of Public Health* 71, No. 3 (March):242–250.

Perera, Frederica, Regina Santella, and Miriam Poirier
1986 "Biomonitoring of workers exposed to carcinogens: Immunoassays to benzo(a)pyrene-DNA adducts as a prototype." *Journal of Occupational Medicine* 28, No. 10 (October):1117–1123.

Perrolle, Judith A., and Michael Rustad
1984 "Industry response to reproductive hazards: A model protection policy for the chemical industry." Paper presented at the Annual Meeting of the American Sociological Association, San Antonio, Texas (August 31).

Perrow, Charles
1984 *Normal Accidents: Living with High-Risk Technologies.* New York: Basic Books.

Pertschuk, Michael
1982 *Revolt against Regulation: The Rise and Pause of the Consumer Movement.* Berkeley: University of California Press.

Peters, George A.
1984 "Chemical risks in the workplace must be minimized." *Legal Times* (September 10).

Peto, Richard
1980 "Distorting the epidemiology of cancer: The need for a more balanced overview." *Nature* 284, No. 5754 (March 27):297–300.

Peto, Richard, and Marvin Schneiderman (editors)
1981 *Quantification of Occupational Cancer, Banbury Report 9.* Cold Spring Harbor, N.Y.: Cold Spring Harbor Laboratory.

Philadelphia Inquirer
1982 "Genes and the working man" (July 3).

Picciano, Dante J., Ray E. Flake, Peter C. Gay, and D. Jack Kilian
1977 "Vinyl chloride cytogenetics." *Journal of Occupational*

References

Medicine 19, No. 8 (August):527–530.

Plumlee, Lawrence, Stanton Coerr, Herbert L. Needleman, and Roy Albert

1979 "Role of high risk groups in the derivation of environmental health standards: Panel discussion." *Environmental Health Perspectives* 29 (April):155–159.

Postol, Lawrence

1988 "Handicap discrimination considerations in treating the impaired worker: Drugs, alcohol, pregnancy, and AIDS in the workplace." *Journal of Occupational Medicine* 30, No. 4 (April):321–327.

Powledge, Tabitha M.

1974 "Genetic screening as a political and social development." In Daniel Bergsma (editor), *Ethical, Social, and Legal Dimensions of Screening for Human Genetic Disease.* Miami: Symposia Specialists.

1976 "Can genetic screening prevent occupational disease?" *The New Scientist* 71, No. 1016 (September 2):486–488.

President's Commission for the Study of Ethical Problems in Medicine and Biomedical and Behavioral Research

1982 *Splicing Life: The Social and Ethical Issues of Genetic Engineering with Human Beings.* Washington, D.C.: U.S. Government Printing Office.

1983a *Screening and Counseling for Genetic Conditions: The Ethical, Social, and Legal Implications of Genetic Screening, Counseling and Education Programs.* Washington, D.C.: Government Printing Office.

1983b *Summing Up: Final Report on Studies of the Ethical and Legal Problems in Medicine and Biomedical and Behavioral Research.* Washington D.C.: U.S. Government Printing Office.

Provost, Glendel J.

1982 "Legal trends in occupational health." *Journal of Occupational Medicine* 24, No. 2 (February):115–119.

Raines, Lisa J.

1986 "Biological testing and occupational disease liability." *Journal of Occupational Medicine* 28, No. 10 (October): 921–923.

Randall, Donna M.

1987 "Protecting the unborn." *Personnel Administrator* 32 (September):88–97.

Randall, Donna M., and James F. Short
  1983   "Women in toxic work environments: A case study of social problem development." *Social Problems* 30, No. 4 (April):411–424.

Rao, K. S., and B. A. Schwetz
  1981   "Protecting the unborn: Dow's experience." *Occupational Health and Safety* (March):53–61.

Rapp, Rayna
  1988   "Chromosomes and communication: The discourse of genetic counseling." *Medical Anthropology Quarterly* 2, No. 2 (June):143–157.

Reich, Michael
  1981   *Racial Inequality.* Princeton, N.J.: Princeton University Press.

Reilly, Philip
  1977   *Genetics, Law, and Social Policy.* Cambridge, Mass.: Harvard University Press.

Reinhardt, Charles
  1978   "Chemical hypersusceptibility." *Journal of Occupational Medicine* 20, No. 5 (May):319–322.

Reiser, Stanley Joel
  1978   "The emergence of the concept of screening for disease." *Milbank Memorial Fund Quarterly/Health and Society* 56, No. 4 (Fall):403–425.

Reskin, Barbara F. (editor)
  1984   *Sex Segregation in the Workplace: Trends, Explanations, Remedies.* Washington, D.C.: National Academy Press.

Ringen, Knut
  1980   "Health risks and equal opportunity: Commentary." *Hastings Center Report* 10, No. 6 (December):25–26.

Robin, Stanley S., and Gerald E. Markle
  1987   "Let no one split asunder: Controversy in human genetic engineering." *Politics and the Life Sciences* 6, No. 1 (August):3–15.

Robinson, James C.
  1984   "Racial inequality and the probability of occupation-related injury or illness." *Milbank Memorial Fund Quarterly/Health and Society* 62, No. 4:567–590.

  1986a   "Hazard pay in unsafe jobs: Theory, evidence, and policy implications." *Milbank Quarterly* 64, No. 4:650–677.

1986b   "Job hazards and job security." *Journal of Health Politics, Policy, and Law* 11, No. 1 (Spring):1–18.

1987a   "Trends in racial inequality and exposure to work-related hazards, 1968–1986." *Milbank Quarterly* 65, Supplement 2:404–420.

1987b   "Worker responses to workplace hazards." *Journal of Health Politics, Policy, and Law* 12, No. 4 (Winter):665–682.

1988a   "Hazardous occupations within the job hierarchy." *Industrial Relations* 27, No. 2 (Spring):241–250.

1988b   "The rising long-term trend in occupational injury rates." *American Journal of Public Health* 78, No. 3 (March):276–281.

Rockey, Paul H., Jane Fantel, and Gilbert S. Omenn
1979   "Discriminatory aspects of preemployment screening: Low-back X-ray examinations in the railroad industry." *American Journal of Law and Medicine* 5, No. 3 (Fall):197–214.

Rom, William N. (editor)
1983   *Environmental and Occupational Medicine.* Boston: Little, Brown.

Rosenberg, Michael J., Paul J. Feldblum, and Elizabeth G. Marshall
1987   "Occupational influences on reproduction: A review of recent literature." *Journal of Occupational Medicine* 29, No. 7 (July):584–591.

Rossi, Alice S.
1977   "A biosocial perspective on parenting." *Daedalus* 106, No. 2 (Spring):1–31.

1984   "Gender and parenthood." *American Sociological Review* 49, No. 1 (February):1–19.

Rossiter, Charles E., and Hans Weill
1974   "Ethnic differences in lung function: Evidence for proportional differences." *International Journal of Epidemiology* 3, No. 1 (March):55–61.

Rothfeder, Jeffrey
1989   "Is nothing private?" *Business Week* (September 4):74–82.

Rothstein, Mark A.
1983   "Employee selection based on susceptibility to occupational illness." *Michigan Law Review* 81, No. 6 (May):1379–1496.

1984   *Medical Screening of Workers.* Washington, D.C.: Bureau of National Affairs.

1986 "Discriminatory aspects of medical screening." *Journal of Occupational Medicine* 28, No. 10 (October):924–929.

1989 *Medical Screening and the Employee Health Cost Crisis.* Washington, D.C.: Bureau of National Affairs.

Rowe, David C.
1986 "Genetic and environmental components of antisocial behavior: A Study of 265 twin pairs." *Criminology* 24, No. 3 (August):513–532.

Rowland, Andrew
1980 "Black workers and cancer: Epidemic proportions." *Labor Occupational Health Program Monitor* 8, No. 1 (January-February):14–16.

Russoniello, Joseph P., and Dorothy Ehrlich
1986 "Mandatory drug tests: Are they fair and legal?" *Golden State Report* 2, No. 12 (December):24–28.

Ruttenberg, Ruth
1982 "Regulation is a boon for business." *Business and Society Review* 41 (Spring):53–57.

Ruttenberg, Ruth, and Randall Hudgins
1981 *Occupational Safety and Health in the Chemical Industry,* 2nd ed. New York: Council on Economic Priorities.

Ruttenberg, Ruth, and Marilyn Powers
1986 "Economics of notification and medical screening for high-risk workers." *Journal of Occupational Medicine* 28, No. 8 (August):757–764.

Ryan, William
1971 *Blaming the Victim.* New York: Random House.

San Francisco Chronicle
1985 "More cancer, murders among minorities." (October 17)

Sahlins, Marshall
1977 *The Use and Abuse of Biology: An Anthropological Critique of Sociobiology.* Ann Arbor: University of Michigan Press.

Salmans, Sandra
1981 "Cotton industry upset by ruling." *New York Times* (June 18).

Salter, Liora
1988 *Mandated Science: Science and Scientists in the Making of Standards.* Boston: Klewer Academic Publishers.

Samuels, Sheldon W.
1983 "Genetic testing of workers." A Technical Report to the Executive Council of the AFL-CIO Industrial Union Department (June 22).

References

1986   "Medical surveillance: Biological, social, and ethical parameters." *Journal of Occupational Medicine* 28, No. 8 (August):572–577.

Savage, David D.
1990   "Court to rule on ban on women in perilous jobs." *Los Angeles Times* (March 27):A1 and A20.

Schiff, Michael, and Richard Lewontin
1986   *Education and Class: The Irrelevance of IQ Genetic Studies.* New York: Oxford University Press.

Schlender, Brenton R.
1980   "Sterilization is main issue in OSHA suits." *Wall Street Journal* (December 9).

Schneiderman, Marvin A.
1982   "Standard setting: Implications of sensitivity, and a search for an ethical base." *Annals of the American Conference of Governmental Industrial Hygienists* 3 (September): 133–138.

Schulte, Paul A.
1987   "Simultaneous assessment of genetic and occupational risk factors." *Journal of Occupational Medicine* 29, No. 11 (November):884–891.

Schuman, Howard, Charlotte Steeh, and Lawrence Bobo
1985   *Racial Attitudes in America: Trends and Interpretations.* Cambridge, Mass.: Harvard University Press.

Schwing, Richard C., and Walter A. Albers, Jr. (editors)
1980   *Societal Risk Assessment: How Safe Is Safe Enough?* New York: Plenum Press.

Sears, David A.
1978   "The morbidity of sickle cell trait: A review of the literature." *American Journal of Medicine* 64 (June):1021–1036.

Severo, Richard
1980a   "The genetic barrier: Job benefit or job bias?" *New York Times* (February 3–6).

1980b   "Genetic screening at DuPont: Blacks only need apply." *The Nation* (September 20).

1980c   "Should firms screen the workplace or the worker?" *New York Times* (September 28).

1981   "DuPont defends genetic screening program for job seekers." *New York Times* (October 8).

1982a   "Caution urged in genetic screening." *New York Times* (October 7).

1982b   "59 top U.S. companies plan genetic screening." *New York Times* (June 23).

Shabecoff, Philip

1979   "Aid found lacking for diseases of job." *New York Times* (December 20).

1981   "Industry and women clash over hazards in workplace: Issue and debate." *New York Times* (January 3).

1983   "A city weighs cancer risk against lost jobs." *New York Times* (July 13).

Shapiro, Irving S.

1980   "DuPont does not deal in scientific racism." *New York Times*, Letter to the Editor (February 7).

Shaw, Margery W.

1980   "The potential plaintiff: Preconception and prenatal torts." In Aubrey Milunsky and George J. Annas (editors), *Genetics and the Law II.* New York: Plenum Press.

1984   "Conditional prospective rights of the fetus." *Journal of Legal Medicine* 5, No. 1 (March):63–116.

Sheridan, Peter J.

1983   "Reproductive hazards: Probing the ethical issues." *Occupational Hazards* (May):72–75.

Sherrington, Robin, Jon Brynjolfsson, Hannes Petursson, et al.

1988   "Localization of a susceptibility locus for schizophrenia on chromosome 5." *Nature* 336, No. 6195 (November 10):164–167.

Shor, Glenn M.

1979   "Occupational disease and compensation: An analysis of the 1972 SSA survey of disabled adults." Prepared for the Office of the Assistant Secretary for Policy, Evaluation, and Research, U.S. Department of Labor (Contract Number B-9-M-8-3652) (October).

1987   Occupational Disease Compensation in California. Berkeley: University of California, California Policy Seminar.

Short, James F., Jr.

1984   "The social fabric at risk: Toward the social transformation of risk analysis." *American Sociological Review* 49, No. 6 (December):711–725.

Shrader-Frechette, K. S.

1985   *Risk Analysis and Scientific Method: Methodological and Ethical Problems with Evaluating Societal Hazards.* Hingham, Mass.: D. Reidel.

References

Smith, Adam
1937 *The Wealth of Nations.* New York: Modern Library [originally published in 1776].

Smith, James P., and Michael P. Ward
1984 *Women's Wages and Work in the Twentieth Century.* Santa Monica, Calif.: RAND Corporation.

Smith, Robert S.
1979 "Compensating wage differentials and public policy." *Industrial and Labor Relations Review* 23, No. 3 (April):339–352.

Society for Occupational and Environmental Health
1977 *Proceedings: Conference on Women and the Workplace,* Washington, D.C., June 17–19, 1976, edited by Eula Bingham. Washington, D.C.

Sontag, Susan
1977 *Illness as Metaphor.* New York: Farrar, Straus, and Giroux.

Sorenson, James R.
1971 *Social Aspects of Applied Human Genetics.* Social Science Frontiers. New York: Russell Sage Foundation.

Stallones, R. A., and T. Downs
1979 "A critical review of K. Bridbord et al." Report prepared for the American Industrial Health Council.

Starr, Paul
1982 *The Social Transformation of American Medicine: The Rise of a Sovereign Profession and the Making of a Vast Industry.* New York: Basic Books.

Stellman, Jeanne Mager
1977 *Women's Work, Women's Health: Myths and Realities.* New York: Pantheon Books.

Stellman, Jeanne M., and Mary Sue Henefin
1982 "No fertile women need apply: Employment discrimination and reproductive hazards in the workplace." In Ruth Hubbard, Mary Sue Henefin, and Barbara Fried (editors), *Biological Woman – The Convenient Myth.* Cambridge, Mass.: Schenkman.

Stephens, J. Clairborne, Mark L. Cavanaugh, Margaret I. Gradie, Martin L. Mador, and Kenneth K. Kidd
1990 "Mapping the human genome: Current status." *Science* 250, No. 4978 (October 12):237–250.

Stevens, William K.
1990 "Measuring workplace impairment." *New York Times* (March 6).

References

Stillman, Nina G.
  1979   "The law in conflict: Accommodating equal employment and occupational health obligations." *Journal of Occupational Medicine* 21, No. 9 (September):599–606.
Stokinger, Herbert E.
  1981   "Genetic screening of employees: Resistance and responsibility." *Dangerous Properties of Industrial Materials Report 1,* No. 7 (September–October):7–11.
Stokinger, Herbert E., and John T. Mountain
  1963   "Test for hypersusceptibility to hemolytic chemicals." *Archives of Environmental Health* 6, No. 4 (April):495–502.
  1967   "Progress in detecting the worker hypersusceptible to industrial chemicals." *Journal of Occupational Medicine* 9, No. 11 (November):537–542.
Stokinger, H. E., and L. D. Scheel
  1973   "Hypersusceptibility and genetic problems in occupational medicine: A consensus report." *Journal of Occupational Medicine* 15, No. 7 (July):564–573.
Stone, Deborah A.
  1986   "The resistible rise of preventive medicine." *Journal of Health Politics, Policy, and Law* 11, No. 4 (Winter):671–697.
Stuller, Jay
  1988   "The price of life." *San Francisco Chronicle* (This World Section, September 4):15–16.
Suzuki, David T., and Peter Knudtson
  1989   *Genetics: The Clash between the New Genetics and Human Values.* Cambridge, Mass.: Harvard University Press.
Swartz, Joel B., and Samuel S. Epstein
  1981   "Problems in assessing risk from occupational and environmental exposures to carcinogens." In *Quantification of Occupational Cancer, Banbury Report 9.* Cold Spring Harbor, N.Y.: Cold Spring Harbor Laboratory.
Syme, S. Leonard, and Lisa F. Berkman
  1986   "Social class, susceptibility, and sickness." In Peter Conrad and Rochelle Kern (editors), *The Sociology of Health and Illness: Critical Perspectives.* New York: St. Martin's Press.
Szasz, Andrew
  1984   "Industrial resistance to occupational safety and health legislation: 1971–1981." *Social Problems* 32, No. 2 (December):103–116.

References

Tesh, Sylvia Noble
  1988   *Hidden Arguments: Political Ideology and Disease Prevention Policy.* New Brunswick, N.J.: Rutgers University Press.
Thaler, Richard, and Sherwin Rosen
  1976   "The value of saving a life: Evidence from the labor market." In Nestor Terlecky (editor), *Household Production and Consumption.* New York: Columbia University Press.
Treiman, Donald, and Heidi I. Hartmann (editors)
  1981   *Women, Work, and Wages: Equal Pay for Jobs of Equal Value.* Washington, D.C.: National Academy Press.
Trost, Cathy
  1985   "Health, safety enforcement at work has eased under Reagan, report says." *Wall Street Journal* (April 18).
  1986   "Plans to alert workers to health risks stir fears of lawsuits and high costs." *Wall Street Journal* (March 28).
Tversky, Amos, and Daniel Kahneman
  1981   "The framing of decisions and the psychology of choice." *Science* 211, No. 4481 (January 30):453–458.
U.S. Congress, House, Committee on Science and Technology, Subcommittee on Investigations and Oversight
  1981   *Hearings: Genetic Screening and the Handling of High-Risk Groups in the Workplace.* Washington, D.C.: U.S. Government Printing Office (October 14 and 15).
  1982a *Hearings: Genetic Screening of Workers.* Washington, D.C.: U.S. Government Printing Office (June 22).
  1982b *Hearings: Genetic Screening in the Workplace.* Washington, D.C.: U.S. Government Printing Office (October 6).
U.S. Department of Health and Human Services, National Clearinghouse for Human Genetic Diseases
  1980   *State Laws and Regulations on Genetic Disorders.* Washington, D.C.: U.S. Government Printing Office.
U.S. Department of Labor
  1980   *Interim Report to Congress on Occupational Diseases.* Washington, D.C.: U.S. Government Printing Office.
U.S. House Subcommittee on Health and Safety, Committee on Education and Labor
  1981   *Hearings: OSHA Oversight Hearings on Proposed Rules on Hazards Identification.* Washington, D.C.: U.S. Government Printing Office (April 7, 28; May 19, 27; July 8, 14, 21; and October 6).

References

1987   *Hearings: High Risk Occupational Disease Notification and Prevention Act of 1987.* Washington, D.C.: U.S. Government Printing Office (March 17, 24, 26, 31; and April 8).

U.S. House Subcommittee on Labor Standards, Committee on Education and Labor

1981   *Hearings: Occupational Disease Compensation and Social Security.* Washington, D.C.: U.S. Government Printing Office.

U.S. President

1982   *Economic Report of the President, 1982.* Washington, D.C.: U.S. Government Printing Office.

Utidjian, Michael D., Morton Corn, Bertram Dinman, Peter F. Infante, and Peggy Seminario

1979   "Role of high risk groups in standard derivation: Panel discussion." *Environmental Health Perspectives* 29 (April): 161–173.

Vainio, Harri, Marja Sorsa, and Kari Hemminki

1983   "Biological monitoring in surveillance of exposure to genotoxicants." *American Journal of Industrial Medicine* 4:87–103.

Venable, John

1978   Statement Issued by Medical Director of Dow Chemical, Texas Division (June 12).

Verespej, Michael A.

1987   "Notifying workers about health risks." *Industry Week* 233 (June 29):15–16.

Viscusi, W. Kip

1979   *Employment Hazards: An Investigation of Market Performance.* Cambridge, Mass.: Harvard University Press.

1983   *Risk By Choice: Regulating Health and Safety in the Workplace.* Cambridge, Mass.: Harvard University Press.

Viscusi, W. Kip, and Charles O'Connor

1984   "Adaptive responses to chemical labeling: Are workers Bayesian decision makers?" *American Economic Review* 74, No. 5 (December):942–956.

Wall Street Journal

1987   "AT and T is urging transfers for some pregnant women." (January 14).

Walsh, Diana Chapman

1987   *Corporate Physicians: Between Medicine and Management.* New Haven, Conn.: Yale University Press.

References

Warner, Richard
  1987   *Recovery from Schizophrenia: Psychiatry and Political Econo-my.* New York: Routledge and Kegan Paul.
Washington Post
  1980a   "Genetics in the workplace." Editorial (March 10).
  1980b   "More on genetic risks." Editorial (March 26).
Wermiel, Stephen
  1991   "Justices bar 'fetal protection' policies." *Wall Street Journal* (March 21).
Wertz, Dorothy C., and John C. Fletcher
  1989a   "An international survey of attitudes of medical genet-icists toward mass screening and access to results." *Public Health Reports* 104, No. 1:35–44.
  1989b   "Disclosing genetic information: Who should know?" *Technology Review* (July):22–23.
West, Susan
  1982   "Genetic testing on the job." *Science 82,* Vol. 3, No. 7 (September):16.
Whorton, Donald
  1983   "Dibromochloropropane health effects." In William N. Rom (editor), *Environmental and Occupational Medicine.* Boston: Little Brown.
Wikler, Daniel I.
  1978   "Persuasion and coercion for health: Ethical issues in government efforts to change life-styles." *Milbank Memorial Fund Quarterly/Health and Society* 56, No. 3:303–338.
Williams, Richard Allen
  1974   "Black-related diseases: An overview." *Journal of Black Health Perspectives* 1, No. 1 (January-February):35–40.
Williams, Wendy W.
  1981   "Firing the woman to protect the fetus: The reconcilia-tion of fetal protection with employment opportunity goals under Title VII." *Georgetown Law Journal* 69, No. 3 (February):641–704.
  1982   "The equality crisis: Some reflections on culture, courts, and feminism." *Women's Rights Law Reporter* 7 (Spring): 175–200.
Williamson, Joel
  1984   *The Crucible of Race.* New York: Oxford University Press.

References

Wilson, Edward O.
  1975 *Sociobiology: The New Synthesis.* Cambridge, Mass.: Belknap Press of Harvard University Press.
  1978 *On Human Nature.* Cambridge, Mass.: Harvard University Press.
Wilson, James Q. (editor)
  1980 *The Politics of Regulation.* New York: Basic Books.
Wilson, James Q., and Richard J. Herrnstein
  1985 *Crime and Human Nature.* New York: Simon and Schuster.
Wilson, William Julius
  1987 *The Truly Disadvantaged: The Inner City, the Underclass, and Public Policy.* Chicago: University of Chicago Press.
Wofsy, Leon
  1986 "Biotechnology and the university." *Journal of Higher Education* 57, No. 5:477–492.
Worrall, John D., and Richard J. Butler
  1983 "Health conditions and job hazards: Union and nonunion jobs." *Journal of Labor Research* 4, No. 4 (Fall):339–347.
Wright, Curtis, Julio C. Rivera, and Joan H. Baetz
  1988 "Liver function testing in a working population: Three strategies to reduce false-positive results." *Journal of Occupational Medicine* 30, No. 9 (September):693–697.
Wright, Michael, D. Jack Kilian, Nicholas A. Ashford, and Paul Kotin
  1979 "Role of the knowledge of high risk groups in occupational health policies and practices: Panel discussion." *Environmental Health Perspectives* 29 (April):143–153.
Yoxen, Edward
  1983 *The Gene Business: Who Should Control Biotechnology?* London: Free Association Books.
Zeckhauser, Richard, and Albert Nichol
  1979 "The Occupational Safety and Health Administration: An overview." In *The Study of Federal Regulation of the Senate Committee on Governmental Affairs,* Vol. 6. Washington, D.C.: U.S. Government Printing Office.
Zeckhauser, Richard, and Donald Shephard
  1976 "Where now for saving lives?" *Law and Contemporary Problems* 40, No. 4 (Autumn):5–45.
Zenz, Carl
  1984 "Reproductive risk in the workplace." *National Safety News* 130 (September):38–46.

Index

Index

chemical safeguards: and workers at risk, 45–6

chemicals: genetic predisposition to, 28–9; government involvement in, 150–1; restrictions on, 52; safety of, 52–3; susceptibility to, 43; see also toxic chemicals (toxins)

Chinese, 94

choice(s), xii, 129; constraints on, 99, 123, 124–5, 128–9; between employment and health, 85, 95, 107–8, 123–4, 129, 184, 233n61; hazard-pay model of, 121–2; issues of, 119, 129; model(s) of, 119–21; questions about, 130–4; and reproductive risk, 81–2; of risk, 119–29

chromosome abnormalities, 11–12, 19, 56, 60, 66, 69, 139, 164, 182; and development of disease, 52, 53, 55; monitoring for, 14, 164; studies of, 19, 57–8

chronic bronchitis, 11, 25, 94

chronic obstructive pulmonary disease (COPD), 31

cirrhosis, 88

Civil Rights Act (1964): Title VII, 77, 78; and EEOC, 165–7

confidentiality, 33, 171; of medical information, 93, 99, 102–3, 105, 117, 118, 133–4

conflict: and workers at risk, 181–2

conflicting interests, 17, 58, 121; in access to medical information, 104; and conceptualization of risk, 7; in fetal exclusion, 79, 80–2; sociological understanding of, 187–8; and susceptibility policies, 139; and workers at risk, 181

congressional hearings, on genetic screening in the workplace, 16, 171

Connecticut, 171, 226n6, 228n19, 248n7

consent, 99, 121, 134–9; see also informed consent

contract research firms, 199n9

control, 46, 121; in industrial medicine, 97–139; of information, 99–107

Cooper, W. Clark, 26

corporate concerns: and future workplace policy, 172–4

corporate officials, 5–6, 32; and genetic monitoring, 54–7; see also management

corporate prerogatives, 107–19

corporate tax rate, 242n22

costs, 80, 83, 107, 153, 168; of changing policy, 185; of chemical hazards, 107, 183; and government regulation, 152; of health insurance, 106, 170; of hiring women, 77; of lawsuits, 76; medical, 145; of occupational disease, 143, 144–53, 177, 180–1; of reducing hazards, 120, 183; shifting to public, 150; social rationality and distribution of, 148–9; who bears, 153

cotton dust, 3, 47; OSHA standard, 91, 160, 161

counseling, 33, 81, 93; availability of, 131–2, 134; in public screening programs, 119

crime, 29, 206n28

cultural bias and technophobia model, 5

cultural factors, 35–6, 198n13; and identification of workers as high risk, 179; about women and minorities, 65

culture, genetic theory of, 206n31

cystic fibrosis, 28, 89, 130–1

Dabney, Betty, 20, 214n38

Daniels, Norman, 233n63

Index

management, 17, 32; and access to information, 105–6; and genetic paradigm, 39; and genetic screening/monitoring, 19; government regulation limiting prerogatives of, 180; and medical information, 102–3, 104, 133; prerogatives of, 107–19; and social issues in testing, 182; women and, 80; see also labor–management conflict

manufacturing industries: blacks in, 85; occupational illness in, 240n5; production workers in, by race, 86–7t; production workers in, by sex, 72t; union membership in, 114t, 115

Manville Corporation, 21, 109, 150

market forces, 121; hazard-pay model of choice in, 121–2; in regulation of risk, 128; and risk by choice, 120

Marsh and McLennan, 211n11

Martin, Charles F., 90

Massachusetts, 75, 100–1

Mazzocchi, Anthony, 37, 106, 196n5

medical ethics specialists, 33

medical exams, 14, 109, 115, 118, 158; preplacement, 99–100, 101, 102, 115–16

medical history, 14, 32, 109, 158

medical information: access to, 134, 135–6, 138, 139, 170, 184; confidentiality of, 133–4; control of, 139; distribution of, 117, 133

medical removal provisions, 136–9, 152, 160, 184–5, 216n52, 239n99

medical surveillance, 153; and employee access to information, 100; government requirements in, 156–9; OSHA rules for, 158–62, 159–60t; programs, 14, 19, 32, 58, 111, 115–16, 136, 137, 155, 174, 180

medical testing/tests: discriminatory effects of, 170; required by government, 168; required by OSHA, 158, 161

medicine; see industrial medicine

Mednick, Sarnoff A., 206n28

men, xi; exclusion from jobs, 74–5; health interests of, 96; mutagenic effects in, 16–17; reproductive hazards to, 47, 69, 70, 74–5, 77; women's conflicting interests with, 82

mental illness, 29, 30

military, 92, 93, 164

Mill, John Stuart, 127

Mills, C. Wright, xii

Milunsky, Aubrey, 141

mineral dusts, 49–50

mining industry, 111

minorities, 172; see also blacks

miscarriages, 74

Monsanto, 66

mortality: child, 66; racial differences in, 88, 221n52

Motulsky, Arno, 21, 205n17, 212n15

Mountain, John T., 24, 44, 45

Muir, Calum, 208n41

mutagens, 16–17, 51, 69, 74, 184

NADH dehydrogenase deficiency, 28

National Academy of Sciences, 24, 31; Committee for the Study of Inborn Errors of Metabolism, 228n18; Conference on Genetic Influences on Responses to the Environment, 59

National Cancer Institute, 24, 203n9

National Institute for Occupational Safety and Health (NIOSH), 19, 68, 91, 105, 169, 190; and monitoring, 244–5n43; National Occupational Exposure Survey,

Index

steel industry, 66, 71, 90, 112, 147
sterility, 69, 74
sterilization, 13, 65, 67, 68, 75, 162; proof of, 107
stigmatization, 51–2, 93
stillbirth, 66
Stokinger, Herbert E., 24, 26, 44, 45, 97
sulfite oxidase deficiency, 28
sulfur dioxides, 28, 59–60
Sun Oil, 66
susceptibility: biological factors and, 50; conceptual shift toward, 4; differential, 24; evidence for, 16–17; individual, 46–7, 177; racial/sexual component of, 7, 65, 83; safety and, 43–7
susceptibility policies, xi–xii, 6, 7, 20, 27, 43, 110; application of, 8; conflict over, 139; corporate enthusiasm for, 173; criticism of, 33–4; dangers of, 135; as discrimination, 95; effectiveness of, 29; emergence of, 11–15; and exclusion of women, 65–83; genetic orthodoxy and, 30–1; government regulation and, 164, 168–9; ideology of, 187–8; informed decisions in, 107; and job placement decisions, 108–9; labor's view of, 59; legal context of, 147–8, 155–6; media coverage of, 171–2; opponents of, 208n42; political environment of, 170–1; potential for abuse, 102, 186; problems with, 48–52; prospects for future, 185–7; and racial stratification, 83; rules affecting, 153–6; safety assumptions of, 39, 56, 58, 60–1; and sex/race/ethnicity, 94; social construction of, 177–81; social context of, 187–8, 189; TLVs and, 45–6; Viscusi endorsement of, 235–6n78

susceptibility practices: ideology in, 39–47, 143; labor's opposition to, 138–9; social costs and, 148–9; in textile industry, 74
susceptibility tests/testing, 7, 32, 48, 99; controversy over, 16; criteria for, 26–7; as example of social construction of risk, 5; for job applicants, 24; opposing views of, 15–20; proponents of, 43–5, 47, 129; purpose of, 108; scientists and, 29
susceptibility theories: conflict over locus of risk and, 39; workplace safety and, 42

tautological arguments, 48
Tay-Sachs, 129, 130, 246n59
technical criteria approach, 34
technological feasibility, 247n2
technological risk, 4–5
technology(ies): for controlling emissions, 123; and controversy over genetic testing, 17; *see also* genetic technologies/techniques
teratogenic risk, 11, 13–14, 15, 80, 184
teratogens, 65, 68
test sensitivity, 27; defined, 205n22
test specificity, 27; defined, 205n22
testicular atrophy, 244n42
testing/tests, 6, 68; initiation of, 130–1, 133; preemployment, 106–7, 130, 133, 134; *see also* genetic tests/testing; medical testing/tests; screening tests
testing data, ambiguous, 52–8
testing programs: company, 57–8; control of, 20
Texas, 101
textile industry, 47, 73, 74, 147; blacks in, 90; exclusionary policies in, 66; testing in, 14, 111; union membership in, 112
thalassemia, alpha/beta, 14, 83, 94

313